Salesforce AppExchange Success Blueprint

Transform your ideas into profitable and scalable
Salesforce applications

Jakub Stefaniak

BIRMINGHAM—MUMBAI

Salesforce AppExchange Success Blueprint

Group Product Manager: Alok Dhuri

Publishing Product Manager: Kushal Dave

Senior Editor: Kinnari Chohan

Book Project Manager: Manisha Singh

Technical Editor: Maran Fernandes

Copy Editor: Safis Editing

Indexer: Pratik Shirodkar

Production Designer: Prashant Ghare

DevRel Marketing Executive: Deepak Kumar and Mayank Singh

Business Development Executive: Puneet Kaur

First published: November 2023

Production reference: 1131023

Published by Packt Publishing Ltd.

Grosvenor House

11 St Paul's Square

Birmingham

B3 1RB, UK

ISBN 978-1-83508-954-5

www.packtpub.com

Dla mojej ukochanej żony, Aleksandry, która jest moim nieustającym źródłem inspiracji i siły.

Dla moich rodziców, którzy zawsze we mnie wierzyli i nauczyli mnie przekształcania marzeń w rzeczywistość.

Bez Was ta książka by nie powstała.

– Jakub

Contributors

About the author

"Jakub is the best Salesforce Expert I know," said Jakub's mom.

Jakub Stefaniak is a Salesforce **Certified Technical Architect** (**CTA**) and the VP of technology strategy and innovation at Aquiva Labs (an expert PDO company), where he assists ISVs in developing products and succeeding in their AppExchange partnerships. Jakub earned his master's in computer science and continued his education firstly at Stanford's Graduate School of Business and then in the Massachusetts Institute of Technology (MIT) Chief Technology Officer program. After delivering presentations about AppExchange across four continents (including at Dreamforce), Jakub got tired of repeating himself, so he penned this book. He's also the author of a self-published AppExchange app.

To my colleagues at Aquiva Labs – your support and insights have been instrumental in developing this book. Whether through our collaboration on various AppExchange projects or invaluable discussions, each of you has enriched the content of these pages. Without the privilege of being a part of a top Product Development Outsourcers like ours, I might never have acquired the necessary experience to undertake this endeavor. Thank you all sincerely.

About the reviewers

Marco Kuster has a diverse professional background, having worked as an architect, web designer, and technical trainer. However, he discovered his true passion when he became a part of the Salesforce ISV team. Working with ISVs has shown him that each one is distinct, and his role is to advise them in developing exceptional software by harnessing the power of Salesforce technologies.

Lawrence Newcombe, a Salesforce CTA and co-founder of Cloud Sundial, is the brains behind FormulaShare, an app revolutionizing record sharing. This tool provides flexible, click-and-configure rules for intricate sharing scenarios, eliminating the need for customization. With free and enterprise editions, FormulaShare is embraced by 100+ production orgs, attesting to its effectiveness.

Aside from app development, Lawrence serves as Lead Technical Architect at Giveclarity.org, where he establishes system architecture and governance for international NGOs. His expertise contributes significantly to meaningful projects, showcasing his dedication to impactful work.

He is also a content creator, sharing insights on identity, OAuth, and cloud sharing on cloudsundial.com. Beyond the digital realm, he finds joy in rock climbing, exploring Bristol's crags and cliffs on sunny evenings.

Krishna Tatta is a Salesforce Certified Technical Architect (CTA) with over 15 years of experience in product engineering, enterprise architecture, SaaS product delivery, and people and organizational leadership. With over a decade of dedicated focus in the Salesforce PDO space, she possesses a profound understanding of the platform and the ISV ecosystem. Notably, she has designed and developed more than 55 Salesforce ISV products and played a pivotal role in shaping the technology strategy for numerous teams of Salesforce consultants. Her guidance empowered these teams to successfully build and deliver over 100 products for the Salesforce AppExchange. Currently, Krishna holds a prominent position at Google, where she leads application engineering for YouTube's global partnerships systems. Apart from her professional accomplishments, she takes immense pride in being a mother of two girls.

Table of Contents

2

Becoming an AppExchange Partner 23

3

Designing Customer-Centric Applications 41

Part 2: Building Blocks

4

Exploring Salesforce Platform Technologies   75

6

Security Review   129

Part 3: Delivering Value

7

Release Management   161

8

Onboarding New Customers   185

Part 4: Scaling for Success

10

11

12

Navigating the Path to Success   275

Index   301

Other Books You May Enjoy   318

Preface

I still recall the days, years ago, when I first delved into creating my very own AppExchange app. My mind buzzed with ideas, but the path to becoming an ISV partner wasn't straightforward. There's a mountain of knowledge you've got to climb, and those early days are rife with opportunities for expensive blunders. Trust me – I've learned some lessons the hard way, which has made me truly understand how crucial it is to get your foundations right and know where your blind spots are.

That's what pushed me to write down everything I've learned in this guide. Think of it as your playbook – packed with lessons, pro tips, and those "*I wish someone had told me this earlier*" insights, all aimed at helping you dodge the bullets I had to face and craft a killer AppExchange app from scratch.

Now, don't get me wrong; this isn't some memoir about my AppExchange escapades. It's all about you – whether you're a seasoned Salesforce developer, an aspiring AppExchange newbie, a visionary start-up founder, or a product manager eager to make your mark in the world of Salesforce. I'm confident that the practical knowledge and unique insights in this book will empower you to turn your ideas into reality and make the Salesforce ecosystem an even more vibrant, innovative space.

In the following chapters, you'll embark on an exciting journey that covers everything, from the fundamentals of AppExchange development to cutting-edge AI opportunities ahead. Along the way, I'll share stories from my personal experiences, highlighting the challenges I've faced and the lessons I've learned. I hope you'll find these anecdotes not only entertaining but also insightful.

Finally, it's my sincere hope that this book will serve as a launchpad for a new generation of AppExchange success stories. As Sir Isaac Newton once said, "*If I have seen further, it is by standing on the shoulders of giants.*" I've been fortunate enough to stand on the shoulders of many great minds in the Salesforce ecosystem, and I'm eager to pass that privilege on to you.

Alright, get ready and get excited! The future of AppExchange development is looking brighter than ever, and I couldn't be more thrilled to have you join us on this amazing journey.

So, dive in and enjoy what's coming your way. Happy reading and happy app building!

Who this book is for

This book has been crafted with a diverse readership in mind, encompassing individuals at various levels of familiarity and expertise within the Salesforce ecosystem. My primary target audience comprises the following personas:

- **Visionary entrepreneurs and start-up founders**: If you have bold ideas and a vision for innovative products and services within the Salesforce ecosystem, this book can help you tap into the thriving AppExchange market and turn your vision into reality

- **Entrepreneurs with existing applications on Heroku or AWS**: If you're a business owner considering an expansion into Salesforce AppExchange, even if you have limited prior experience with Salesforce, this book offers insights and guidance to navigate the platform effectively

- **Salesforce developers and architects**: If you're already immersed in the Salesforce ecosystem, and you're eager to expand your knowledge and skills in AppExchange development, this book is a valuable resource for you

- **Product managers, Chief Product Officers (CPOs), and other stakeholders**: Not everyone in this category is a developer, but if you play a pivotal role in shaping the direction and strategy of AppExchange applications, this book provides valuable insights to inform your decision-making processes

No matter where you stand within the Salesforce ecosystem, this book has something to offer you. It's your gateway to enhancing your expertise and harnessing the potential of the Salesforce platform.

What this book covers

Chapter 1, Introduction to Salesforce Ecosystem and AppExchange, is the starting point of our journey where we dive into the Salesforce ecosystem. In this chapter, we will explore the vastness of Salesforce, discover the benefits of creating applications for AppExchange, assess whether the Salesforce Platform aligns with your application idea, examine ISV partnership options, and weigh the advantages and responsibilities of being a Salesforce ecosystem partner.

Chapter 2, Becoming an AppExchange Partner, discusses the AppExchange Partner Program structure and benefits, effective utilization of the AppExchange Partner Community, key partnership agreements, crafting tailored business plans for the Salesforce ecosystem, and leveraging the AppExchange Partner Toolkit (Partner Business Org, License Management App, Feature Management App, and so on), helping you to establish a solid foundation for a successful partnership in the Salesforce ecosystem.

Chapter 3, Designing Customer-Centric Applications, covers the art of creating applications that truly meet customer needs and provide value. It emphasizes understanding customer pain points, aligning value propositions, mapping customer journeys, and selecting effective pricing models. By the end of this chapter, you'll possess the knowledge and insights needed to craft user-centric applications that leave a lasting impression in the AppExchange marketplace, helping customers solve their problems effectively.

Chapter 4, Exploring Salesforce Platform Technologies, is a journey into the lesser-known but highly valuable ISV-specific features of Salesforce. It sheds light on managed packages, Dynamic Apex, flows, custom property editors, Platform Cache, and the Salesforce Lightning Design System, offering insights into their functionalities and how they can be used to solve specific problems in AppExchange development.

Chapter 5, Seamless Integration with External Systems, is a comprehensive guide that equips you with the skills and tools needed to build robust bridges, connecting your Salesforce applications to external systems. This chapter covers technical architecture, integration patterns, Salesforce APIs, Salesforce Connect, the Canvas SDK, and connected apps, providing you with the knowledge to seamlessly integrate your applications with external platforms and navigate the Salesforce ecosystem with confidence.

Chapter 6, Security Review, equips you with the knowledge and tools to navigate the security review process, maintain high-security standards, comply with Salesforce security requirements, use scanning tools, document false positives, and continuously improve security for your Salesforce application.

Chapter 7, Release Management, is an exploration of the critical aspects of managing software releases within the Salesforce ecosystem. It serves as a vital bridge between the development phase and the end users, ensuring the smooth and consistent delivery of your software applications. In this chapter, we will delve into topics such as understanding the core principles of release management, identifying different types of software versions, utilizing push upgrades to facilitate seamless application updates, staying up to date with the latest package version, and determining the optimal frequency to release and deploy your software. By the end of this chapter, you will have gained the expertise to effectively guide your software applications from the development stage into the hands of your end users.

Chapter 8, Onboarding New Customers, is where we will learn the art of welcoming and retaining new customers in the Salesforce landscape. We'll explore the strategies to craft a compelling AppExchange listing, the techniques for engaging and fun onboarding experiences, the secrets of creating cinematic demos, providing interactive trial experiences, offering clear installation instructions, and embracing customer customization while ensuring a smooth transition into your software's world. By the end of this chapter, you'll have the tools to create an effective onboarding process that encourages potential users to become long-term residents in the house of your software.

Chapter 9, Operational Excellence, embarks on an adventurous journey through the Salesforce wilderness to discover the riches of customer satisfaction and revenue growth. Along the way, we'll explore the choice between the **Checkout Management App (CMA)** and the **Channel Order App (COA)**, all in pursuit of the treasure of operational excellence.

Chapter 10, Leveraging Analytics and Insights, embarks on an archaeological journey through the AppExchange ruins to uncover the wisdom hidden in data, exploring Partner Intelligence, Marketplace Analytics, and App Analytics to optimize AppExchange listings and enhance user experiences. We'll also delve into CRM Analytics, combining in-house data with Salesforce insights, and learn how to make data-driven decisions on our path to AppExchange success.

Chapter 11, *Managing Technical Debt*, covers the concept of technical debt, similar to financial debt, and its implications on security, the identification of warning signs, tools, and strategies for management. We will also learn how to always be ready for security review re-submissions.

Chapter 12, *Navigating the Path to Success*, explores the significance of innovation as a competitive edge, the importance of collaboration with Salesforce, the impact of external expertise, the opportunities and challenges of AI in the AppExchange domain, and the essential success metrics to validate strategies, in the culmination of our journey through the Salesforce AppExchange ecosystem.

Disclaimer: The illustrative images in this book have been generated using MidJourney, a digital visualization tool. These images are entirely artificial and do not represent real people or events. They are artistic creations designed to enhance the reader's experience.

Conventions used

There are a number of text conventions used throughout this book:

Bold: Indicates a new term, an important word, or words that you see on screen. For instance, words in menus or dialog boxes appear in bold. Here is an example: "Your debugging session terminates when you click **Return to subscriber overview**."

> **Tips or important notes**
> Appear like this.

Get in touch

Feedback from our readers is always welcome.

General feedback: If you have questions about any aspect of this book, email us at customercare@packtpub.com and mention the book title in the subject of your message.

Errata: Although we have taken every care to ensure the accuracy of our content, mistakes do happen. If you have found a mistake in this book, we would be grateful if you would report this to us. Please visit www.packtpub.com/support/errata and fill in the form.

Piracy: If you come across any illegal copies of our works in any form on the internet, we would be grateful if you would provide us with the location address or website name. Please contact us at copyright@packtpub.com with a link to the material.

If you are interested in becoming an author: If there is a topic that you have expertise in and you are interested in either writing or contributing to a book, please visit authors.packtpub.com.

Share Your Thoughts

Once you've read *Salesforce AppExchange Success Blueprint*, we'd love to hear your thoughts! Scan the QR code below to go straight to the Amazon review page for this book and share your feedback.

https://packt.link/r/1835089542

Your review is important to us and the tech community and will help us make sure we're delivering excellent quality content.

Download a free PDF copy of this book

Thanks for purchasing this book!

Do you like to read on the go but are unable to carry your print books everywhere? Is your eBook purchase not compatible with the device of your choice?

Don't worry, now with every Packt book you get a DRM-free PDF version of that book at no cost.

Read anywhere, any place, on any device. Search, copy, and paste code from your favorite technical books directly into your application.

The perks don't stop there, you can get exclusive access to discounts, newsletters, and great free content in your inbox daily

Follow these simple steps to get the benefits:

1. Scan the QR code or visit the link below

https://packt.link/free-ebook/978-1-83508-954-5

2. Submit your proof of purchase
3. That's it! We'll send your free PDF and other benefits to your email directly

Part 1:
Setting the Stage

Ah, the Salesforce ecosystem and AppExchange. Think of them as the grand ballroom of tech where you're not just a guest but the star performer. Before you take the stage, however, you need to know your lines, your props, and which way the exit is (just in case). Before our show begins, we need to do a dress rehearsal.

First, we'll embark on a behind-the-scenes tour of the Salesforce ecosystem and AppExchange, to familiarize ourselves with the spotlight and where not to step. Then, as you transform into the **Independent Software Vendor (ISV)** partner you were destined to be, we'll share secrets (shh!) on crafting apps that not only dazzle but also resonate with the audience... I mean, customers.

By the time the curtain falls on this part, you'll have your performance mapped out, ready to receive a standing ovation on AppExchange.

Our setlist includes the following:

- *Chapter 1, Introduction to Salesforce Ecosystem and AppExchange*
- *Chapter 2, Becoming an AppExchange Partner*
- *Chapter 3, Designing Customer-Centric Applications*

1

Introduction to the Salesforce Ecosystem and AppExchange

Welcome, trailblazers, to the exciting adventure of Salesforce and its AppExchange marketplace! As you embark on this journey through the uncharted territories of the Salesforce ecosystem, I'll be your trusty guide, helping you navigate the twists and turns and uncover hidden treasures along the way.

The stakes are high, as this expedition could lead to unprecedented opportunities for businesses seeking to create and distribute innovative applications that solve real-world challenges. So, grab your metaphorical hiking boots because in this chapter, we'll be exploring the following topics:

- The expansive landscape of Salesforce and its ecosystem, allowing you to fully comprehend the platform's potential

- The untapped value of building applications for AppExchange, enabling you to make informed decisions about joining the expedition

- Determining if the Salesforce platform is the right basecamp for your application idea, ensuring a strong foundation for your venture

- Venturing into the unknown territories of the **independent software vendor** (**ISV**) partnership, empowering you to map out the best route for your business

- Evaluating the rewards and responsibilities that come with becoming a partner in the Salesforce ecosystem, including various contractual arrangements such as **Original Equipment Manufacturer** (**OEM**) and ISVforce, preparing you to conquer the diverse landscape of opportunities

These topics are critical for every trailblazer such as you because they will help you make informed decisions about your involvement in the Salesforce ecosystem and capitalize on the unique opportunities that AppExchange provides. By understanding the roles and responsibilities associated with ISV partnership, you will be able to choose the right path for the success of your business.

Now, strap on your backpack and prepare for a thrilling journey into the wilds of Salesforce and AppExchange. It's time to blaze a trail to success! Let's get started!

Salesforce and its ecosystem

Picture this: it's 1999, and you're struggling to keep track of your customer interactions, manage your sales pipeline, and monitor your sales team's performance. What do you do? Well, luckily for you, a group of visionaries founded Salesforce, a cloud-based **customer relationship management (CRM)** platform. And voilà! Salesforce saves the day, growing into one of the world's leading CRM platforms, boasting over 150,000 customers[1] and a whopping 23%[2] market share.

Nowadays, Salesforce's ecosystem is like an all-you-can-eat buffet of products, services, and features, allowing businesses to mix and match to create a customized, mouth-watering platter. The key components of this smorgasbord include the following:

- **Sales Cloud**: Think of it as the CRM butler, assisting businesses in managing their sales pipeline, customer interactions, and sales team performance

- **Service Cloud**: Offers efficient and tailored customer service support across various channels

- **Community Cloud**: A digital platform where customers, partners, and employees collaborate, exchange ideas, and solve problems, enhancing engagement and loyalty within the Salesforce environment

- **Marketing Cloud**: Your very own marketing maestro, orchestrating campaigns across email, social, and mobile channels like a seasoned conductor

- **Tableau**: A data visualization and analytics platform that allows businesses to create interactive dashboards and reports from their data, gaining deeper insights into customer data to drive growth and innovation

- **Slack**: A collaboration hub that streamlines communication and file-sharing, with integration with Salesforce providing real-time notifications and updates to enable seamless teamwork across platforms

---

1   https://www.salesforce.com/campaign/worlds-number-one-CRM/
2   https://www.salesforce.com/news/stories/idc-crm-market-share-ranking-2023/

- **MuleSoft**: An integration platform that connects different systems and applications, streamlining workflows, reducing manual data entry, and automating business processes, with deep integration with Salesforce providing a unified view of customer data across systems
- **Commerce Cloud**: The e-commerce genie, granting businesses the power to create personalized shopping experiences across multiple channels
- **Platform**: A **platform as a service** (**PaaS**) playground that lets developers build and deploy custom applications atop Salesforce
- **Trailhead**: Salesforce's online platform that offers interactive training for users, developers, and administrators

One of the key features of Salesforce is its cloud computing platform. Now, I know what you're thinking—"Cloud computing? Isn't that just where all the data goes when you delete it?" But fear not, dear reader, for cloud computing is much more than that. It allows businesses to access computing resources and software applications over the internet, rather than having to install and manage them on their own physical servers. This enables businesses to reduce IT costs, increase scalability, and improve flexibility and accessibility. Plus, it sounds much cooler than saying "I store everything on a USB drive."

But what sets Salesforce apart from other cloud-based platforms is its multi-tenant architecture. In this setup, multiple customers share the same underlying infrastructure, much like living in an eco-friendly apartment building. Each customer's data and resources are securely isolated, just like having separate rooms and personal belongings in an apartment. This approach enables Salesforce to optimize resource utilization and easily scale its platform to cater to the diverse needs of its users, all while maintaining stringent data security and privacy protocols.

And let's not forget about AppExchange—the marketplace for third-party applications and solutions that integrate with Salesforce.

AppExchange

If you've secured a copy of this book, chances are you're no stranger to AppExchange and already have aspirations of crafting an app on this platform. But, for the slight possibility that this tome landed in your hands courtesy of a Christmas surprise from your tech-savvy grandma who thought you could use a new hobby, allow me to elaborate on what AppExchange truly is. AppExchange is a marketplace where over 91%[3] of Salesforce customers use the various digital tools available. They benefit from the capabilities of the Salesforce Customer 360 platform, which provides them with all the resources they need for digital success. The AppExchange marketplace offers a wide range of tools, significantly

---

3   https://www.salesforce.com/news/stories/link-appexchange-migration/

influencing the Salesforce economy. According to an **International Data Corporation (IDC)** study[4], it's expected to generate a mouthwatering $1.6 trillion in new business revenue by 2026. The cherry on top? For every dollar Salesforce earns this year, the ecosystem will make $4.96, and by 2026, that number will rise to $6.19. With over 5,000 solutions and with over more than 10 million[5] installs under its belt, this bustling marketplace is a testament to the power of collaboration in the world of enterprise software, a vital component for 150,000 customers in 100 countries.

Innovation is the secret ingredient that keeps AppExchange exciting. ISVs are investing in developing new products and enhancing existing ones, incorporating cutting-edge technologies such as **artificial intelligence (AI)**, automation, and data analytics to create a remarkable experience for users.

Looking forward, the potential for growth in the AppExchange marketplace is as vast as an expansive landscape. The ongoing success of the Salesforce economy shows there's always room for new and innovative ideas, providing both new and established AppExchange partners with a unique opportunity to add their own remarkable offerings to the menu.

Embarking on the AppExchange journey – familiarizing yourself with the interface

As a new AppExchange partner, it's essential to acquaint yourself with the AppExchange interface. By understanding how potential customers navigate and search for apps, you can better position your app for success. To access the AppExchange marketplace, visit the official link at `https://appexchange.salesforce.com` or find it within the Salesforce platform.

The AppExchange marketplace is organized into various categories, including solutions by type, products, and industries, making it easy for users to find what they're looking for. Spend time exploring these categories and observe how other solutions are presented, as it will help you tailor your app's listing to appeal to your target audience.

By immersing yourself in the AppExchange experience, you can gain valuable insights into what customers seek and expect. This knowledge will not only help you develop a competitive app but also ensure its discoverability and relevance in the marketplace.

Salesforce Labs

In the vast landscape of the AppExchange marketplace, Salesforce Labs stands out. This segment of the marketplace features over 260[6] apps developed by Salesforce employees, offering an assortment of free apps and solutions designed to cater to a wide range of Salesforce users' needs.

---

4   `https://www.salesforce.com/content/dam/web/en_us/www/documents/platform/idc-platform-bv-report-2020.pdf`

5   `https://appexchange.salesforce.com/`

6   `https://appexchange.salesforce.com/category/salesforce-labs-apps`

The apps vary in their complexity, meeting diverse business requirements, from straightforward tools to intricate solutions. Salesforce Labs acts as a testing ground, giving users the opportunity to try out new features without the necessity of custom development or in-depth testing. Additionally, it's a community-centric initiative, welcoming feedback and contributions to continuously improve and refine the apps.

Exploring the value and potential of building applications for AppExchange

As you venture deeper into the wilds of the Salesforce ecosystem, it's time to survey the landscape and unearth the hidden treasures that await in building applications for AppExchange. Just as every explorer seeks riches on their journey, partners have discovered bountiful rewards by participating in the AppExchange program.

The Valoir report on AppExchange[7], August 2022, revealed four gleaming gems of benefits experienced by partners: accelerated sales cycles, reduced security, and due diligence efforts, reduced infrastructure management costs, and increased marketing reach with fewer internal marketing resources.

Imagine discovering a shortcut to your destination, accelerating sales cycles by up to 20% as you traverse the AppExchange terrain. The validation of your solution in the eyes of Salesforce customers is like having a trusty compass that guides prospects toward your offerings.

As you navigate the treacherous cliffs of security and due diligence, fear not! The rigorous review required for AppExchange listings helps partners slash the time and resources associated with these challenges by up to 80%.

The Salesforce platform is assisting ISVs in reducing infrastructure management costs by up to 75%. By leveraging its pre-built capabilities and components, you can focus your investments on product innovation, scaling the heights of success.

Finally, the Salesforce **AppExchange Marketing Program** (**AMP**) and co-marketing opportunities allow you to blaze a trail with fewer marketing resources, achieving similar or better outcomes with 30% less effort. We will dive deeper into AMP in *Chapter 12*.

Aren't you convinced yet? Let's turn our attention to another source: *The Business Value of Salesforce Platform for Application Development*[8], published by IDC in October 2020. This report investigates the value of Salesforce tools and technologies in the context of application development. Keep in mind, fellow explorers, that AppExchange partners wield the same tools as they forge their path through the Salesforce wilderness.

---

7   https://valoir.com/blog-1/salesforceappexchange
8   https://www.salesforce.com/content/dam/web/en_us/www/documents/
    platform/idc-platform-bv-report-2020.pdf

The platform's key benefits for both Salesforce customers and AppExchange partners are impressive, as we can see here:

- **Increased efficiency in application development**: Like discovering a secret shortcut, the Salesforce Platform reduces application development life cycles by 68%, boosting productivity by 56% and leading to more apps and features released annually

- **Improved application quality and reliability**: The platform is like a trusty adventurer's gear, ensuring high levels of application reliability, reducing unplanned downtime by 89%, and enhancing productivity for business end users

- **Optimized access, adoption, and use of business-critical applications**: Chart a course to better customer satisfaction, improved business results, and greater revenue, with an average of $5.7 million additional new revenue generated per year

- **Enhanced efficiency of application management teams**: Like a well-organized expedition, the Salesforce platform enables teams to manage applications 63% more efficiently, streamlining workflows and cutting overhead

The IDC report indicates that 35,086 internal IT users utilize tools akin to those used by ISV developers, underscoring the report's pertinence for AppExchange partners. Given this insight, it's evident that the Salesforce Platform provides significant business value for partners in the realm of application development. Notably, while the report primarily focuses on Salesforce customers, the shared tool usage with ISV developers makes it pertinent to AppExchange partners.

What exactly do ISVs do on AppExchange?

Picture yourself strolling through the bustling Salesforce neighborhood, admiring the shiny skyscrapers of business functionality. The streets are filled with AppExchange partners, the superheroes of this metropolis, working tirelessly to make Salesforce an even better place to be.

So, what exactly do these ISV partners do on AppExchange? Let's take a look:

- **Enhancing Salesforce's capabilities**: ISVs work to augment Salesforce's existing functionalities. They focus on helping customers derive more value from the platform by extending and refining its features.

- **Addressing specific needs**: These partners identify and address areas where Salesforce's offerings might be limited or lacking. By developing solutions for these areas, they ensure that users have a more comprehensive and seamless experience with Salesforce.

- **Providing industry-specific solutions**: ISVs specialize in creating apps tailored to particular industries or market segments. They offer targeted solutions that benefit businesses, regardless of their familiarity with Salesforce.

But to truly succeed on AppExchange, partners must focus on three essential ingredients, as follows:

- **Whipping up intellectual property (IP)**: By collaborating with Salesforce, partners have the flexibility to create innovative applications utilizing APIs or building their applications solely with Salesforce technology

- **Packaging the app for success**: Like a beautifully wrapped gift, partners must market and sell their apps effectively to drive customer adoption

- **Assembling a dream team**: By joining the partner program, partners need to allocate resources and personnel to ensure their apps reach their full potential, developing a long-term marketing, sales, and support strategy

In the end, ISV partners are the lifeblood of the Salesforce ecosystem.

Different types of partners

Salesforce categorizes its partners into different types, so let's get some terms straight.

Firstly, Salesforce recognizes two primary types of partners: ISVs and Consulting Partners. In this book, when I use the term *"Partner"*, I'm referring to ISVs by default. So, if you come across the term *"Salesforce Partner"* online and find information that doesn't seem to pertain to you, this distinction is likely the reason.

The line separating these two categories is straightforward: ISVs focus on developing AppExchange products, while Consulting Partners, often referred to as **System Integrators** (**SIs**), offer consulting and implementation services tailored for Salesforce customers.

But there's another partner type worth noting: **Product Development Outsourcers** (**PDOs**). PDOs provide consulting services specifically for ISVs. Essentially, if you're an ISV looking for expertise in product development, a PDO is who you'd reach out to.

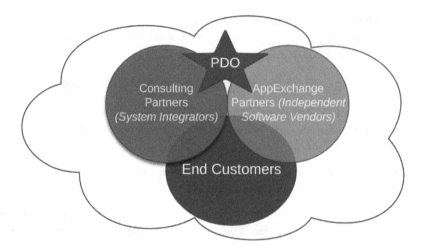

Figure 1.1: Salesforce Partners landscape

Delving deeper into collaboration dynamics, *Chapter 12* of this book will explore how you can effectively collaborate with both PDOs and SIs.

Evaluating the suitability of the Salesforce Platform for your application idea

Is the Salesforce platform the ideal lair for your application idea? After all, even superheroes need the perfect base of operations to suit their powers.

Salesforce is a powerful platform, brimming with tools and features for constructing and deploying custom applications. However, not all solution ideas may find their perfect sidekick within Salesforce. Suit up and consider these factors when evaluating if Salesforce is the right choice for you:

- **Application requirements**: Consider the specific powers of your application, such as functionality, scalability, and integration needs. Assess if Salesforce's arsenal of tools and features can meet these requirements or if you need to seek aid from a different platform or technology.

- **User experience (UX)**: Determine if the Salesforce platform can deliver the UX your application needs to save the day. Salesforce offers a multitude of tools for crafting custom **user interfaces** (**UIs**), but you may need to call upon additional technologies to create a truly extraordinary and unique UX. On the flip side, Salesforce apps tend to excel when they mirror the appearance and functionality of the standard Salesforce interface, delivering a seamless UX.

- **Integration needs**: Evaluate if Salesforce can form a seamless alliance with your existing systems and data sources. Salesforce provides various integration options, such as APIs and connectors, but you may need to enlist other tools or technologies to achieve total integration harmony.

- **Security and compliance**: Ponder the security and compliance demands of your application. Salesforce boasts powerful security and compliance measures, but you may need to take extra steps to ensure your app meets the specific requirements of your industry or region. Additionally, you will need to consider the requirement for the app to operate within what Salesforce determines to be a secure environment. This might result in some app ideas being disqualified entirely.

- **Time and resource constraints**: Weigh up whether constructing your application on Salesforce aligns with your time and resource constraints. Building an app for Salesforce can demand significant investments, so it's crucial to assess if it syncs with your business goals and priorities.

By examining these factors, you can determine if the Salesforce platform is the ideal choice for your idea.

Examples of existing AppExchange apps and their use cases

The following examples demonstrate the breadth and diversity of applications available on AppExchange, including electronic signature solutions, document generation, and reporting tools, professional services automation solutions, field service management solutions, and data aggregation and calculation tools:

- **FormulaShare**[9]: FormulaShare is an advanced dynamic sharing rules app on Salesforce that allows admins to dynamically share standard and custom objects with roles, groups, or users identified in the formula, lookup, or text fields. With FormulaShare, admins can easily create sharing rules based on the contents of fields they control without the need for coding or complex configurations. FormulaShare offers a freemium model that allows users to use up to 3 standard rules and 1 cross-object rule, and share up to 10,000 records. For larger organizations with more complex sharing needs, FormulaShare offers two premium versions: Enterprise and Unlimited.

- **Ask Your Document**[10]: Your Salesforce Documents AI - like ChatGPT but for your Documents, Files, and Attachments. This smart app integrates with Salesforce for easy on-platform file processing and inquiries. Leverage AI to ask and answer questions about any file content, simplifying data analysis. With a user-friendly interface, robust data security, and quick installation from AppExchange, it's perfect for businesses of all sizes wanting to streamline file tasks.

- **Kaptio Travel Platform**[11]: Kaptio is a travel and tourism management solution. It provides a comprehensive set of features for managing travel bookings, reservations, and itineraries, all within the Salesforce environment. Kaptio allows travel agents and operators to streamline their workflow, automate their processes, and provide exceptional customer service. With Kaptio, users can manage their entire travel business, from sales and marketing to customer service and support, all from one unified platform.

---

9   https://appexchange.salesforce.com/
    appxListingDetail?listingId=a0N3A00000FR5TCUA1

10 https://askyourdocument.aquivalabs.com/

11 https://www.kaptio.com/

- **IPfolio**[12]: IPfolio is an IP management solution. It allows users to manage, track, and collaborate on their IP assets, such as patents, trademarks, and licenses, all within the Salesforce platform. IPfolio streamlines the IP management process by providing a centralized and organized system, enabling organizations to make informed decisions and protect their valuable IP assets.

- **Hapi**[13]: Hapi combines deep hospitality experience with Salesforce platform expertise. The result is expert guidance, best practices and proven methodologies when implementing Salesforce solutions for hotel companies.

These applications provide unique solutions and benefits for Salesforce users, enabling them to streamline their business processes, increase efficiency, and improve customer satisfaction. By leveraging the Salesforce platform and ecosystem, these applications offer customized solutions to businesses of all sizes and industries.

Meet your new best friend – Formula Debugger

Throughout the upcoming chapters, I'll refer to the Formula Debugger app, which I developed and self-published a while ago, to provide examples of how AppExchange partners can implement particular tools and features. This will give you a hands-on understanding of the development process and the benefits of creating and publishing apps on AppExchange.

Who uses it? Typically, Salesforce administrators, who are knee-deep in formula fields, are trying to make sense of it all. Suddenly, they find themselves wishing for a magical helper that could make their lives easier. Well, their wish is granted! Here's what the Formula Debugger app brings to the (debugging) table:

- **Syntax analysis**: The app highlights matching parentheses like a syntax fairy, making it easier to understand and correct formula field syntax

- **Easy test data preparation**: Formula Debugger streamlines the process of preparing test data, eliminating the need for any **Data Manipulation Language** (**DML**) wizardry

- **AI integration**: The app harnesses the power of AI to detect potential issues with formula fields and kindly provides suggestions on how to fix them

---

12 https://ipfolio.com
13 https://www.hapicloud.io/

Here's what the interface of the application looks like:

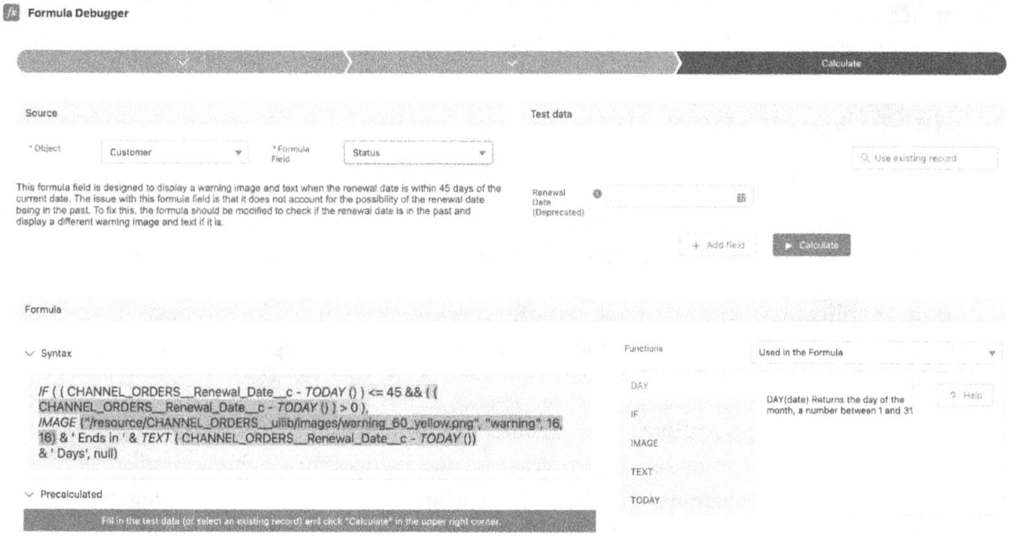

Figure 1.2: Formula Debugger

If you want, you can install it for free by searching for "`formula debugger`" on AppExchange, or use the following link to teleport there directly: `https://formuladebugger.jakubstefaniak.com`.

Happy debugging!

The AppExchange sweet spot – where applications thrive

Based on the examples and discussions in this chapter, the ideal applications for AppExchange are those that do the following:

- Provide unique solutions and benefits for Salesforce users. You cannot just build a clone of Sales Cloud or Service Cloud!

- Streamline business processes, increase efficiency, and improve customer satisfaction.

- Leverage the Salesforce platform and ecosystem to deliver customized solutions to businesses of all sizes and industries.

- Meet Salesforce's security, privacy, and usability standards.

- Align with the Salesforce platform's strengths and limitations, such as web-based applications, integrations with other systems, and cloud-based solutions.

By building applications that meet these criteria, you can take advantage of the benefits of becoming an ISV partner and leverage the potential of AppExchange to expand your customer base, generate recurring revenue streams, and gain visibility and credibility within the Salesforce ecosystem.

Examples of applications that are not a good fit for the Salesforce platform

While Salesforce offers a range of tools and features for building custom applications, some application types may not align with the Salesforce platform's strengths or limitations. Here are some examples:

- **Gaming applications**: The Salesforce platform is primarily designed for business applications and may not be the best fit for gaming applications that require high-performance graphics and processing capabilities.

- **Resource-intensive applications**: The Salesforce platform may not be suitable for applications that require extensive computing resources or real-time processing, such as complex **machine learning** (**ML**) or data analysis applications. AppExchange products should not attempt to carry out this processing on-platform but rather integrate with systems better positioned to handle complex processing use cases. Just so you know, in the Salesforce ecosystem, there are other options available. For instance, Heroku provides a robust platform specifically designed to handle resource-intensive computing tasks. Additionally, Salesforce offers its own proprietary AI solutions that are capable of effectively addressing advanced data processing needs.

- **Standalone desktop applications**: The Salesforce platform is cloud-based and primarily designed for web-based applications. Standalone desktop applications that require offline functionality may not be a good fit for the Salesforce platform.

- **Custom hardware applications**: Applications that require custom hardware or integration with physical devices may not be a good fit for the Salesforce platform, as it primarily focuses on software-based solutions.

By understanding the limitations of the Salesforce platform, you can make informed decisions about whether it is the right choice for your application idea. If your application falls outside the scope of the Salesforce platform, you may need to explore alternative technologies or platforms that better align with your requirements.

Software-as-a-Service products for Salesforce customers

Additionally, the AppExchange marketplace accepts **Software-as-a-Service** (**SaaS**) products that integrate with Salesforce and provide unique solutions for Salesforce users. These SaaS companies can also become AppExchange partners and list their products on the marketplace, highlighting their partnership with Salesforce and the security of their applications. However, becoming an AppExchange partner with a paid-for app listing requires sharing a **percentage of net revenue** (**PNR**) with Salesforce, which is why some companies have chosen not to become partners. Companies need to evaluate the business implications of becoming a partner despite the straightforward technical aspect of going through a security review. While this book focuses on building applications on the Salesforce platform, integrating with Salesforce through SaaS products offers businesses a variety of solutions and applications, both on and off the platform, to customize and extend their Salesforce instance based on their unique requirements.

Understanding ISVforce and OEM differences

The Salesforce ISV partnership world is like an ice cream shop, and you're here to choose the perfect flavor for your business. In one corner, we have ISVforce contracts, and in the other, we have OEM contracts. Both are delicious, but which one suits your taste buds best? Let's dig into the details to help you make the right choice.

Program build type – ISVforce

ISVforce partners are like the classic vanilla flavor of the Salesforce dessert world. They whip up applications built on the Salesforce platform, ready to be savored on the AppExchange menu. ISVforce partners can sprinkle in tasty toppings (think third-party integrations) and serve up a delightful customer experience. However, they must share a scoop of their revenue with Salesforce and comply with the platform's development guidelines.

ISVforce encompasses several key aspects, which include the following:

- Crafting and selling appetizing applications on the Salesforce platform to *existing* Salesforce users
- Customizing and extending applications within the Salesforce ecosystem
- Sharing a PNR with Salesforce
- Complying with Salesforce's development guidelines and best practices

Why choose ISVforce?

ISVforce is like the crowd-pleasing main course at a Salesforce banquet. These applications typically expand Salesforce's functionality in some way—namely, they're the delectable side dishes that complement the main entrée within the ecosystem. Many app creators realize that a significant number of their customers and prospects are already feasting at the Salesforce table, and they want to bring their culinary creations where their target market is. Typically, this involves enhancing the Salesforce Cloud offering (such as Sales, Service, Community, or Industry Clouds) in a manner that benefits both the partner and Salesforce.

Another tantalizing aspect of ISVforce is that customers of ISVforce can whip up their own creative concoctions by extending their application through custom objects. This added flexibility and scalability act as a secret ingredient that significantly expands your total market opportunity, providing a level of versatility that is not typically achievable with the OEM Embedded solution. While OEM customers can create up to 10 custom objects for integration purposes, the usage of these custom objects is strictly regulated to ensure that OEM customers are not building custom applications beyond established boundaries.

If you're crafting an application that relies on functionality within specific licenses (for example, Customer Communities), the customer must purchase the license from Salesforce before they can savor your app.

Program build type – OEM Embedded

OEM is like a unique, customizable cookie dough ice cream. These partners embed Salesforce technology into their own solutions, creating custom-branded offerings for their customers. The beauty of OEM partnerships lies in the freedom to create unique UXs and sell solutions directly without the obligation to list them on AppExchange. However, it's important to mention that while ISV partners are not obligated to publish on the AppExchange marketplace, some OEM partners do opt to have their applications listed on AppExchange. Regardless of listing status, OEM partners are still required to share a portion of their revenue with Salesforce.

OEM Embedded encompasses several key aspects, which include the following:

- Embedding Salesforce technology into custom-branded solutions
- Building on top of the Salesforce platform, *without any references* to other products such as Sales, Service, Marketing, Commerce, or Industry clouds
- Sell directly to customers (even without an AppExchange listing!)
- Share a higher PNR with Salesforce

As you savor these two flavors, keep in mind your business goals and requirements. For example, some successful Salesforce partners have opted for the OEM flavor, gaining the opportunity to resell additional technologies and add-ons unavailable to classic ISVforce.

Why choose OEM Embedded?

OEM Embedded applications have a primary focus on revolutionizing the infrastructure within specific industry verticals such as healthcare, finance, manufacturing, and more. These applications have the ability to attract a diverse range of customers, whether or not they are currently using the Salesforce platform. It's important to highlight that OEM Embedded solutions can also generate interest from new users within existing Salesforce customer organizations. For example, an HR department that is not currently utilizing Salesforce may opt to purchase an OEM product to meet their specific needs, while other departments such as Sales may already be regular users of Sales Cloud.

The benefit of OEM-embedded applications is the freedom to sell not only to existing Salesforce customers but also to a broader audience. Existing Salesforce customers can easily discover, purchase, and install OEM Embedded applications from the AppExchange marketplace, similar to how they would with an ISVforce application. Furthermore, for new customers, it is possible to provision a new Salesforce org for them using the Trialforce technology, without the requirement of directly connecting them to Salesforce. It's important to note that OEM customers receive an OEM Salesforce platform license, which is specifically tailored for the use of the OEM application.

Unlike ISVforce solutions that require the purchase of an additional license from Salesforce, OEM Embedded applications only have two specific types of licenses that can be made available to customers, as follows:

- **Lightning Platform (required)**: Allows customers to utilize the Salesforce platform, which is also identified as the Salesforce Platform license. However, it's important to note that licenses obtained from OEM partners are specifically intended for accessing and utilizing the partner solution. In order to broaden the capabilities of the partner solution, end users are permitted to create, access, and employ an additional 10 custom objects per solution. However, these custom objects are restricted to use solely with the partner solution. Please note that these contractual limits aren't automatically enforced. It's on the customer to make sure they don't set up more than 10 custom objects or use them in ways that aren't permitted.

- **Customer Community (optional)**: Enables customers or partners of the OEM customer to access a designated portion of the OEM application, facilitating interactions with their data.

Ultimately, the decision between ISVforce and OEM contracts depends on various factors, including your business's appetite for customization, access to additional technologies, revenue sharing, and the existing user base within your **go-to-market** (**GTM**) strategy. It's crucial to consider whether your target users already have Salesforce licenses or not, as this can significantly impact the suitability and alignment of either option with your business objectives. However, the decision comes with a trade-off: OEM partners are required to share a higher PNR with Salesforce, compared to ISVforce.

Programs comparison

In the following table, we will explore and compare the key features and distinctions between ISVforce and OEM Embedded, covering aspects such as their overview, target market, pricing, payment basis, products, reselling eligibility, and restrictions on Salesforce objects:

Feature	ISVforce	OEM
Overview	Extend functionality of Salesforce products and build integrations with CRM objects	Apps sold to both current Salesforce and non-Salesforce customers
Target market	Sold exclusively to Salesforce users	Sold to both Salesforce and non-Salesforce customers
Pricing	By default 15% PNR*	By default 25% PNR*
Products	Package installed on top of Salesforce-sold licenses (for example, Sales/Service Cloud)	App sold as a standalone solution with a restricted OEM Embedded license
Reselling eligibility	Partners not eligible to resell Salesforce products	Partners may resell certain add-on products to non-Salesforce customers
Restrictions on Salesforce objects	None	Cannot extend or replicate standard Salesforce objects
Configuring and Maintaining Salesforce Orgs for Customers	No	Potentially yes, especially if you're providing a dedicated Salesforce org
Customers' Training and Support Expectations	Your app only	Your app and Salesforce platform

*As of today (FY24), the PNR rates are as described. It's important to keep in mind that these pricing terms may change in the future. For the most accurate and current information, please visit the Salesforce Partners website at https://partners.salesforce.com.

Marginal PNR Program

In the past, ISVs paid fixed royalty rates for each license type: 25% for OEM and 15% for ISVforce. However, the year 2020 brought a game-changing update, rewarding larger and more successful app developers with reduced royalty rates. Generally, partners joining the AppExchange Partner Program[14] after March 1, 2020, are automatically enrolled in this benefit, while existing partners can also apply.

---

14 https://partners.salesforce.com/s/education/appinnovators/
  AppExchange_Partner_Program?language=en

Partners become eligible for reduced PNR rates on future and add-on bookings when their **Annual Order Value (AOV)** reaches or exceeds $1,000,000. As partners progress through AOV bands, their PNR rates decrease accordingly. As of today (FY24), the Marginal PNR Program is outlined in the following table. However, it is important to note that Salesforce has the authority to make updates or changes to the Marginal PNR Program Benefit at its own discretion, without necessarily providing prior notice. The Marginal PNR Program Benefit is one of the Program Benefits offered under the **Salesforce Partner Program Agreement (SPPA)**, and you will gain a more comprehensive understanding of it in the upcoming chapter:

AOV band	OEM Program PNR rate	ISVforce Program PNR rate
<$1,000,000	25%	15%
$1,000,001 - $2,500,000	23%	14%
$2,500,001 - $5,000,000	21%	13%
$5,000,001 - $10,000,000	19%	12%
$10,000,001 - $20,000,000	17%	11%
$20,000,001+	15%	10%

Note that only partners with an AOV above $1,000,000 will experience a reduction in PNR rates on new and add-on businesses. Certain non-standard terms may disqualify partners from enrolling in the Marginal PNR Program Benefit.

Choosing the right contract for your business

Welcome to the Great Ice Cream Debate: ISVforce versus OEM contracts! Now that you've had a taste of both flavors, it's time to choose the perfect scoop for your business. Let's weigh up the sprinkles and cherries of each option so that you can make an informed decision on which contract suits you best.

First, let's consider the nature of your application and your target audience. If your app is the cherry on top of the Salesforce sundae, catering mainly to existing Salesforce customers, then the classic ISVforce contract is your go-to flavor. As an ISVforce customer, you can craft and sell your sweet creations on AppExchange, dipping into a variety of Salesforce technologies and resources. Plus, with lower revenue-sharing requirements and more flexibility in product development and support, the ISVforce route is a tempting treat.

But what if your app isn't strictly a Salesforce topping? If your target audience includes those who haven't tasted the Salesforce goodness, then the OEM—our customizable cookie dough ice cream—might be the one for you. OEMs can resell a wider range of technologies and add-ons, whipping up custom-branded solutions to be sold directly to their customers. However, this unique flavor comes with a higher price tag in the form of revenue-sharing requirements and contractual sprinkles. When targeting customers who are not yet Salesforce users, it's important to consider the additional responsibilities that come with org and environment setup and maintenance.

As you ponder which partnership model to indulge in, consider the level of customization and integration needed, the support and maintenance requirements, and the marketing and sales resources provided by Salesforce. It's crucial to taste-test the pros and cons of each model, as well as the revenue-sharing obligations and contractual nuts.

Ultimately, the ideal partnership model is not a static choice but a dynamic decision tailored to your evolving business goals, needs, and resources. As you understand your application's nature, target audience, and the level of customization and support required, you can adopt a partnership model that best propels your business forward. It's noteworthy that partnerships aren't rigid structures. They can, and sometimes do, evolve over time. Some partners have been seen to shift their contracts from one model to another, such as moving from OEM to ISVforce or vice versa, or even adopting both contracts simultaneously, to better align with their business needs. Just as in an ice cream empire, the key to successful growth and expansion is the flexibility to adapt to changing tastes and demands.

Blended model

Sometimes, when you're facing the tough decision between ISVforce and OEM Embedded contracts, you may feel like you have to choose between chocolate fudge and caramel swirl. But what if I told you that you could have both, in one delicious cone?

In fact, ISVforce and OEM Embedded partnerships can work together in harmony to provide a comprehensive solution for your business (if the technical design of your application satisfies the constraints of both models). By leveraging the strengths of both partnership models, you can create a custom solution that caters to both existing Salesforce customers and those new to the platform.

It's important to carefully consider the technical implications of each partnership model before making a decision. Moreover, it's strongly advised to have a conversation with the Salesforce ISV sales team about this issue since they possess valuable insights and can offer helpful guidance while selecting a contract. Ultimately, the right partnership model will depend on your business goals, needs, and resources, and may impact your technical architecture and application design in unique ways.

Summary

In this chapter, fellow trailblazers, we traversed the vast landscape of Salesforce and its AppExchange marketplace, uncovering the value and potential that building applications for this platform can bring to your business. We scaled the peaks of evaluating the suitability of the Salesforce platform for your application idea and navigated the winding paths of ISVforce and OEM.

Gaining a deep understanding of the Salesforce ecosystem and the benefits and responsibilities of becoming an ISV partner is vital for making informed decisions about your involvement, ensuring you can forge a successful route through this wild terrain. With the knowledge you've gained, you're now better prepared to tackle the challenges that lie ahead and capitalize on the unique opportunities that AppExchange offers.

As we venture into the next chapter, I'll guide you through the process of becoming a successful AppExchange partner. You'll learn about partner agreements, crafting a comprehensive business plan, navigating the AppExchange Partner Portal, and leveraging the AppExchange Partner Toolkit. By mastering these tools and processes, you'll lay a strong foundation for your AppExchange expedition and be well-equipped to conquer the partnership landscape.

Further reading

- IDC report: `https://www.salesforce.com/content/dam/web/en_us/www/documents/platform/idc-platform-bv-report-2020.pdf`

- Valoir report: `https://valoir.com/blog-1/salesforceappexchange`

2

Becoming an
AppExchange Partner

Gather round, fellow trailblazers! Our expedition through the Salesforce ecosystem and AppExchange marketplace continues as we delve into the process of becoming a successful AppExchange partner. In this chapter, I'll guide you along the rugged terrain of partner agreements, business plans, and partner portals, ensuring you have a strong foundation for your AppExchange adventure.

By the end of this chapter, you will have learned about the following:

- The structure and benefits of the AppExchange Partner Program, helping you understand the value of joining the Salesforce expedition

- How to effectively explore and utilize the AppExchange Partner Community for managing partnership activities and accessing valuable resources

- Key agreements that govern AppExchange partnerships, such as a map of the territory you'll traverse

- How to craft a comprehensive business plan tailored to the Salesforce ecosystem, ensuring your success as an AppExchange trailblazer

- The importance of leveraging the AppExchange Partner Toolkit as your trusty compass to support and grow your partnership

Armed with this knowledge, you'll be well-equipped to navigate the Salesforce ecosystem confidently and lay the groundwork for a flourishing AppExchange partnership. So, let's continue our journey into the wilds of Salesforce and AppExchange and uncover the secrets to conquering the partnership landscape!

Overview of the AppExchange Partner Program

Becoming an AppExchange partner offers a wealth of advantages that can help your application thrive within the competitive Salesforce ecosystem. In this section, you will find some of the key benefits you can expect by joining the AppExchange marketplace, such as the following:

- **Access to a large customer base**: As a partner, your application gains exposure to Salesforce's extensive network of diverse customers, increasing your potential for sales and engagement.

- **Partner ecosystem collaboration**: Joining the AppExchange marketplace opens up collaboration opportunities with other Salesforce partners, allowing you to expand your network, share knowledge, and generate leads.

- **Comprehensive development tools and resources**: Salesforce provides a variety of tools and resources that support application development, testing, and deployment on the platform.

- **Platform security and trust**: By building your application on the Salesforce platform, you benefit from its robust security infrastructure and gain customer trust.

- **Go-to-market (GTM) support**: Salesforce offers resources and support to help partners market their applications effectively, including marketing best practices, co-marketing opportunities, and access to Salesforce events.

- **Technical support and training**: AppExchange partners gain access to Salesforce's technical support resources, such as documentation, webinars, and dedicated support teams, helping them stay current and overcome technical challenges.

- **Revenue-sharing opportunities**: Selling your application on the AppExchange marketplace allows you to generate additional revenue while leveraging the extensive Salesforce ecosystem.

- **App awareness**: Salesforce offers various opportunities to boost the visibility of your application, such as AppExchange listings, sponsorships, and guest blog contributions, helping you reach a wider audience and build your brand's reputation.

- **Business management**: Salesforce provides a range of tools and resources, including the Environment Hub, **Channel Order App (COA)**, **License Management App (LMA)**, **Partner Business Org (PBO)**, and Marketplace Analytics, to help you effectively manage your AppExchange business.

- **Demand generation**: By becoming an AppExchange partner, you gain access to resources and programs such as the **AppExchange Marketing Program** (**AMP**), which support you in generating demand for your application and driving conversions. We are going to discuss AMP in *Chapter 12*.

Joining the AppExchange marketplace as an ISV partner provides numerous advantages that can contribute to your application's success within the Salesforce ecosystem. From gaining access to a vast customer base to leveraging Salesforce's brand reputation and comprehensive support resources, the benefits of partnering with Salesforce on the AppExchange marketplace are significant and can pave the way for your application's growth and success.

Navigating the AppExchange Partner onboarding lifecycle

Becoming an AppExchange partner might seem like a daunting dance, but I'm here to guide you through the three main tracks to ensure your success as an ISV partner: the technical track, the GTM track, and the business track. Think of these tracks as your dance instructors, guiding you through each step of your journey to AppExchange stardom.

Technical track

Put on your coding shoes and dive into the development and security aspects of your app. Key milestones in this track include the following:

- **Discovery**: Unravel the mysteries of technical requirements for both your application and the Salesforce platform
- **Defining a strategy**: Choreograph your development and security processes to create a harmonious app
- **Kicking off a security review**: Initiate the security review process, ensuring your app's compliance with Salesforce's strict standards
- **Passing the security review**: Earn a gold star by successfully completing the security review and addressing any identified concerns

GTM track

Get ready to dazzle the crowd with marketing and sales strategies for your app. This track is typically led by a Salesforce Partner Account Manager and involves two milestones, as follows:

- **Setting up an overall GTM strategy**: Craft a master plan to promote and sell your application to eager customers
- **Implementing a marketing plan**: Execute marketing initiatives, such as online promotions, events, and co-marketing with Salesforce, to put your app in the spotlight

Business track

Lastly, focus on the operational and contractual aspects of becoming an AppExchange partner, ensuring your business runs as smoothly as your dance moves. Key milestones in this track include the following:

- **Partner opportunity registration**: Make your interest in becoming a Salesforce partner official by registering and submitting your application

- **Joining the Partner Community**: Gain exclusive access to Salesforce's Partner Community, where resources, support, and networking opportunities await

- **Signing the agreements**: Review and sign on the dotted line for necessary contracts, such as the **Salesforce Partner Program Agreement (SPPA)** and the **Partner Application Distribution Agreement (PADA)**

- **Drafting the technology strategy**: Plan your technology roadmap and development plans for future performances

- **Publishing the app on the AppExchange marketplace**: Take center stage by publishing your application on the AppExchange marketplace, making it available to Salesforce customers

While the onboarding process may not always follow this exact order, these milestones will serve as a handy guide to navigating your journey as a Salesforce partner. By focusing on the technical, GTM, and business aspects of becoming an AppExchange partner, you can build a successful and thriving business within the Salesforce ecosystem—and look like a dance pro while doing it. The following diagram provides a visual representation of the three main tracks to ensure your success as an ISV partner:

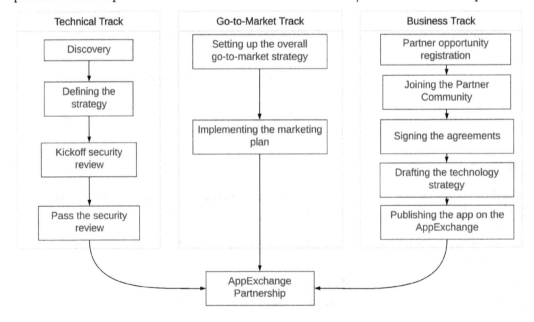

Figure 2.1: AppExchange Partner onboarding process

Joining the AppExchange Partner Community

Joining the AppExchange Partner Community is like getting a golden ticket to Willy Wonka's chocolate factory but for Salesforce enthusiasts. Becoming an AppExchange ISV partner starts with this magical hub, which gives you access to resources, support cases, events, and forums.

So, how do you snag this ticket to the Salesforce world? Follow these simple steps:

- Visit `partners.salesforce.com` and click **Become a Salesforce Partner**—no need for a candy bar purchase here.

- Proceed with the sign-up process. Even if you are already a Salesforce user, it's recommended to avoid using your Salesforce customer credentials. Instead, create an entirely new username for your partner instance. Complete the form, hit **Submit**, and wait for that sweet confirmation email.

- Click the link in the email to set a permanent password and verify your account, thus unlocking your 12-month PBO trial.

- Return to `partners.salesforce.com`, log in with Salesforce, and grant access to the identity URL service as though you're opening the door to a whole new world.

And there you have it—you've got access to your PBO, the Enterprise Edition of Salesforce, with a 12-month trial.

Just one more thing to note—you're going to have to activate your PBO licenses. This is done by logging a case in the Partner Community, and it's something you'll need to do after you sign the PADA (don't worry; we're going to cover that in the next section). If you don't, your trial PBO will expire after 12 months, and you don't want that to happen. The easiest and most straightforward way to sidestep this potential hassle is to set a reminder in your calendar for a few months from now. That way, you can check to ensure your PBO trial is still active and hasn't been deactivated due to the expiration of the trial period. Now that you're part of the Partner Community, get ready to maximize your partnership with Salesforce and the AppExchange ecosystem.

It's worth highlighting that joining the AppExchange Partner Community is completely free, and it comes with the unparalleled benefit of obtaining a PBO at no cost—a refreshing contrast to the industry's typical high licensing fees.

Partner agreements – the fun part (seriously)

Welcome to the exciting world of Salesforce AppExchange Partner Program legalities! While the thought of legal agreements may make you want to curl up and binge-watch your favorite TV show, I promise to make this section as entertaining and informative as possible. So, grab a cup of coffee (or tea, if you're fancy), and let's dive into the delightful realm of partner agreements!

SPPA

Picture the SPPA as the treasure map to your Salesforce partnership success. It's not just any click-through agreement—it's the one that guides you through the maze of Salesforce Partner Programs and the Partner Community. And let's not forget the exciting sidekick—the Salesforce Partner Program Policies, providing specific guidance tailored to each partner program type.

Embarking on your Salesforce partnership adventure

As a new Salesforce partner, your thrilling adventure begins when you accept the SPPA while logging in to the Partner Community for the first time. You'll need an authorized representative from your company to review and accept the SPPA, but don't worry—they don't need a law degree to get the job done.

The SPPA – a one-way ticket to the Partner Community

The SPPA is like the golden ticket that grants you access to the Partner Community. But remember, it's non-negotiable. Just as you can't change the rules of gravity, you can't change the terms of the SPPA.

Navigating the partnership terrain

The SPPA lays the groundwork for accessing the Partner Community and joining the Partner Program, while the Policies act as a trusty compass, providing more detailed guidance for specific partner programs. Make sure you read both documents thoroughly —after all, you wouldn't start a road trip without a map and a sense of direction, would you?

Business approval for your AppExchange solution

The next crucial stage in launching your AppExchange solution involves submitting it for business approval. This process necessitates that every ISV Partner planning to bring a new application to market submit a business plan.

Crafting a business plan for the AppExchange marketplace – the recipe for app-tastic success

If the AppExchange marketplace were a delicious cake, your business plan would be the secret ingredient that makes it a showstopper. To excel in this competitive marketplace and ensure you meet Salesforce's high standards for ethics and integrity, let's bake a mouth-watering business plan together. This section will serve as your recipe, guiding you through the essential ingredients of an AppExchange-tailored business plan and how to use the AppExchange publishing console to whip up a plan that'll impress Salesforce.

Business plan submission and approval process – the kitchen prep

Before your masterpiece graces the shelves of the AppExchange marketplace, Salesforce needs a taste of your business plan. The business plan consists of three sections, as follows:

- **Business Details**: Aim for concise yet comprehensive answers. As a new partner, it might be tempting to provide exhaustive details, but Salesforce typically appreciates direct and to-the-point responses.

- **Product Architecture**: Again, clarity is key. Offer a clear overview without diving too deep into technical jargon.

- **Compliance Certification**: This is required only for paid AppExchange listings.

Once your business plan is ready, submit it for review. Salesforce will give you feedback to perfect your recipe, either approving it or suggesting improvements. If needed, you can resubmit it after addressing the comments.

Business details – the foundation layer

This section is the base of your cake, helping Salesforce understand how your company fits into its product ecosystem. It includes the following aspects:

- **Market research and analysis**: Get to know your target market, competition, and existing solutions in the AppExchange marketplace. This knowledge will help you identify market gaps and position your product effectively.

- **Application development strategy**: Address the technical aspects, challenges, and solutions for developing your app and integrating it with Salesforce. In *Chapter 4*, you'll get a handle on ISV-specific technologies.

- **Defining your value proposition**: What makes your app the cherry on top? Articulate the unique features and benefits that set your application apart from competitors. The strategies covered in *Chapter 3* will assist you with this.

- **Revenue model and pricing strategy**: Choose a revenue model that fits your app and market, and decide on a competitive pricing strategy. This is also addressed in *Chapter 3*.

- **Marketing and sales strategy**: Whip up a comprehensive plan to promote your app within the Salesforce ecosystem, including creating a compelling AppExchange listing. We'll be delving into that in *Chapter 8*.

- **Customer support and success plan**: Keep your customers satisfied by offering various support channels and resources to help them get the most from your app. In *Chapter 9*, you'll get to explore a few options.

- **Financial projections and key performance indicators (KPIs)**: Estimate potential revenue, expenses, and profitability, and define KPIs to track your app's success. *Chapter 12* delves into the most prevalent KPIs.

- **Implementation timeline and milestones**: Plan your development, launch, and maintenance timeline, including key milestones and deadlines.

Product architecture

In the spirit of the cake metaphor, let's consider the Product Architecture section as the intricate cake structure hidden beneath the frosting. It's time to put on your hard hat and dive into the technical nitty-gritty of your app's construction. Just as with any good architect, you'll need to provide Salesforce with a comprehensive blueprint of your product's design.

This section should cover the following aspects:

- **How your app stores credentials, passwords, and other sensitive data**: Think of this as the secret vault within your cake castle, keeping all the important treasures safe and secure

- **The architecture and design of your product**: Your app's floor plan, if you will, including technology stack, programming languages, frameworks, and any third-party libraries or services

- **Integration with other systems and applications**: It's like the plumbing and wiring that connects your app to the greater Salesforce landscape

- **Handling security and data privacy concerns**: The ever-vigilant guards protecting the realm of your app

The purpose of this section is to demonstrate that your app follows Salesforce best practices for architecture and design—like a well-designed, earthquake-resistant cake tower.

Compliance certification

For paid AppExchange listings, it's time to convince Salesforce that your company is a reliable and ethical business partner. Consider the Compliance Certification section as the Michelin star of the app world. To earn this prestigious accolade, you need to present your company's business practices and relationships in the best light.

Include the following ingredients:

- **Legal structure, ownership, and financial stability**: The foundational pillars of your app bakery.

- **Any past legal or regulatory issues**: If any mishaps occurred in the kitchen, it's time to address them and show how you've improved.

- **Data privacy and security practices**: How you protect customer data and comply with applicable laws and regulations. It's like having a top-notch sanitation rating for your bakery.

- **Third-party relationships or partnerships**: Showcase how these collaborations align with Salesforce's values and policies, such as teaming up with the best pastry chefs in town.

Overall, the Compliance Certification section should demonstrate that your company is a trustworthy and reliable partner for Salesforce and its customers—the proof is in the pudding, after all.

Voilà! A well-crafted business plan is ready! By addressing each section of the business plan, you'll ensure that your app meets Salesforce's standards and contributes to your business's growth. With careful planning and execution, your app can become the *pièce de résistance* of the Salesforce ecosystem. *Bon appétit!*

Call with the AppExchange ISV Partner team

After submitting your business plan, the ISV AppExchange Partner team meticulously reviews your proposal. Following its review, they may reach out for feedback or to request additional information. This is when an initial, informal discussion takes place. This call is not just a review; it's a valuable opportunity for you to ask questions, explore opportunities, and understand how the team can assist and support you in your journey as a potential partner.

During the conversation, the ISV AppExchange Partner team might identify areas that require your attention. If any issues arise, you're provided with an opportunity to rectify them and resubmit your plan. After this discussion, having gained a thorough understanding of your submission and development timeframe, the team might arrange further calls, if necessary, and will guide you toward the next steps.

The next phase of this process involves the execution of the PADA. This agreement sets out the specifics of your partnership with Salesforce and the distribution of your application through the AppExchange marketplace.

PADA

Think of the PADA as the secret sauce in the Salesforce AppExchange Partner Program sandwich. It governs partners participating in the ISVforce and OEM categories and outlines the terms and conditions for distributing applications. The PADA is like the chef's special that brings all the ingredients together, making it a must-have before sharing your app with the Salesforce ecosystem.

A dash of flexibility – security review first, sign later

The PADA has a unique flavor—it allows partners to submit their applications for a security review even before signing the agreement. It's like getting a sneak peek at dessert before finishing your appetizer. However, partners can't start selling until they've savored every bite of the PADA process with Salesforce.

Here are three key ingredients of the PADA:

- **Percentage Net Revenue (PNR)**: It's the amount and type of revenue that partners share with Salesforce, like splitting the bill after a fancy dinner

- **Partner application description (or combined solution description)**: It's the legal description of the partner's application, which helps calculate PNR, just like reading the menu to know what you're ordering

- **Product Catalog**: It's the list of products and services offered by the partner within the Salesforce ecosystem, like a shopping list for your Salesforce pantry

Understanding these elements can help partners cook up a successful partnership with Salesforce, even if they're not the ones directly negotiating the PADA.

The ISVforce Addendum

When partners decide to build an app for the AppExchange marketplace using the ISVforce app distribution model, they need to add the ISVforce Addendum to their PADA. This extra ingredient covers various aspects, such as partner relationships, customer relationships, fees, and marketing.

The PADA's shelf life

The PADA, with its ISVforce Addendum, initially has a 3-year term, and like a fine wine, it auto-renews for additional 1-year periods unless either party decides it's time for a new vintage or terminates the agreement earlier.

Leveraging the AppExchange Partner Toolkit

As an AppExchange partner, having the right tools at your disposal is instrumental in navigating your journey successfully. Just as a seasoned adventurer wouldn't venture into the wilderness without a reliable compass, a sturdy pair of boots, and a well-stocked backpack, you wouldn't want to delve into the dynamic landscape of the AppExchange marketplace without your own set of tools.

In this section, we are going to unveil the AppExchange Partner Toolkit, an assortment of resources designed to empower partners such as you. The aim is to familiarize you with the key tools available, each serving its unique purpose, to help you streamline your operations, manage your customers, and effectively deploy your applications.

Armed with the knowledge of these tools, you'll be well-equipped to scale the heights of the AppExchange ecosystem. So, let's embark on this exciting expedition to uncover the AppExchange Partner Toolkit.

PBO features and capabilities

Dear reader, welcome aboard the magical mystery tour of the PBO, your very own Salesforce command center, where dreams of managing your business operations come true. No need to pinch yourself—this is real, and it's time to explore the PBO's features.

Your PBO is your versatile sidekick, ready to do the following:

- Woo new customers with Salesforce CRM apps
- Manage scratch orgs and second-generation managed packages efficiently with the **Developer Hub** (**Dev Hub**)
- Create test orgs using the Environment Hub
- Keep your leads and licenses in check with the **License Management App** (**LMA**)
- Manage application features effectively with the **Feature Management App** (**FMA**)
- Slay the order submission game with the **Channel Order App** (**COA**)
- Seamlessly manage payments with Checkout
- Be the superhero your customers need with the Subscriber Support Console

The Environment Hub – your secret laboratory for app testing and packaging

Picture this: you're a mad scientist (in the most endearing way, of course) concocting the perfect AppExchange potion. Your laboratory? The Environment Hub. It's here that you can perfect your app's recipe by creating test orgs, streamlining packaging, fostering collaboration, and keeping track of all your experiments. Let's dive into the benefits of this fantastic laboratory of yours.

Here are some benefits of using the Environment Hub:

- **Easily create test orgs**: Much as with a master chef testing out different ingredients, the Environment Hub allows you to whip up test orgs for various Salesforce editions and configurations. This ensures your app is fully compatible and performs optimally in every kitchen (ahem, environment) it lands in.

- **Streamline app packaging**: Consistency is key, whether it's in your secret sauce or app packaging. The Environment Hub helps ensure that your app is packaged uniformly across environments, making it a breeze to deploy and distribute.

- **Improve collaboration**: Cooking is always more fun with friends. The Environment Hub lets you share environments with your team members, making the testing process a collaborative and efficient endeavor. Together, you'll identify and resolve issues faster than a soufflé can rise.

- **Centralized tracking**: Keep your laboratory organized with the Environment Hub's centralized view of all your environments. Easily track vital information such as creation date, edition, and expiration date, ensuring your environments stay up-to-date and compliant with Salesforce requirements.

Accessing the Environment Hub – finding your way to the lab

Ready to put on your lab coat and goggles? Here's how to access the Environment Hub:

1. Log in to your PBO.
2. Click the **App Launcher** icon in the top-left corner.
3. Search for **Environment Hub** and select it from the search results.

Now that you've found your way to this secret laboratory, it's time to channel your inner mad scientist and start experimenting.

LMA – your personal bouncer for app licenses

You're going to be the proud owner of an exclusive club (your app) on the bustling AppExchange street. The LMA is your trusty bouncer, keeping track of all the guests (licenses) entering and leaving your establishment. In this section, we'll learn about the benefits of having the LMA as your bouncer, give you a tour of the **License Management Org** (**LMO**), and explain the relationship between the LMO and your PBO.

Overview of the LMA

The LMA is designed to keep your club's guest list (licenses) in check, and with the LMA, you can do the following:

1. Monitor and manage your clientele, including those on trial visits and VIPs with paid access.
2. Control the guest list by enabling or disabling licenses like a velvet rope.
3. Track customer attendance and app popularity.
4. Access customer orgs for support purposes using the Subscriber Support Console.

The LMA incorporates three custom objects: Package, Package Version, and License. The Package object serves as the foundational entity, encompassing all LMA data. Each Package object can encompass multiple Package Versions, which in turn can be associated with numerous Licenses. Every License corresponds directly to a single Lead. Notably, when a Lead undergoes manual conversion into an Account and Contact, the associated License seamlessly links to the newly converted records. The following **entity relationship diagram (ERD)** provides a visual representation of these intricate connections between custom and standard Salesforce objects:

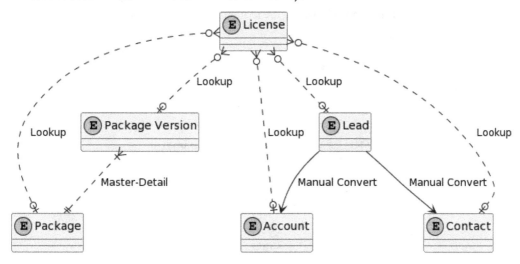

Figure 2.2: Entity relationship diagram of LMA system entities and their relationships

The LMO

The LMO is like the exclusive backstage area of your Salesforce organization, where you can track all Salesforce users that install your managed package on Salesforce AppExchange. Whenever a user installs or uninstalls your package, the LMO gets notified with a lead record, like an autograph from each guest. The LMO tracks each package uploaded on Salesforce AppExchange and can be any Salesforce Enterprise or Unlimited organization that has installed the free LMA from AppExchange.

The best option is to have LMO installed in your PBO. This means that your PBO serves as the central repository for all license information related to your app installations, keeping everything neatly organized behind the scenes.

FMA for managing app features

You can think of the FMA as a maestro ready to orchestrate a memorable experience for each guest at your club. We'll explore the core concepts, use cases, and the two FMA parameters: LMO-to-Subscriber feature parameters, and Subscriber-to-LMO feature parameters.

Understanding the FMA

The FMA is not mandatory to use, but it can be the mastermind behind your app, orchestrating the perfect blend of features and functionality for each customer. Built on top of the LMA, the FMA allows you to fine-tune **user experiences (UXs)** by controlling what users see and how they interact with your app. Consider the FMA the conductor of your app's symphony, guiding every note to create a harmonious experience.

Here is an Entity relationship diagram, illustrating the relationships between various entities in the FMA:

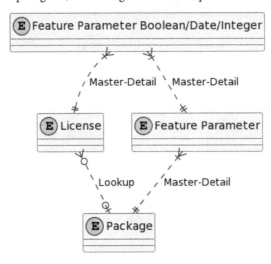

Figure 2.3: Entity relationship diagram of FMA entities and their relationships

FMA use cases

The FMA can perform various tunes to cater to your guests' preferences. Here are a few examples:

- **Freemium model**: Customize features based on whether a client has a paid or free license type
- **Piloting betas**: Release new features to a select group of customers for testing without affecting current users
- **Streamlining development**: Reduce development time and overhead by managing multiple applications using the FMA, strategically aligning features to leverage the existing code base

Enabling and disabling features with LMO-to-Subscriber feature parameters

LMO-to-Subscriber feature parameters are like the maestro's wand, enabling or disabling features with a simple flick. These parameters are writable on your end and read-only for your subscribers, and can be used to control access to certain features or set limits on resource usage. Want to offer a sneak peek of a new feature? No problem! Enable it for a limited trial period and watch the excitement unfold. Just update the related feature parameters in your LMO, and let the magic happen in your code.

Tracking preferences and activation metrics with Subscriber-to-LMO feature parameters

Subscriber-to-LMO feature parameters are the maestro's attentive ears, listening to the feature activation preferences of your subscribers. With values assigned by your subscribers and sent to your LMO, you can collect insights and adapt your performance to their liking. Just update the feature parameters in your subscriber's org using Apex code, and you're good to go.

FMA considerations

While designing your FMA strategy, it's essential to keep a few things in mind, as follows:

- A fully managed package cannot be hidden or revealed using the FMA. However, you can provide a **call to action** (**CTA**) for users to access the features.

- Testing can be challenging as there's no test LMO, and the documentation might be unclear. Developers need to perform a dark launch to the packaging environment for testing.

- Develop a features strategy, keeping in mind the 200-feature limit per managed package.

- Only three types of FMA flags are available: **Boolean**, **Integer**, and **Date**.

- You can adjust feature parameters in your LMO manually. However, suppose your solution has many feature parameters that must be changed from their default settings for paying customers upon installation. In that case, it might be a good idea to automate this process. Consider setting up a record-triggered flow on the License object to make things smoother.

Unlocking the full potential of your PBO

As you already know, your PBO is a standard Salesforce org, which means it can be customized and extended to meet your specific needs through local development or by installing managed packages. To help you unlock your PBO's full potential, let's discuss three primary ways of extending it: installing an AppExchange app (either generic or dedicated to ISVs, such as Package Visualizer), using an open-source project (like ISV Cockpit), or custom development.

Package Visualizer

The Salesforce Labs-created Package Visualizer[1] app is a free managed package that improves your AppExchange experience by giving you a convenient way to view your packages, version ancestry, and subscriber data. You can install it directly from AppExchange. With its seamless integration with LMA, Package Visualizer allows you to manage your apps with ease and efficiency. Furthermore, Package Visualizer simplifies obtaining detailed logs for package usage. It offers valuable insights, empowering informed decisions in package development and management. We will explore this further in *Chapter 10*.

The Package Visualizer app features a split-view design that simplifies navigation, allowing you to explore package details, versions, and subscribers in a graphical manner. With the upgrade scheduling functionality, efficiently planning and executing upgrades ensures that your customers always have access to the latest version of your app.

Salesforce ISV Cockpit

The Salesforce ISV Cockpit[2] app is an open source native Salesforce app that extends the functionality of the LMA in your PBO. It allows you to monitor the health of your apps and provide proactive support to subscribers experiencing errors. When an error occurs in a managed package, your app can send error notifications to a specified email address. ISV Cockpit leverages this feature by receiving and parsing those emails. By combining this information with data from the LMA, the ISV Cockpit app can accurately assign each incoming error to a customer account, package, package version, and license. Additionally, it extracts information about the error type and location.

All this data is stored in a single Custom Object, enabling easy reporting and the creation of sophisticated support workflows.

Custom development

One of the significant advantages of using your PBO is the flexibility to customize and extend its capabilities. In your PBO, everything is built upon Salesforce objects, including standard objects such as Accounts, Leads, and Contacts, as well as custom objects related to LMA such as Licenses, Packages, and Package Versions. This flexibility allows you to create customizations that support your business goals.

Let's take a look at two examples of local customizations that can improve your customer retention and sales processes.

---

1 https://appexchange.salesforce.com/
   appxListingDetail?listingId=a0N4V00000FNBc0UAH
2 https://github.com/rsoesemann/salesforce-isv-cockpit

Alert sales reps before a license expires

To ensure that your customers' licenses are renewed on time and prevent potential losses, you can set up a flow to automatically email a sales rep on your team before the license expires. To do this, proceed as follows:

- Create an email template for the notification.
- Use Salesforce Flow's **Get Records** element to fetch licenses nearing expiration. Set up a condition to specify enough time before the expiration date to discuss renewal options.
- Use the **Send Email** element in the flow to send an email notification. Here, choose the email template you created in the first step and specify a sales rep or team member as the recipient.
- Activate your flow to start notifying sales reps before a license expires.

Notify customer-retention specialists when an offering is uninstalled

Understanding why a customer uninstalls your offering can help improve your offering or restore the business relationship. By setting up another flow, you can notify a customer-retention specialist on your team when an offering is uninstalled. To do this, proceed as follows:

1. Create an email template for the notification.
2. In Salesforce Flow, create a new Record-Triggered Flow. Choose the **A record is an updated** option for the trigger. Specify the offering object and set the condition to trigger the flow when the **License Status** field equals **Uninstalled**.
3. In the flow builder, add a **Send Email** action. For this action, choose the email template you created in the first step and specify the customer retention specialist as the recipient.
4. Save and activate your flow. Now, the customer retention specialist will be automatically notified whenever an offering is uninstalled.

Many ISVs focus primarily on building their managed packages but often overlook the potential of customizing their PBOs to support their business goals. By leveraging the power of Salesforce objects and combining AppExchange apps with open-source solutions and custom development, you can create a powerful, flexible PBO tailored to your specific needs. As a result, you will be better equipped to drive better customer experiences and improve business processes. Don't make the same mistake as others; take advantage of the customization opportunities that Salesforce offers to maximize your PBO's potential.

Summary

Throughout this chapter, fellow trailblazers, we've journeyed deeper into the Salesforce ecosystem, exploring the secrets of becoming a successful AppExchange partner. We've trekked through the wilderness of crafting tailored business plans and deciphered the maps that are the key partnership agreements.

Together, we've navigated the AppExchange Partner Community and learned how to use its resources to enhance our expedition. We've also discovered the value of the AppExchange Partner Toolkit, our trusty compass guiding us toward success in the Salesforce landscape.

But, adventurers, don't rest on your laurels yet! Our journey is far from over. Ahead, we see the green valley of designing customer-centric applications. We'll dive into the vibrant flora and fauna of customer needs, mapping their journeys, and crafting applications that align with their hidden desires. Plus, we're going to learn the ins and outs of strategic pricing models. This isn't just important; it's the link between our customer-focused apps and the customers themselves. Onward, trailblazers!

Further reading

- *AppExchange ISV Onboarding Guide*: https://www.appexchangeguides.com/e/appexchange-isv-onboarding-guide-jcvehuiiqzjsr/g9IpAtAM

- *Managing Licenses for Managed Packages*: https://developer.salesforce.com/docs/atlas.en-us.workbook_lma.meta/workbook_lma/lma_intro.htm

3

Designing Customer-Centric Applications

Welcome back, steadfast pioneers! As our thrilling journey through the winding Salesforce ecosystem and bustling AppExchange marketplace unfolds, we focus on the exciting challenge of designing customer-centric applications and optimal pricing strategies.

You might be wondering, "Why is all this so important?" Well, let's lean on the wisdom of two thought leaders. Harvard Business School marketing professor Theodore Levitt famously said, "People don't want to buy a quarter-inch drill. They want a quarter-inch hole!" He was stressing that people don't buy products; they buy solutions to their problems. Similarly, Clayton Christensen asserts, "People buy products and services to get a job done". Their insights underline our direction in this chapter— understanding what job your customer needs done and how your application can be the drill to achieve it.

In this exploration, we'll cover the following:

- Identifying customer needs and pain points to truly understand the "hole" your customers need

- Creating value propositions aligned with customer needs to design the "drill" that makes the perfect "hole"

- Mapping customer journeys to visualize and improve the path your customers take to get their job done

- Unravel the ancient art of selecting the right pricing model for your AppExchange application, an endeavor rivaling the thrill of a treasure hunt

- Learn the wisdom of understanding customer willingness to pay, a talent as vital as brewing the perfect cup of coffee on a Monday morning

- Decode the cryptic process of identifying your app's core value and aligning pricing with customer segments, a task as intricate and exciting as assembling IKEA furniture without the manual

With the acumen gathered from this chapter, you'll be well-prepared to devise applications that deliver not just solutions, but memorable user experiences. Use this newfound knowledge to create standout applications that resonate with customers in the AppExchange marketplace. So, put on your explorer hats, fellow pioneers, as we delve deeper into the Salesforce ecosystem and unearth strategies for crafting captivating user-centric applications!

Identifying customer needs and pain points

Picture this: you've spent countless hours brainstorming, designing, and developing an application that you believe is the next big thing on the AppExchange. You're confident that it will revolutionize the way people do business. But then, when you finally launch it, you're met with... crickets. What went wrong?

Reasons why innovation projects fail

Innovation is a crucial aspect of any business that wants to remain competitive and relevant in today's fast-paced world. However, despite the importance of innovation, many companies struggle to come up with successful innovation projects. One of the main reasons why innovation projects fail is because there is no agreement on what a "need" even is. Different people have different definitions of what constitutes a need, and this can lead to confusion and miscommunication within an organization. For example, some people might define a need as something that solves a specific problem, while others might define it as something that fulfills a desire or want. This lack of clarity can make it difficult for companies to identify unmet customer needs and develop solutions that address those needs.

Another reason why innovation projects fail is that many companies take an "ideas-first" approach to innovation. In this approach, companies brainstorm or come up with product or service ideas and then test them with customers to see how well the ideas address their needs. While this approach may seem logical at first glance, it has several flaws.

First, generating more ideas does not meaningfully improve the probability that someone will come up with the optimal idea to satisfy unmet customer needs. People are in effect brainstorming ideas without ever knowing what all the customers' needs are or which of those needs are most important.

Second, when companies start with an idea rather than a need, they risk developing solutions that don't actually solve any real problems for customers. This can result in wasted time and resources, as well as missed opportunities for growth.

In contrast to the "ideas-first" approach, some companies take a "needs-first" approach to innovation. In this approach, companies first learn what customers' needs are by conducting research and gathering data from various sources. They then identify which needs are unmet and devise a solution that addresses those unmet needs. This approach is more effective because it ensures that companies are developing solutions that actually solve real problems for customers.

To implement a "needs-first" approach to innovation, companies need to have a clear understanding of the different types of customer needs. The **jobs-to-be-done** (**JTBD**) framework is useful for categorizing, defining, capturing, and organizing the six types of customer needs. These are functional needs, emotional needs, social needs, situational needs, supporting needs, and epistemic needs.

Your ideal customer profile

Before delving into the nuances of designing customer-centric applications, it's imperative to establish a foundational understanding of the ideal customer profile (ICP). The ICP isn't merely an introductory concept; it's the cornerstone upon which successful, customer-focused designs are built.

What is an ICP?

An ICP is a detailed description of the most suitable customer for a particular product or service. It's not just a target market or a buyer persona; it's a precise profile of the company or individual that would get the most value from your product and, in turn, provide the most value to your business.

There are several reasons why it's beneficial to have a well-defined ICP:

- **Focused marketing and sales efforts**: With a clear ICP, ISVs can direct their marketing and sales resources more efficiently, ensuring that they're reaching out to prospects that are more likely to convert

- **Higher conversion rates**: When you know who your ideal customer is, your messaging resonates better, leading to higher conversion rates and shorter sales cycles

- **Improved product development**: Understanding your ICP can provide insights into feature development, ensuring that the product evolves in a direction that continues to serve and delight the ideal customer

- **Better customer relationships**: When you're serving your ideal customers, they're more likely to be satisfied and become long-term, loyal users of your product

A meticulously defined ICP ensures that the product or service being offered resonates and aligns with the desires and needs of those who stand to derive the most benefit from it.

However, there's a common trap that many fall into, especially during the early stages of a product's lifecycle: the allure of the "sell to all" approach. While it might seem advantageous to cater to a broad spectrum of potential customers, this strategy often backfires. It can dilute the core value of the product, leading to wasted resources and a scattered focus.

Moreover, the clarity of a product's strategy is closely tied to the ICP. Without a clear understanding of and focus on the ICP, the product's strategic direction can become convoluted. While the idea of serving a vast audience has its appeal, it often poses challenges in maintaining the product's market positioning and evolutionary path.

Beyond just conceptualizing the ICP, it's crucial to document it. A mere mental image or abstract idea of the ideal customer isn't sufficient. Having a written representation of the ICP serves as a beacon for the entire team, ensuring a unified understanding and approach toward the target audience.

By defining and understanding your ICP, you're now in the position to effectively apply the JTBD framework to define jobs related to the right customers. This approach ensures that you cater to the actual needs of your target group, rather than trying to please everyone and running the risk that your app doesn't truly resonate with any specific audience.

Navigating the JTBD framework

The JTBD theory is like an adventurer's compass, guiding us toward the hidden treasures of customer needs. It provides a framework for categorizing, defining, capturing, and organizing the six types of customer needs, which are essential for creating innovative and successful products and services.

The core functional JTBD

Imagine the core functional job as the treasure we seek on our map. It's the primary task your customers aim to accomplish or the chief challenge they desire to overcome with your AppExchange application. For example, a task management app may address the core job of managing tasks efficiently. Grasping this core functional job equips us to create applications that directly tackle our customers' main needs and enhance their user experience.

Desired outcomes on the core functional job

Having found our treasure, i.e., the core functional job, we focus on the desired outcomes. Think of these as the jewels encrusting our treasure —these are the criteria your customers use to gauge success while executing the core functional job. For example, there are a few AppExchange apps that aid in improving sales performance – a desired outcome for sales-driven organizations. Recognizing and catering to these desired outcomes helps us fashion applications that not only meet but exceed customer expectations.

Related jobs

Related jobs are akin to the side quests our customers undertake either before, during, or after the core functional job. Identifying these quests, such as tracking time spent on each task in a task management app, and incorporating them into our application design can enrich our offerings, making them more comprehensive, valuable, and enticing to customers.

Emotional and social jobs

Beyond sheer functionality, customers harbor emotional and social needs associated with using your application. Emotional and social jobs illustrate how customers aspire to feel or be perceived while carrying out the core functional job. An app, which enhances document generation, could make customers feel more efficient and productive, addressing their emotional job. Meeting these needs can foster solid emotional connections and breed customer loyalty.

Consumption chain jobs

Consumption chain jobs are tasks performed by your support team throughout your application's lifecycle, from installation to maintenance, and eventual disposal. Taking care of these jobs, such as Ask Your Document does with its easy setup and integrations for their tool, can boost the overall customer experience, crafting a sense of lasting satisfaction.

Financial desired outcomes

Finally, the financial desired outcomes serve as the monetary and performance metrics your customers depend on when choosing which AppExchange application to install. By understanding these outcomes, we can construct compelling value propositions that resonate with our target audience, ensuring our application is the treasure they've been seeking on their AppExchange map.

Why would someone hire your product?

The JTBD framework helps you understand that customers "hire" products or services to get a job done in their roles. These jobs can be functional, social, or emotional in nature. Understanding the job that customers are trying to accomplish, rather than focusing solely on their demographic information or preferences, can help ISVs innovate and improve their offerings.

The framework encourages you to ask questions such as:

- What is the fundamental problem or need that customers are trying to solve?
- What progress are customers trying to make in their lives?
- What obstacles or challenges do customers face in achieving their desired progress?

By deeply understanding the job that customers are trying to accomplish, partners can develop products, services, and experiences that better align with those needs. This approach can lead to more successful innovation, customer satisfaction, and, ultimately, business growth.

Innovating for customers who (at this moment) don't hire any product

When considering customers who do not hire any product to get a job done, the JTBD framework can still be valuable in several ways:

- **Identifying latent needs**: Sometimes customers may not be aware of existing solutions or may not find existing products satisfactory for their needs. By understanding the job they are trying to accomplish, you can uncover latent needs and identify opportunities for innovation. This allows them to develop new products or services that better address those unmet needs.

- **Market segmentation**: Examining customers who don't currently hire any product to do a specific job can provide insights into untapped market segments. By understanding why these customers haven't found a suitable solution yet, you can tailor their offerings to cater to these segments and capture new market opportunities.

- **Disruptive innovation**: The JTBD framework is particularly helpful for disruptive innovations. Disruptive innovations often emerge by addressing jobs that traditional products or services fail to adequately address. By understanding the job that customers are struggling to accomplish, partners can develop disruptive solutions that meet those needs more effectively and potentially disrupt existing markets.

- **Product iteration and improvement**: Even if customers are currently using products to get a job done, the JTBD framework can help identify areas for improvement. By understanding the job in more detail, you can refine their products or services to better align with customer needs, enhance the user experience, and create more value.

Leveraging JTBD for essential features

In today's fast-paced and competitive business landscape, it's crucial to keep your product lean and focused on its core purpose. The temptation to add numerous features and functionalities can be overwhelming, but it often leads to unnecessary complexity and dilution of the product's value proposition. To avoid this pitfall and ensure that your product remains focused on its core idea, leveraging the JTBD framework is essential.

This framework provides a customer-centric approach that emphasizes understanding the fundamental job customers are trying to accomplish with your product. By focusing on this core job, you can identify the essential features required to address customers' needs effectively. This approach helps you prioritize and streamline the development process, avoiding the inclusion of nonessential features that may distract from the core purpose of your product.

By adopting the mindset of keeping your product lean and focused, you can enhance its usability, relevance, and value to customers. This approach not only prevents unnecessary feature overload but also enables you to deliver a streamlined and purposeful product that directly addresses customers' needs. It allows you to avoid the pitfalls of feature creep and maintain a clear and compelling value proposition.

The JTBD framework can be a powerful tool in helping businesses focus on the core meaning of their products and avoid adding nonessential features. Here's how it helps in this regard:

- **Customer-centric approach**: The framework puts the customer and their job at the center of product development. Instead of getting caught up in adding features based on assumptions or internal preferences, partners using the JTBD framework actively seek to understand the core functional job that customers are trying to accomplish. This customer-centric approach helps prioritize features that directly contribute to fulfilling that core job, avoiding unnecessary additions.

- **Desired outcomes focus**: Within the framework, there is an emphasis on understanding the desired outcomes that customers have while trying to accomplish their core job. By deeply understanding these desired outcomes, you can align your product development efforts with what truly matters to customers. This allows you to concentrate on developing features and functionalities that directly support those outcomes while eliminating nonessential features that may not contribute to the core purpose of the product.

- **Clear problem-solving perspective**: The JTBD framework encourages partners to view their product as a solution to a specific problem customers are facing. This problem-solving perspective helps maintain focus on addressing the core problem effectively and efficiently. It helps you continually question and evaluate whether additional features or functionalities are necessary to solve the problem at hand or if they are just adding unnecessary complexity.

- **Minimizing scope creep**: Scope creep refers to the tendency of a project to expand beyond its original boundaries, often resulting in feature overload. By using the JTBD framework, you can define the boundaries of their product based on the core job customers need to accomplish. This clearly defined scope helps prevent the inclusion of nonessential features that may dilute the product's value proposition and distract from its primary purpose.

- **Continuous validation**: The JTBD framework promotes an iterative and customer-centric approach to product development. By continuously gathering customer feedback and insights throughout the product lifecycle, you can validate and refine their understanding of the core job and the essential features required. This ongoing validation helps ensure that the product remains focused on its core meaning and avoids the addition of unnecessary features that may not align with customer needs.

In conclusion, adopting a lean and focused approach to product development helps ISVs create applications that resonate with customers and provide real value. By leveraging this approach, you can ensure that your product remains focused on its core purpose and avoid the addition of unnecessary features. As we transition to the next section, we will explore the concept of feature shock and discuss strategies to prevent it from negatively impacting your application's job specification.

Avoiding feature shock

As we explore the art of designing customer-centric applications, it's essential to address the potential pitfall of feature shock. Feature shock occurs when an application becomes bloated with too many features, leading to complexity and confusion for users. To create applications that resonate with customers and provide real value, we must focus on essential features that directly address customer needs.

Prioritize core functionality

Start by identifying the primary job your customers need to accomplish with your application. Focus on developing features that directly contribute to solving that core problem and avoid adding unnecessary features that may dilute the value proposition or confuse users.

Understand desired outcomes

Analyze the desired outcomes your customers expect while executing the core functional job. Align your application's features to meet or exceed these expectations, ensuring that your product delivers value and enhances the user experience.

Keep it lean and focused

Resist the temptation to add numerous features to your application. Instead, adopt a lean and focused approach to product development, prioritizing features that directly address customer needs and contribute to the core purpose of your product.

Iterate and validate

Continuously gather customer feedback throughout the product development process. Use this feedback to validate your understanding of customer needs and refine your application's features accordingly. This iterative approach helps ensure that your product remains relevant and valuable to customers.

Monitor and adjust

Regularly review your application's features and performance, looking for opportunities to simplify, streamline, or enhance the user experience. Be prepared to make adjustments as needed to keep your application focused on its core purpose of delivering value to customers.

Creating value propositions aligned with customer needs

Now, we will delve into a powerful tool called the Value Proposition Canvas. The Value Proposition Canvas enables ISVs to uncover and design value propositions that align with customer needs. By connecting the JTBD framework with the Value Proposition Canvas, we can gain deeper insights into customer desires and create compelling offerings. In this section, we will provide a step-by-step guide to help you prepare a Value Proposition Canvas tailored explicitly for your AppExchange app.

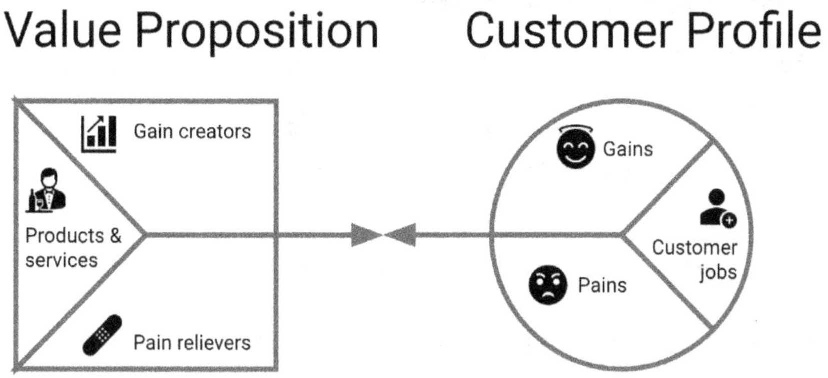

Figure 3.1: An example of a Value Proposition Canvas template

By following the instructions in the next subsections, you will gain a deeper understanding of your target customers, their needs, and how your app can deliver unique value.

Step 1: Define your target customer segments

Having established your ICP, it's time to delve deeper by segmenting within that ICP on the Salesforce platform. Recognize that customer segments are essentially subsets of your broader ICP. By considering variables such as industry, company size, job roles, and specific challenges that your app addresses, you can identify and cater to these nuanced segments. This approach not only sharpens your focus but also allows for a tailored and impactful value proposition for each segment.

For those in the early stages of product development, it's common to have a single segment that mirrors your ICP. This is because, initially, the focus is on a more generalized target to gain traction. However, as your product matures and you aim to reach new markets, it's crucial to revisit this chapter. With growth, the need to define multiple segments becomes apparent, allowing you to cater to the evolving and diverse subsets of your initial ICP. This iterative process ensures that your product remains relevant and continues to meet the needs of a wider audience.

Step 2: Understand customers' JTBD

Delve into the jobs that your target customers are trying to accomplish with your app. Conduct interviews, surveys, or market research to gain insights into their specific challenges, goals, and desired outcomes. By understanding the JTBD, you can better align your app's features and functionalities to address those needs effectively.

Step 3: Create the customer profile

Building on the specific segment identified in *step 1*, you can now craft a detailed customer profile that encapsulates the unique characteristics, motivations, and preferences of this narrower audience. While your ICP provides a broader overview, this profile dives deep into the nuances of the segment, offering insights into demographics, behavioral tendencies, psychographics, and other pertinent details. This in-depth understanding aids in truly empathizing with their specific needs. Ensure that this rich information is visualized and documented within the customer profile section of the Value Proposition Canvas, emphasizing its tailored focus on the segment derived from your overarching ICP.

Step 4: Identify pain points and desired gains

Pinpoint the pain points your target customers experience while trying to accomplish their jobs. These pain points represent the challenges, frustrations, or inefficiencies they face. Simultaneously, identify the desired gains that customers hope to achieve when using your app. These gains can include increased productivity, cost savings, improved decision-making, or enhanced user experience. Make a note of these pain points and desired gains within the Value Proposition Canvas.

Step 5: Design the value map

Now, shift your focus to the value map section of the canvas. Identify the core features and functionalities of your app that directly address the pain points and desired gains identified in the previous steps. Highlight how your app's capabilities alleviate specific pain points and deliver desired gains to customers. Additionally, consider any additional features, pain relievers, or gain creators that can enhance the value your app provides.

Step 6: Validate and iterate

Validate your value proposition by seeking feedback from potential customers, conducting user testing, or engaging in conversations with AppExchange users. Gather insights on how well your app aligns with their needs and refine your Value Proposition Canvas based on this feedback. Continuously iterate and improve your value proposition to ensure that it resonates with your target audience.

If you've already got some users on hand, you can simply get in touch with them using the contact details from your LMA. Reach out and ask if they'd be interested in taking part in a survey or interview.

Now, if we're looking at the period before the product launch, there are two main approaches to consider. If your product is being developed based on your consulting background or expertise in a certain domain, chances are you already have a network of potential customers that you can directly approach.

On the other hand, if you're entering an entirely new market, I'd suggest creating a landing page even before the product exists. This serves as a placeholder for the non-existent product. Then, engage in marketing efforts to persuade potential customers to sign up. After that, you can follow up with them for further engagement.

If you're facing difficulty in finding these initial potential customers, it could be a sign that locating actual, paying customers down the line might prove even more challenging. In such cases, it's worth considering whether pursuing this idea is truly viable.

By following this step-by-step guide, you can effectively prepare a Value Proposition Canvas specifically tailored for your AppExchange app. The canvas will provide a visual representation of how your app aligns with customer needs, highlights its unique value, and differentiates it from competitors.

At its heart, the well-defined value proposition should answer the following fundamental questions:

- **Purpose and functionality**: What is your app designed to do? This is the foundational aspect of your product, the primary function it serves.

- **Problem-solving**: What specific challenges does your app address for businesses? Every product should solve a tangible problem or fill a gap in the market.

- **Clarity and directness**: To effectively market and sell your app, it's crucial to articulate its value in clear, direct terms. This clarity is not just for potential customers but also for internal teams and partners such as Salesforce.

- **Uniqueness**: In a market saturated with similar products, what makes your app stand out? This uniqueness could stem from innovative features, superior performance, or even exceptional customer support.

- **Competitive edge**: Why should anyone choose your app over others? It's essential to pinpoint what you're doing better than anyone else. Ideally, there should be a unique problem that your product addresses better than any other solution in the market.

- **Features and benefits**: Beyond just functionality, what are the key features and benefits that your app offers? These could be technical aspects, user-friendly designs, or even cost-effectiveness.

- **Differentiation**: What is the distinct value that sets your product apart from similar applications in the market? This differentiation is the crux of your value proposition and should be prominently highlighted.

In conclusion, a well-defined value proposition is the narrative that will guide your product's journey. It's the story you tell potential customers, partners, and even your team. As you progress, this narrative will shape your marketing and sales strategies, ensuring your product not only finds its audience but also thrives in a competitive environment.

Remember to regularly review and update your Value Proposition Canvas as you gain new insights and feedback from AppExchange users. By consistently refining your value proposition, you will enhance your app's chances of success and maximize its impact on the AppExchange platform.

Mapping customer journeys

Having understood customers' JTBD and crafted a compelling Value Proposition using the Value Proposition Canvas, the next step is to map out the customer journey. Mapping customer journeys allows ISVs to gain a deep understanding of the customer's interactions, emotions, and touchpoints throughout their experience with your product. In this section, we will explore the process of mapping customer journeys and how it helps clarify the customer experience, shape the product roadmap, and inform the overall business strategy.

The significance of mapping customer journeys

Mapping customer journeys provides partners with a comprehensive view of a customer's end-to-end experience. It goes beyond individual touchpoints and interactions, allowing organizations to understand a customer's holistic journey and the emotions they experience throughout.

Understanding the complete customer experience

Customer journey mapping enables ISVs to gain a deep understanding of the complete customer experience. It helps identify all the touchpoints, from initial awareness to post-purchase support, across various channels and platforms. By mapping out this journey, you can visualize the entire customer lifecycle and gain insights into the customer's interactions with the product or service.

Identifying pain points and opportunities

Mapping customer journeys helps identify pain points and areas of opportunity for improvement. By understanding customers' emotions, challenges, and frustrations at each touchpoint, you can pinpoint areas where the experience falls short. This identification of pain points provides valuable insights for designing solutions that address customer needs and enhance the overall experience.

Enhancing customer-centricity

Customer journey mapping is a key tool for fostering a customer-centric mindset within organizations. By gaining a comprehensive view of the customer's journey, you can align your strategies, processes, and operations to better serve customer needs. It helps shift the focus from internal processes to the customer's perspective, leading to improved customer satisfaction and loyalty.

Driving continuous improvement

Mapping customer journeys enables organizations to continuously improve the customer experience. By visualizing the entire journey, you can identify opportunities for optimization and innovation. The insights gained from mapping customer journeys inform decision-making, allowing organizations to prioritize initiatives that will have the most significant impact on customer satisfaction and business outcomes.

Aligning cross-functional teams

Customer journey mapping facilitates cross-functional collaboration within organizations. It brings together teams from marketing, product development, sales, customer support, and other departments to understand the customer experience as a whole. By aligning these teams around the customer journey, you can break down silos, improve communication, and work together towards a shared goal of delivering exceptional customer experiences.

Identifying customer touchpoints and interactions

To effectively map the customer journey, you must identify and document all the touchpoints and interactions that customers have with your product or service. Identifying these touchpoints is crucial for gaining a comprehensive understanding of a customer's journey.

Defining key customer touchpoints

Start by identifying the key touchpoints where customers engage with your product or service. These touchpoints can be both online and offline, such as website visits, social media interactions, customer service calls, visiting your stand during conferences, or email communications. Consider all the channels and platforms through which customers interact with your business.

Mapping the customer's journey flow

Once the key touchpoints are identified, map out the flow of the customer's journey. This entails understanding the sequence of touchpoints and the transitions customers make between them. Visualize the customer's path from the initial point of contact to conversion and subsequent interactions. This mapping helps uncover the natural progression of a customer's journey and potential gaps or overlaps in the experience.

Documenting customer interactions at each touchpoint

For each touchpoint, document the specific interactions customers have with your product or service. This includes the actions they take, the information they seek, and the challenges they encounter. Consider both the functional aspects, such as product usage or website navigation, and the emotional aspects, such as how customers feel during each interaction. This documentation helps identify the strengths and weaknesses of each touchpoint.

Considering cross-channel interactions

In today's omnichannel landscape, customers often engage with ISVs across multiple channels. Consider how different touchpoints connect and influence each other. For example, a customer may start their journey by researching online, then connect with you during a conference, and later contact customer support. Understanding these cross-channel interactions provides insights into the holistic customer experience and helps ensure consistency across touchpoints.

Analyzing customer expectations and needs at each touchpoint

For each touchpoint, analyze customer expectations and needs. Consider what customers are looking to achieve or accomplish at each stage of their journey. Are they seeking information, making a purchase decision, seeking support, or experiencing post-purchase satisfaction? Understanding customer expectations helps tailor touchpoints to meet those needs effectively.

Visualizing the customer journey map

Once touchpoints, interactions, emotions, and pain points have been identified, it's time to visualize the customer journey map. Visual representation allows stakeholders to grasp the customer experience holistically and facilitates communication and collaboration within the organization. Here's how you can effectively visualize the customer journey map:

Choose the right visualization format

Select a visualization format that best suits your needs and effectively communicates the customer journey map. Common options include diagrams, flowcharts, infographics, or digital tools specifically designed for customer journey mapping. Consider the level of detail you want to display and how easy it will be for stakeholders who will be interacting with the map to understand it.

Map the customer journey stages

Start by mapping out the different stages of the customer journey, such as awareness, consideration, purchase, and post-purchase. These stages provide a high-level overview of the customer's progression and allow stakeholders to understand the overall flow of the journey. Use visual elements, such as swimlanes or columns, to separate each stage.

Plot customer touchpoints and interactions

Within each stage, plot the identified touchpoints and interactions that customers have with your product or service. Represent these touchpoints as visual markers or symbols on the map. Connect the touchpoints to show the customer's path and the sequence of interactions. This visualization provides a clear picture of the customer's journey and the various touch points they encounter along the way.

Depict customer emotions and pain points

Integrate customer emotions and pain points into the visualization to enhance understanding. Use visual cues, such as color codes or icons, to represent positive and negative emotions at each touchpoint. Similarly, indicate pain points with symbols or callouts to highlight areas that require attention or improvement. This visual representation adds depth to the map and aids in identifying areas for enhancement.

Include supporting data and insights

Supplement the visual representation with supporting data and insights related to each touchpoint and stage of the customer journey. This can include customer feedback, analytics data, or survey results. By incorporating quantitative and qualitative information, stakeholders gain a more comprehensive understanding of a customer's experience and can make data-driven decisions.

Share and collaborate

Share the customer journey map with relevant stakeholders across different departments within the organization. Encourage collaboration and discussion to gain diverse perspectives and insights. This collaborative approach fosters a shared understanding of the customer journey and promotes a customer-centric mindset throughout the organization.

Update and evolve the customer journey map

Remember that the customer journey is dynamic and subject to change. Continuously update and evolve the customer journey map as you gather new insights and feedback. Regularly revisit the map to identify emerging touchpoints, modify existing ones, and refine the visualization based on evolving customer needs and market trends.

Visualizing the customer journey map is a powerful way to communicate and understand the customer experience. By selecting the right visualization format, mapping the stages and touchpoints, depicting emotions and pain points, including supporting data, and fostering collaboration, you can gain a comprehensive view of the customer journey. This visualization aids in identifying areas for improvement, aligning stakeholders, and driving customer-centric strategies. Regularly updating and evolving the customer journey map ensures that you stay in tune with customer needs and deliver exceptional experiences throughout the journey.

Analyzing and prioritizing improvements

After creating the customer journey map, the next crucial step is to analyze the findings and prioritize improvements. This analysis helps identify pain points, areas of opportunity, and moments that matter most to customers. By prioritizing improvements based on their impact and feasibility, you can focus your efforts on initiatives that will enhance the customer experience effectively. Here's how you can analyze and prioritize improvements based on the customer journey map:

Identify pain points and moments of friction

Review the customer journey map and identify pain points or moments of friction that customers encounter throughout their journey. These could be instances where customers face challenges, experience frustrations, or encounter obstacles that hinder their progress. Prioritize addressing these pain points as they directly impact the customer experience.

Evaluate moments of delight and differentiation

Identify moments within the customer journey where customers experience delight or where your product can differentiate itself from competitors. These are instances that evoke positive emotions, exceed customer expectations, or provide unique value. By understanding these moments, you can further enhance them and leverage them as competitive advantages.

Assess customer needs and expectations

Analyze the customer needs and expectations at each touchpoint and stage of the journey. Consider whether the current offerings meet those needs and expectations effectively. Look for gaps or areas where improvements can be made to align more closely with customer requirements. Prioritize improvements that directly address significant customer needs and expectations.

Evaluate impact and feasibility

Assess the potential impact and feasibility of each improvement opportunity. Consider factors such as resources required, technological feasibility, and alignment with business goals. Identify improvements that have the potential to deliver significant benefits to the customer experience while being feasible to implement within your organization's constraints.

Prioritize based on importance and urgency

Rank the identified improvements based on their importance and urgency. Consider the impact on customer satisfaction, revenue generation, retention, or competitive advantage. Prioritize improvements that have a high impact and are time-sensitive to ensure that you address critical issues and opportunities promptly.

Create an action plan

Develop a clear action plan that outlines the prioritized improvements, timelines, and responsible stakeholders. Break down each improvement into actionable steps and assign accountability. Establish clear goals and **key performance indicators** (**KPIs**) to measure the impact of the implemented improvements.

Continuously monitor and iterate

Implement the prioritized improvements and continuously monitor their effectiveness. Gather feedback from customers, track relevant metrics, and evaluate the impact on the customer experience. Iterate and refine your approach based on the insights gained, ensuring that your actions align with evolving customer needs and business objectives.

Analyzing and prioritizing improvements based on the customer journey map is essential for enhancing the customer experience effectively. By identifying pain points, assessing moments of delight, evaluating customer needs and expectations, and considering impact and feasibility, you can prioritize improvements that deliver the most significant benefits. Creating an action plan and continuously monitoring the implemented improvements allows for ongoing optimization and alignment with customer needs. By prioritizing improvements based on their importance and urgency, you can make strategic decisions that result in improved customer satisfaction, loyalty, and business success.

Pricing model options

Choosing the right model can catapult your application from an unknown entity to the "talk of the town," much like an unknown food truck that becomes an overnight sensation. In our trusty adventurer's kit, we have a myriad of options, akin to a Swiss army knife in terms of pricing. Let's whip them out and examine them, shall we?

Pricing based on licenses

The license structure you choose has a direct influence on your pricing model. Broadly, there are two types of licenses you can consider: per-user and per-company.

- Per-user licenses: With the per-user model, you base your pricing on the number of individuals using the app. This model's scalability and simplicity have made it popular among many app developers.

- Site/per-company licenses: Unlike the per-user model, the per-company license grants access to all users within a customer's business. This model may be more suitable for applications that offer benefits at a company-wide level.

For customers that operate with multiple Salesforce organizations, it's essential to determine how the license is applied. There might be flexibility for the license to cover either a single organization or all of a customer's organizations. Therefore, it is crucial that you provide clear specifications in their Terms and Conditions (Ts&Cs) regarding the coverage of the license for multi-organization customers. This ensures both parties have a shared understanding of the licensing scope.

Payment terms and frequency

While deciding on your app's price is essential, so is determining the frequency of payments. There are two common payment terms to consider: monthly and annual subscriptions.

Monthly subscriptions: For apps that offer regular updates and provide continuous support, a monthly subscription could be the best way to secure ongoing revenue

Annual subscriptions: If your app requires less frequent support or provides slower ROI for customers, an annual subscription might be more suitable

Free elements and trial periods

Even if your app is free or offers a trial period, understanding the appropriate license to issue is vital:

- Free licenses: If your app is free, you'll still need to issue a license. Typically, a standard site license is issued in such cases.

- Free trial licenses: Offering a free trial is a great way to introduce customers to your app. However, it's crucial to set the length of the free trial and understand how charges will apply once the trial ends.

As we navigate these winding paths, remember that your chosen pricing model must harmoniously align with your app's service type and target audience. Much like how the right key fits the perfect lock, AppExchange empowers you to control your app's usage by revoking the license of anyone who hasn't paid the agreed-upon fee.

Understanding customers' willingness to pay

Dive into the complexities of understanding customer willingness to pay, a task as delicately balanced as brewing the perfect cup of java on a Monday morning. No, we're not talking about throwing a coin into a wishing well and hoping for the best. Instead, we're talking about the fine art of figuring out just how much your customers are willing to uncork from their wallets for your app.

Think of pricing like your morning cup of coffee. If you forget to add it to your morning routine (the app design process), you're going to be walking around like a caffeine-deprived zombie. Pricing isn't the pesky fly you swat away; it's an integral part of your application's DNA, as vital as the beans are to your coffee.

Starting your day (or your design process, as it may be) with pricing considerations ensures that your app isn't just a shiny new toy. It's a shiny new toy that people want to buy and have the means to do so. You're not just creating an app with fantastic features; you're crafting a tool designed for a specific market with a particular price point in mind.

By bringing pricing into the mix early on, you're in sync with your customers' expectations, much like a barista knows just how much foam goes into your latte. This alignment not only helps you design an app that does the salsa with your customers' perceived value but also shimmies its way into being seen as worth its price.

So, don your barista apron, fire up the espresso machine, and let's delve into the art of understanding customer willingness to pay. It's a skill that, once mastered, can make your app the equivalent of the perfect Monday morning coffee—absolutely indispensable.

Incorporating pricing into the design process

The path to a successful AppExchange app starts at the concept stage, with pricing serving as one of the cornerstones in the app's design and development. Pricing isn't just a label you attach to your app; it's a strategic aspect that affects everything from development decisions to your app's positioning in the market.

Understanding what customers value

The first step in this process involves understanding what features and functionalities your customers value the most. In the context of an AppExchange app, this could involve market research, customer interviews, surveys, or beta testing with a small group of users. During this stage, it's important to identify the core value your app provides and how that translates into a dollar amount in the eyes of your customers.

Developing a hypothesis around pricing

Based on the insights gathered from your market research, you can then develop a hypothesis around pricing. For instance, if you discover that customers place a high value on a particular feature of your app, you might hypothesize that they'd be willing to pay more for a version of your app that includes this feature.

Test the hypothesis and iterate

Once you've formulated a hypothesis, the next step is to test it in the market. This might involve releasing a version of your app at the hypothesized price and gauging the response. Depending on the market's response, you can then adjust your hypothesis and pricing strategy as necessary. This could involve adding, removing, or modifying features, or adjusting the price itself.

Through this process, pricing becomes a guiding principle, informing your design decisions and helping you focus on features that deliver the most value to your customers. Moreover, by incorporating pricing into your app's design process, you ensure that the final product is one that customers are willing to pay for, thereby maximizing the financial viability and success of your app on the Salesforce AppExchange.

Identifying the product's core value

Determining the core value of your AppExchange application is a fundamental step in formulating a successful pricing strategy. Your app's core value is that unique proposition that separates it from the rest and provides tangible or significant value to your users.

Here are a few steps to guide you in identifying your app's core value:

1. Understand your customers. Use techniques from the first part of this chapter to understand your customers' needs and pain points. What issues does your app solve for them? How does it make their lives or businesses better or easier? The answers to these questions often point directly to the core value of your app.

2. Define unique features. Identify the unique features or functionalities of your app that customers can't get elsewhere. These unique features often carry a significant portion of your app's value.

3. Evaluate impact. Consider the tangible impact of your app on a customer's business. This could be measured in terms of increased revenue, decreased costs, time saved, or other quantifiable metrics. The greater the impact, the more value your app provides.

4. Conduct surveys and get feedback. Get direct feedback from your customers. Use surveys, interviews, or other forms of direct communication to get your customers' perspective on what they value most about your app.

The identified core value serves as a strong foundation for your pricing model, as it directly correlates with what customers are willing to pay for. The more clear and quantifiable this value is, the easier it will be for customers to understand and accept the pricing of your AppExchange application. With this core value in mind, you can align your pricing strategy accordingly, ensuring that the price you set reflects the value your customers receive.

Understanding the customers' perception of value

Identifying your app's core value is crucial, but understanding how customers perceive this value is even more important. Their perception directly influences their willingness to pay, thereby shaping the effectiveness of your pricing strategy.

Here are several strategies to gain insights into your customers' perception of value:

- **Customer interviews and surveys**: Conducting interviews and surveys allows you to collect direct feedback from your customers. Through these interactions, you can learn what features or aspects of your app customers value the most and how they perceive the value of these features.

- **Competitor analysis**: By looking at how similar apps in the market are priced and how customers respond to them, you can infer how customers might perceive the value of your app. This is particularly helpful when you're introducing a new app to the market or if you're considering a price change for an existing app.

- **Usage data**: Analyzing usage data can provide insights into what features customers use most frequently or spend the most time on. This data can be an indicator of what parts of your app customers find most valuable. I'm going to elaborate on this in *Chapter 10*.

- **Beta testing and early adopter feedback**: Beta testers and early adopters can provide valuable feedback on how they perceive the value of your app. Their feedback can guide you in setting an initial price or making adjustments to your pricing strategy.

By understanding how customers perceive the value of your app, you can better align your pricing strategy with their expectations. This alignment helps ensure that your customers perceive your pricing as fair and commensurate with the value they receive, increasing their satisfaction and willingness to pay. Remember, the price a customer is willing to pay is ultimately a reflection of the value they perceive they're receiving. By carefully understanding and aligning with this perception, you can effectively maximize your pricing strategy's success.

Using pricing as a strategic tool

Pricing isn't simply a mechanism to generate revenue; it's a powerful strategic tool that can influence customer behavior, drive application adoption, and maximize revenue. To utilize pricing in this strategic capacity, it's important to understand the different ways it can impact your business objectives and customer behavior. Here are some ways to strategically employ pricing:

- **Pricing to drive adoption**: Especially when launching a new application, setting a lower introductory price can be an effective way to drive adoption. Once the app has a user base, the price can be gradually increased. This strategy helps overcome the initial resistance to trying a new app.

- **Tiered pricing**: Offering different pricing tiers with varying feature sets is a popular strategy that can cater to a wide range of customers with different needs and willingness to pay. Customers who only need basic features can opt for a lower-priced tier, while those who need more advanced features can choose a higher-priced tier.

- **Freemium model**: In this model, the basic version of the app is offered for free, while advanced features are accessible only in the paid version. This strategy can help attract a large user base, some of whom may later upgrade to the paid version.

- **Volume discounts**: Offering discounts for purchasing licenses in bulk can encourage customers to buy more, potentially leading to higher total revenue.

- **Pricing for customer retention**: Offering discounts for long-term contracts can encourage customer loyalty and retention, ensuring a consistent revenue stream.

- **Dynamic pricing**: Adjusting prices based on demand, customer segments, or market conditions can maximize revenue and ensure competitiveness.

By understanding these strategies, you can leverage pricing as a tool to guide customer behavior and achieve specific business objectives. Remember, pricing is much more than just setting a number; it's a strategic decision that requires thoughtful consideration of various factors. In the end, the key is to set a price that reflects the value of your app while also aligning with your business goals and market dynamics.

Aligning pricing with customer segments

Understanding the unique needs, values, and purchasing power of your different customer segments is crucial for setting an effective pricing strategy. In this section, we'll delve into how to align pricing with your customer segments, ensuring each segment perceives your app as valuable and priced appropriately.

- **Identify your customer segments**: Your customers may vary in terms of industry, company size, role, and need. For example, a small start-up might use your app differently than a large enterprise. Understand these different segments and their unique needs.

- **Understand value perception**: Each customer segment may perceive the value of your app's features differently. A feature that's critical for one segment might be unimportant for another. Understand what features each segment values the most and why.

- **Assess willingness to pay**: Different customer segments may have different budgets and willingness to pay for your app. Larger companies may be willing to pay more for an app that can scale, while smaller businesses may be more price-sensitive.

- **Develop segment-specific pricing**: Based on your understanding of each segment's value perception and willingness to pay, develop a pricing strategy that's tailored to each segment. This could involve tiered pricing, where each tier is designed for a specific segment, or offering segment-specific discounts or packages.

- **Communicate value effectively**: For each segment, communicate the specific value they will get from your app in terms they understand and care about. Show them why your app is worth the price you're asking for.

By aligning your pricing strategy with your customer segments, you can ensure that your app is perceived as valuable and priced appropriately across all segments. This will maximize your app's adoption and revenue potential while also enhancing customer satisfaction. Remember, when it comes to pricing, one size does not fit all. Your pricing strategy should be as diverse and tailored as your customer base.

Validating willingness to pay through customer feedback

Listening to your customers is pivotal in confirming their willingness to pay. In this section, we will talk about the importance of gathering customer feedback on your app's pricing and how to go about it effectively.

- **Engage in direct conversations**: Whenever possible, engage your customers in direct conversations. This could be through customer interviews, surveys, or focus groups. Ask open-ended questions about their perceived value of your app and how much they feel it's worth.

- **Observe behavioral cues**: Customers may not always explicitly state their views on pricing, but their behavior can provide vital clues. Monitor usage patterns, feature adoption, and churn rates. Are customers downgrading or canceling their subscriptions? This might suggest that they do not perceive sufficient value for the price.

- **Beta testing and early adopters**: Utilize beta testing and early adopters to gather feedback on pricing. Early adopters, in particular, can provide invaluable insights, as they often represent highly engaged users who see significant value in your app.

- **Analyze feedback and adjust**: Carefully analyze the feedback you gather. If many customers feel your app is overpriced, it may be necessary to adjust the price or better communicate the value provided. On the other hand, if customers say they would happily pay more for your app, you may have room to increase your price.

- **Continuous iteration**: The process of validating willingness to pay is not a one-time event. Continuously solicit and analyze feedback, adjusting your pricing strategy as necessary.

Validating the willingness to pay through customer feedback can significantly increase your chances of pricing your app correctly. By understanding the perceived value and price sensitivity of your customers, you can set a price that maximizes both customer satisfaction and your app's revenue potential.

Developing a comprehensive pricing plan

Brace yourselves for a journey into developing a comprehensive pricing plan that's as thrilling and intricate as piecing together IKEA furniture without the manual. If you've ever wrestled with the FJÄLLBO or navigated the enigma that is the BILLY bookcase, you know what I'm talking about.

Where do we start? With the pricing strategy, of course. The first step in developing a comprehensive pricing plan is to determine the appropriate pricing strategy for your app. Do you prefer to use value-based pricing or competitive pricing? Your decision should be based on your understanding of your customers, the value your app provides, and your market position.

Value-based pricing

Value-based pricing focuses on the perceived value your app provides to customers rather than the cost of production. This pricing strategy requires a deep understanding of your customers and their needs, as well as the value your app brings to their business processes. Value-based pricing can result in higher profits, as customers are often willing to pay more for a solution that addresses their specific pain points.

For example, imagine a Salesforce AppExchange partner developing a sales analytics app that helps sales teams identify and prioritize high-value leads. They determine that their app can save an average sales rep $10,000 per year in lost revenue. Based on this value, they decided to price their app at $5,000 per user per year.

Competitive pricing

Competitive pricing involves setting your app's price based on the prices of similar apps in the market. This strategy requires a thorough understanding of your competitors, their offerings, and their pricing structures. Competitive pricing can help you position your app effectively in the market, but it may not always capture the unique value your app provides.

Now imagine a Salesforce AppExchange partner developing a customer support app with features similar to those of other apps on the market. They analyze the pricing of their competitors and decide to price their app at a slightly lower price point to attract price-conscious customers.

In conclusion, choosing the right pricing strategy for your app depends on several factors, including your understanding of your customers, the value your app provides, and your market position. It's essential to carefully consider each pricing strategy and choose the one that best aligns with your app's unique value proposition and target audience.

Understanding the product–market fit

Whoever said decoding the core value of your app and aligning pricing with customer segments was as easy as pie, well, they probably never tried to assemble IKEA furniture without the manual. Oh, yes. You heard that right. Think of it as a thrilling escapade that requires both a discerning eye and the precision of a master craftsperson.

In the world of AppExchange, understanding your product–market fit is akin to standing in a room with a flat pack of unassembled furniture and an Allen wrench in your hand, with the picture on the box as your only guide. You have a vision of the final product and your target customers, and it's your job to piece together the various parts, or features of your app, in a way that fits their needs and pain points.

"Does this widget go here or there?" you might wonder, much like pondering which customer segment values which feature of your app. It's a tricky business, aligning the nuts and bolts, or should I say, the features and the pricing. But when the last bolt is tightened and you stand back to behold your masterpiece, you realize the process was worth it.

Understanding the product–market fit, dear reader, isn't just about putting a price tag on your app. It's about ensuring that the price reflects the true value of your app to your target customers, just like that stylish and functional IKEA bookshelf sitting pretty in the corner of your room. There's satisfaction in that, isn't there?

Evaluating your app's value proposition

Your app's value proposition is the unique combination of features, benefits, and pricing that sets it apart from competitors and makes it attractive to your target customers. To evaluate your app's value proposition, consider the following questions:

- What unique features does your app offer?
- How do these features address your target customers' needs and pain points?
- How does your app's pricing compare to competitors' and the value it provides?

By understanding your app's value proposition, you can develop a pricing plan that accurately reflects the value your app delivers to your target customers.

For example, a Salesforce AppExchange partner develops a sales forecasting app that uses artificial intelligence to provide more accurate predictions than other apps in the market. Their app's value proposition includes the unique AI-driven forecasting feature, the time and revenue savings it provides, and its competitive pricing.

Designing product bundles

Product bundling is a powerful strategy that can significantly enhance the perceived value of your app. This section will explore the concept of product bundling and how you can use it in your pricing strategy. It will discuss different types of bundles (such as feature-based bundles and customer segment bundles), their benefits, and how to design them effectively.

Feature-based bundles

Feature-based bundles group together specific features or functionalities of your app into different packages. This allows customers to choose the package that best meets their needs and budget. To create feature-based bundles, consider the following steps:

1. Identify the core features of your app that address your customers' primary needs.
2. Group additional features based on their value and relevance to specific customer segments.
3. Create tiered packages that include different combinations of core and additional features.
4. Set the pricing for each package based on the value it provides to customers.

Customer segment bundles

Customer segment bundles tailor your app's features and pricing to specific customer segments, such as different industries, company sizes, or job roles. To create customer segment bundles, consider the following steps:

1. Identify your primary customer segments and their unique needs and pain points.
2. Determine the features and functionalities that are most relevant to each segment.
3. Create customized packages that cater to the specific needs of each segment.
4. Set the pricing for each package based on the value it provides to the segment.

For example, a Salesforce AppExchange partner develops a document management app. They create customer segment bundles for legal, finance, and human resources departments, each with features tailored to the unique needs and workflows of those industries.

Product bundling offers the following benefits for your app and your customers:

- Enhanced perceived value: Bundling features together can make your app appear more valuable and comprehensive, increasing its appeal to customers
- Simplified decision-making: Offering a limited number of well-defined bundles makes it easier for customers to choose the package that best fits their needs, reducing decision fatigue
- Increased revenue: By offering tiered packages with different pricing levels, you can capture more value from customers who are willing to pay more for additional features
- Customization and flexibility: Bundles allow you to cater to different customer segments and needs, making your app more versatile and adaptable

In conclusion, product bundling is a powerful pricing strategy that can help you enhance the perceived value of your app, simplify decision-making for your customers, and increase your revenue. By designing feature-based or customer segment bundles, you can create tailored offerings that cater to the specific needs and preferences of your target customers.

Understanding and leveraging price sensitivity

Price sensitivity, or elasticity, is a crucial concept to understand when setting prices. This section will explain what price sensitivity is, how to measure it, and how to leverage this understanding to optimize your pricing plan.

What is price sensitivity?

Price sensitivity refers to the degree to which a change in price affects the demand for a product or service. When customers are highly price-sensitive, a small change in price can significantly impact their willingness to purchase your app. Conversely, when customers are less price-sensitive, they may be more willing to pay higher prices for your app, allowing you to capture more value.

Measuring price sensitivity

To measure price sensitivity, you can use the following techniques:

- Surveys and interviews: Ask customers directly about their willingness to pay for your app at different price points

- Conjoint analysis: Use statistical methods to estimate customer preferences and price sensitivity based on their choices among different product options

- Price experiments: Test different prices for your app and observe the impact on demand and sales

By understanding your customers' price sensitivity, you can optimize your pricing plan to maximize revenue and customer satisfaction.

Leveraging price sensitivity in your pricing plan

Once you have a clear understanding of your customers' price sensitivity, you can use this information to inform your pricing plan:

- Set prices that capture maximum value: If your customers are less price-sensitive, you may be able to set higher prices without negatively impacting demand. This allows you to capture more value from your app.

- Offer discounts and promotions strategically: If your customers are highly price-sensitive, offering limited-time discounts or promotions can help drive demand and increase sales.

- Adjust pricing for different customer segments: Different customer segments may have different levels of price sensitivity. By adjusting your pricing for each segment, you can capture more value from customers who are less price-sensitive while still appealing to those who are more price-sensitive.

In conclusion, understanding and leveraging price sensitivity is crucial for developing an effective pricing plan for your AppExchange app. By measuring price sensitivity and using this information to inform your pricing strategy, you can optimize your pricing plan to maximize revenue and customer satisfaction.

Setting prices for different market segments

Your customers are likely diverse, and different customer segments may have different perceived values and price sensitivities. This section will explain how to segment your market and set different prices for different segments, a strategy known as price discrimination.

Segmenting your market

Market segmentation involves dividing your customers into distinct groups based on shared characteristics, such as industry, company size, or job role. To segment your market effectively, consider the following steps:

1. Identify the key characteristics that differentiate your customers
2. Analyze the needs, preferences, and price sensitivities of each group
3. Determine the features and pricing that best align with each segment's needs and willingness to pay

For example, a Salesforce AppExchange partner develops a sales enablement app. They segment their market into small businesses, mid-sized companies, and large enterprises, each with different sales team structures, workflows, and budgets.

Setting prices for different segments

Once you have segmented your market, you can set different prices for each segment based on their unique needs and price sensitivities. This approach, known as price discrimination, can help you capture more value from customers who are willing to pay more while still appealing to price-sensitive segments. To set prices for different segments, consider the following steps:

1. Determine the value your app provides to each segment and their willingness to pay.
2. Set prices that reflect the value that your app delivers to each segment and align this with their price sensitivities.
3. Communicate the benefits and pricing of your app clearly to each segment, highlighting the features and value that are most relevant to their needs.

For example, a Salesforce AppExchange partner offers a customer support app with three pricing tiers: a basic tier for small businesses, a professional tier for mid-sized companies, and an enterprise tier for large organizations. Each tier is priced based on the value it provides to the respective segment and their willingness to pay.

In conclusion, setting prices for different market segments can help you optimize your pricing plan and capture more value from your AppExchange app. By segmenting your market and setting prices based on the unique needs and price sensitivities of each segment, you can appeal to a broader range of customers

Discounting for nonprofits

Nonprofit organizations are an important segment to consider. Nonprofits often have unique needs and budget constraints that may not align with traditional business models. Given this, offering special nonprofit discounts can be a valuable strategy to cater to this segment.

To effectively offer nonprofit discounts, consider doing the following:

- Identify and understand the specific needs of nonprofit organizations

- Design special packages or tiers tailored to nonprofit requirements

- Clearly communicate the availability and benefits of nonprofit discounts to attract this segment

It's worth noting that on the Salesforce AppExchange, it's possible to filter apps that offer such nonprofit discounts, making it easier for these organizations to identify solutions that cater to their needs.

Reviewing and revising your pricing plan

As you already know, pricing your AppExchange app is a complex, ongoing process, similar to assembling a piece of IKEA furniture. It's not a one-off task, but a recurring one that requires regular adjustments to align with your evolving business strategy and the competitive landscape. This involves revisiting your pricing strategy, which can be likened to adding a fresh coat of paint or tightening a few screws on your IKEA furniture.

Actively seek customer feedback about your app's pricing, value, and overall satisfaction. This can be done through surveys, customer interviews, or monitoring online reviews and social media discussions. For instance, if users find your pricing structure too complicated, consider simplifying it.

Keep an eye on changes in the competitive landscape, including new entrants, competitor pricing changes, and market trends. If new competitors enter the market with similar offerings at lower prices, you may need to re-evaluate your pricing strategy or highlight your unique value proposition to justify your current pricing.

As your business evolves, your pricing plan may need to be revised to align with new strategic objectives, such as expanding into new markets, targeting new customer segments, or launching new product features. For instance, when Salesforce started, they had one product with multiple editions and a single price per user. Now, Salesforce offers multiple products addressing diverse user needs, with various editions and pricing structures that include per-user and transactional costs.

Regularly analyze your app's performance and usage data to identify trends or patterns that may indicate the need for pricing adjustments. If you notice a high churn rate among users who have signed up for the highest pricing tier, this could be a sign that the value delivered at that price point is not meeting customer expectations, prompting you to re-evaluate the features and pricing of that tier. You are going to learn how to do this in *Chapter 10*.

Finally, establish a regular schedule for reviewing and revising your pricing plan, such as quarterly or semi-annually. This helps ensure that your pricing remains relevant, competitive, and aligned with your business objectives. For Salesforce, while they don't alter their prices frequently, they showcase innovation in their approach; new features might be launched as free additions in a new release or initially as paid features that may later become free.

By regularly reviewing and revising your pricing plan, you can ensure that it remains aligned with your customers' needs, the competitive landscape, and your business strategy. This proactive approach to pricing management will help you capture the maximum value from your app, ensure fair pricing for your customers, and contribute to your app's long-term success in the Salesforce AppExchange ecosystem.

Summary

And so, our jaunt through understanding the needs of our customers, identifying the job they wish to get done, and crafting our AppExchange applications accordingly comes to a close. This chapter has equipped us with the ability to align our applications to the tasks our customers need to accomplish, making our offerings not just relevant, but essential. It's clear, now more than ever, that our understanding of customer needs, their pain points, and the journey they undertake, form the lifeblood of our success on the AppExchange platform. We gained insight into customers' willingness to pay and designed pricing strategies that aligned with perceived value and maximized revenue. Ultimately, we learned to incorporate pricing considerations from the earliest stages of product design. This knowledge isn't just vital—it's the bridge that connects our customer-centric applications to the customers themselves.

As we prepare for the next leg of our adventure, we'll delve into the unique Salesforce features and technologies essential for AppExchange development. We'll master the art of Flow, **Lightning Web Components** (**LWC**), Apex with Dependency Injection, and Platform Cache, ensuring we have the skills to conquer the challenges ahead and build innovative, robust AppExchange applications. Onward, trailblazers!

Further readings

For a deeper understanding of customer-centric app design, you can read *Competing Against Luck: The Story of Innovation and Customer Choice* by Clayton M. Christensen, Taddy Hall, Karen Dillon, and David S. Duncan.

If you're interested in navigating the intricacies of pricing your AppExchange app, *Monetizing Innovation: How Smart Companies Design the Product Around the Price* by Madhavan Ramanujam and Georg Tacke can be your guide on this exciting journey.

Part 2:
Building Blocks

If *Part 1* was the appetizer (delicious, wasn't it?), welcome to the main course. Imagine you're an architect – not the Salesforce kind (well, yes, that too) but one who designs tall, breathtaking skyscrapers. What would be more important than having a sturdy blueprint and the right kind of bricks? This is where we roll up our sleeves, toss on a metaphorical hard hat, and get into the architectural intricacies of building a stellar AppExchange product.

Before you know it, you'll emerge from this part with your digital tool belt fully loaded, ready to craft your own AppExchange marvel.

Plans on deck:

- *Chapter 4, Exploring Salesforce Platform Technologies*
- *Chapter 5, Seamless Integration with External Systems*
- *Chapter 6, Security Review*

4

Exploring Salesforce Platform Technologies

Greetings once more, fellow trailblazers! Our exciting odyssey through the Salesforce ecosystem continues, as we embark on an expedition to uncover the lesser-known, yet incredibly valuable, ISV-specific features that shape the AppExchange landscape. Fret not, for this chapter isn't about learning how to become a developer – it's not a goal of this book. Instead, I want to highlight the unique features and technologies often overlooked by Salesforce developers and architects.

As we traverse this chapter, we'll shed light on how specific technologies work and what kind of problems can be solved thanks to them. Even if you're not a developer, don't shy away from this adventure—just ensure that your Salesforce architect and lead developer join you in reading this chapter.

In this leg of our journey, we'll delve into the following topics:

- Unraveling the enigmatic world of managed packages and their pivotal role in protecting and distributing your applications.

- Dynamic Apex, the powerful backbone that enables customizable Salesforce applications to cater to unique business requirements.

- The art of Flow, where streamlining processes and enhancing **user experiences** (**UXs**) within your application are brought to life.

- The realm of **Custom Property Editors** (**CPEs**), a place of boundless flexibility and customization for **user interfaces** (**UIs**).

- Scaling the heights of Platform Cache, where optimizing performance in managed packages becomes a mastered skill.

- Crafting a UI and UX with **Salesforce Lightning Design System (SLDS)** to create an engaging and intuitive interface for your app. Even if you're not a designer, don't step back from this adventure—just make sure that your UI/UX expert is along for the ride on this chapter's expedition.

With the insights gained from this chapter, your team will become well-versed in the unique aspects of Salesforce and AppExchange development. Harness this newfound knowledge to create innovative, robust, and secure applications that stand out in the AppExchange marketplace. So, gather your fellow explorers, and let's continue our extraordinary adventure through the Salesforce ecosystem, as we master essential technologies for AppExchange success!

Unraveling the mystery of packages

Imagine managed packages as locked treasure chests containing precious gems—your **intellectual property (IP)**. These chests allow you to securely deliver your valuable creations to your customers while protecting the treasures within from prying eyes. In this section, we'll explore the concept of packages, highlighting their role in delivering and safeguarding your applications on the AppExchange marketplace. I'll also guide you through the evolution from **first-generation (1GP)** to **second-generation (2GP)** managed packages and explore the benefits of using the **Developer Hub (Dev Hub)** in managing 2GP packages.

Managed packages – safeguarding your IP

Managed packages act as a protective layer, ensuring that your IP remains safe and secure when delivering your Salesforce applications to your customers. They help you do the following:

- **Obscure your Apex code**: Like hiding the key to a treasure chest, managed packages conceal the source code of your Apex classes and triggers, making sure subscribers cannot view or modify it

- **Protect custom settings and custom metadata**: Managed packages provide an extra layer of security around custom settings and custom metadata, preserving the confidentiality and integrity of your application's data

- **Control component visibility**: Like a customizable lock, managed packages allow you to define the visibility and accessibility of your components, such as objects, fields, and Visualforce pages, preventing undesired modifications by subscribers

1GP managed packages

1GP managed packages were the pioneers in Salesforce packaging technology. Although they laid the foundation for the secure delivery of applications, they lacked the flexibility and efficiency required for modern development practices. Consequently, new projects should use and embrace the improved capabilities of 2GP managed packages.

2GP managed packages

2GP managed packages represent the next generation of Salesforce packaging, offering a more nimble and streamlined approach to developing and distributing Salesforce applications. They enable seamless updates and upgrades for your customers while retaining the core function of protecting your IP.

Namespace – the unique identifier of your treasure chest

Think of a namespace as the ornate carving on the exterior of your treasure chest, making it easily distinguishable and unique among countless other chests. In the world of Salesforce managed packages, a namespace serves as a unique identifier, ensuring that your application components don't collide with other components in your customers' Salesforce orgs.

In the grand scheme of managed packages, namespaces perform a role of paramount importance. They act as a blueprint for the structure, organization, and protection of your app. Let's take a look at how:

- **Component isolation**: Namespaces provide an extra layer of isolation for your components, such as objects, Apex classes, and Visualforce pages, by adding a unique prefix to each component's name. This prevents naming conflicts and ensures that your application components coexist harmoniously with those of other managed packages or custom components in your customers' orgs.

- **Code protection**: Namespaces contribute to the protection of your IP by making it more challenging for others to reference your components directly in their code unless you explicitly allow them to do so. This extra safeguard helps maintain the integrity of your application and its components.

- **Branding and recognition**: A namespace, much as with the ornate carving on a treasure chest, can also serve as a branding element, giving your application a distinct identity in the vast Salesforce ecosystem. By choosing a meaningful and unique namespace, you can make your application stand out and be easily recognizable by your customers.

Package extensions – tailoring applications for multiple products and editions

Package extensions offer a flexible approach for AppExchange partners to build applications that cater to customers using different Salesforce products, such as Health Cloud and Financial Services Cloud, as well as different Salesforce editions such as Professional. By utilizing a base managed package and an extension package, you can create a modular application that satisfies diverse customer requirements without maintaining multiple code bases.

Consider your application as a multifaceted puzzle, where the base managed package constitutes the central pieces, forming the core functionality suitable for all customers. Extension packages, on the other hand, are like specialized puzzle pieces that enhance the base package with additional features and functionalities, tailored to specific Salesforce products or editions.

In the context of 2GP, you can create a base 2GP package containing the core features and then develop one or more extension 2GP packages that depend on the base package. In line with the organizational structure and needs, these extension packages can encompass layered functionalities, ranging from the data model, and logic, to the UI. These packages might also incorporate features specific to certain Salesforce products or editions, allowing partners to explore and extend their offerings effectively. This modular approach allows you to maintain a single code base while offering tailored solutions to different customers.

When designing your application and the interfaces between the packages, consider the entire application life cycle. It's crucial to ensure updates to the base package do not break the extension package. When adding new features, include them in the appropriate package and make the necessary components `@namespaceAccessible` components if they are referenced by the extension package.

Leveraging package extensions in 2GP enables you to create scalable and modular applications that cater to a diverse range of customers while simplifying the upgrade process. As your customers' needs grow, you can easily upsell them by introducing the appropriate extension package to enhance their application experience.

Package extensions versus feature parameters

When developing on the Salesforce AppExchange marketplace, you might often find yourself in a dilemma: should you build an extension package or use the **Feature Management App** (**FMA**), described in *Chapter 2*? Both approaches have their own advantages and uses. Here's a handy comparison:

Criteria	Package extensions	Feature parameters
Scope	These are designed to extend the functionality of a base package. They have a dependency on the base package and can't be installed independently.	This is more about controlling the visibility and access to specific features within a package. It doesn't add new functionality but rather manages existing ones.
Flexibility	This approach provides a great deal of flexibility because it enables you to add new objects, fields, logic, and dependencies on Salesforce features that are not required by your base package. It's like building a new app but with a dependency on the base package.	Limited to toggling features on or off. New components must be added to the base package.
Use case	Ideal for scenarios where you have different versions of your app for different industries or when you have add-on modules that not every customer might need.	This approach is ideal for beta testing features or for gradually introducing new features to your customers. It also allows for control over usage allowance allocations and the disabling of features in a freemium or tiered-access model.
Complexity	Requires more development and testing effort as you're essentially building a new (albeit smaller) app.	Easier to implement as you're just controlling access to existing features.
Technical debt	Can reduce technical debt due to better separation of concerns (SoC).	Can increase technical debt due to added complexity in the core code base.

Feature parameters are particularly suited for gradual feature deployments, gaining insights through A/B testing, allowing end users to customize product functionality dynamically, and ensuring efficient maintenance when enhancements are closely tied to the core product. Importantly, they don't introduce the overhead of maintaining and releasing separate packages, making them a streamlined solution for managing features within the core package. However, this approach, while offering flexibility in feature evolution, can increase the complexity of the core code base.

Conversely, package extensions are designed to augment the functionality of an existing product by creating separate packages. They are the preferred choice when there's a need for modular functionality, managing complexities that might interfere with the core product, or when new features demand a different versioning and release rhythm. Package extensions, while promoting better SoC and reducing technical debt due to their modular nature, come with their own challenges. They require creating, maintaining, and releasing separate packages, which can introduce additional overhead. Their compartmentalized design ensures a cleaner code base but demands more rigorous management.

In making a decision, you should weigh the nature of your product, its strategic objectives, and technical challenges. While package extensions are apt for modular and intricate enhancements, feature parameters are adaptable and versatile. The final decision should resonate with your distinct trajectory and goals.

Dev Hub

Dev Hub is an essential tool for Salesforce developers and AppExchange partners, providing a centralized environment to manage, develop, and deploy Salesforce applications, particularly 2GP managed packages. In this section, we will discuss the relationship between Dev Hub and 2GP managed packages, emphasizing critical information you need to know.

The managed package in a 2GP packaging model is owned by Dev Hub, but the packaged metadata is not stored in it. To use a 2GP package, it is recommended to enable Dev Hub in your **Partner Business Org** (**PBO**). In a 2GP packaging model, a single Dev Hub instance can own one or more packages, streamlining the management process for multiple applications.

It's recommended to register the namespace in a separate Developer Edition org, which can then be linked to your Dev Hub instance. This process allows you to use a namespace and associate multiple namespaces with a single Dev Hub instance, enhancing organization and flexibility. To achieve this, you would need to do the following:

1. Create a separate Developer Edition org if you don't already have one with a registered namespace.

2. Register the namespace in the Developer Edition org. It's important to select namespaces wisely, considering they cannot be changed or reused once associated with an org.

3. Log in to your Dev Hub org as a system administrator or as a user with Salesforce DX Namespace Registry permissions.

4. From the **App Launcher** menu in your Dev Hub org, select **Namespace Registries**.

5. Click **Link Namespace** and log in to the Developer Edition org using the system administrator's credentials.

Please be aware that before you can link the namespace, it's necessary to define and deploy a **My Domain** name in your Dev Hub org, if not already done.

Localization best practices for managed packages

In the dynamic world of Salesforce ISV development, thinking about localization, even for a small managed package, is crucial. The right approach from the beginning may not be much of an effort, but trying to fix localization issues for a large managed package later can be extremely time-consuming. Here are some tips and best practices for managing localization in your Salesforce managed packages.

The importance of localization

Localization is all about ensuring your app can effectively support multiple languages and cultural contexts. In a global market, this is not just a nice-to-have feature—it's a requirement. Being able to present all user-facing information in a way that's culturally appropriate and understandable to the user ensures a seamless UX. Furthermore, Salesforce AppExchange listings support multiple languages, making it even more important to implement effective localization strategies.

Deciding what becomes a label

A simple rule: every piece of text presented to the user, whether it's UI components or API responses, should be localized. This includes everything from screen flow text, custom tabs, objects, and fields to exception messages that might be presented to the user.

Managing redundancy and dependencies

You might come across redundancy in your labels, especially if your app is large. However, it's important not to worry too much about it. The same phrase may have different connotations in different languages, and what might seem redundant in one language might not be so in another. Therefore, treating each label as unique and giving each its appropriate context can be beneficial.

Modularizing labels and versioning

Labels should ideally be kept in a single `CustomLabels` XML file per package, maintained in alphabetical order by API name. You should manually incorporate new labels into your package metadata, specifically within the `CustomLabels.labels-meta.xml` file. This entails utilizing an **integrated development environment** (**IDE**) rather than relying on the Salesforce UI. Using a prefix on each label API name to define the module it belongs to and categories to group labels together can further help with organization.

Translation tools

The translation process can be outsourced to a professional translation service. Exporting labels to XLF format can simplify the process for them, and they will maintain a catalog of what they have already translated, making it easier to identify new or modified entries each time.

Allowing subscribers to adjust your translations

In namespaced packages, end customers can override metadata translations for custom objects. For instance, they can override the label on a custom field or a workflow task using Translation Workbench. If they do so, updates to your application are not going to override local translation. Although you can't restrict subscribers from providing translations, this feature allows them to tailor your app to their specific context and needs.

Apex – the backbone of customizable Salesforce applications

Apex is a powerful, strongly typed programming language used for developing custom business logic on the Salesforce platform. It is designed to execute server-side operations, allowing developers to create dynamic and versatile Salesforce applications that cater to specific business requirements.

One of the challenges faced by AppExchange partners is creating applications that meet the unique needs of their customers. As a managed package, a Salesforce application core cannot be modified by a subscriber after installation. However, end customers may have diverse requirements, prompting the need for customization and extensibility. *Forbes* reports that 71% of customers feel frustrated by the lack of customization options in apps.

To address this intricacy, the Salesforce platform provides substantial opportunities for customization, even within managed packages. End customers can tweak a partner application extensively via the Salesforce platform to align with their business needs. They can utilize custom fields, flows, Apex, and other tools to personalize the application. Additionally, Dynamic Apex empowers developers to produce applications that, while having a fixed core, provide extra room for customization, enhancing the end user's experience and fulfilling their specific requirements.

Dynamic Apex – the power of adaptability in AppExchange applications

Dynamic Apex, a crucial aspect of Apex programming, provides Salesforce developers with a toolset for crafting highly customizable and adaptable applications. It includes **Dynamic Salesforce Object Query Language (Dynamic SOQL)**, **Dynamic Salesforce Object Search Language (Dynamic SOSL)**, and **Dynamic Data Manipulation Language (Dynamic DML)**, all of which are key to addressing unique business requirements and complexities in AppExchange development.

What is Dynamic Apex?

Apex is Salesforce's proprietary, strongly typed programming language, primarily used for building custom business logic. Traditional Apex offers a robust set of features for developing applications, but it typically doesn't support runtime alterations based on dynamic conditions. This is the gap that Dynamic Apex fills.

In essence, Dynamic Apex[1] allows developers to construct applications that can reference SOQL, SOSL, and DML strings at runtime, thereby enabling the creation of adaptable queries, searches, and data operations.

---

1   https://developer.salesforce.com/docs/atlas.en-us.apexcode.meta/apexcode/apex_dynamic.htm

The components of Dynamic Apex are set out here:

- **Dynamic SOQL**: Dynamic SOQL lets you build a SOQL string at runtime using Apex code. This permits the creation of complex, flexible queries based on specific runtime conditions or parameters, thereby enabling applications to interact with data in a versatile and adaptable manner.

- **Dynamic SOSL**: Much like Dynamic SOQL, Dynamic SOSL allows you to create a SOSL search string at runtime with Apex code. This capability helps create search strategies based on user inputs or other dynamic parameters, facilitating more customized and powerful search functionality.

- **Dynamic DML**: Dynamic DML operations allow developers to build and execute data manipulation tasks dynamically. This can include insert, update, delete, and upsert operations. Dynamic DML thus supports highly adaptive data handling within Salesforce applications.

The importance of Dynamic Apex in AppExchange development

Developing applications for the Salesforce AppExchange marketplace often requires a high level of customization to cater to diverse customer needs. Here, the inherent flexibility and adaptability of Dynamic Apex are of immense value.

Dynamic Apex can help you build applications that support various Salesforce features based on the specific configurations of a customer's org. For instance, some orgs may have Person Accounts enabled, while others might not. An application built with Dynamic Apex can dynamically check for the presence of Person Accounts and adjust its functionality accordingly.

This flexibility is not restricted to standard Salesforce features alone. Dynamic Apex opens the door for applications to seamlessly integrate with a subscriber's local custom objects and fields. This means that, rather than being restricted by the limits of predefined configurations, your product can now be built to work in harmony with unique customizations that an organization might build on top of your managed package.

Similarly, features such as Advanced Currency Management, which might be enabled in some orgs and not in others, can be dynamically supported using Dynamic Apex. The application can detect the status of such features in the org and modify its operations to align with the available functionalities.

Dynamic SOQL example

The `LookupController` class, a component of the Formula Debugger managed package, exemplifies the versatility of Dynamic SOQL. This controller enables users to search and retrieve records from both standard Salesforce objects and local custom objects using a dynamic query. You can see an example of it in use here:

```
public with sharing class LookupController {
    public static List<sObject> search(String searchTerm, string
searchObject) {
        String searchCondition = '%' + String.
escapeSingleQuotes(searchTerm) + '%';
```

```
        String searchQuery = 'SELECT Id, Name FROM ';
        searchQuery+=String.escapeSingleQuotes(searchObject);
        searchQuery+=' WHERE Name LIKE :searchCondition ';
        searchQuery+='WITH SECURITY_ENFORCED ORDER BY Name LIMIT 5';
        return Database.query(searchQuery);
    }
}
```

It's crucial to note that while the use of Dynamic SOQL adds flexibility, it also introduces potential vulnerabilities, notably SOQL Injection. This attack allows malicious actors to "inject" their SOQL code into a query. To guard against this, the `LookupController` class ensures user input is sanitized with the `String.escapeSingleQuotes` method, escaping single quotes and preventing potential SOQL Injection threats. You are going to learn more about this vulnerability in *Chapter 6*.

Dynamic Apex or extension package?

Salesforce ISV developers often encounter the challenge of integrating specific features that are not universally enabled across all customer orgs. A significant decision in these scenarios is whether to leverage Dynamic Apex within the core package or develop an additional extension package. Both methodologies have their distinct advantages and disadvantages, and the choice depends on various factors such as the specific use case, scalability expectations, and application complexity.

The need for this decision

Let's take the case of supporting both Person Accounts and Business Accounts. Person Accounts are a specific Salesforce feature primarily used in B2C contexts, while Business Accounts cater to B2B relationships. Not all Salesforce organizations enable the feature of Person Accounts.

If your solution needs to cater to both types of accounts, a crucial challenge is to avoid creating a package dependency on Person Accounts, as it would restrict your package's compatibility. Hence, you must develop a package that operates effectively regardless of whether the Person Accounts feature is enabled or not. This is when the decision between using Dynamic Apex or creating an extension package becomes pivotal.

Let's look at the pros and cons of each option in a tabular format, as follows:

Method	Advantages	Disadvantages
Extension packages	Clear segregation of business logic Facilitates standard SOQL queries Allows incremental updates specific to the added feature A single security review can include one base package and up to four extension packages	Additional security reviews are required if more than four extension packages are created Extra security reviews may be required for extension packages developed after the initial review of the base package Increased management effort due to separate packages
Dynamic Apex	Supports additional features within the core package Single security review Offers flexibility with Dynamic SOQL, Dynamic SOSL, and Dynamic DML	Cannot create dynamic declarative components Scalability issues with growing features Potential performance impacts due to lack of precompilation for Dynamic SOQL queries Risks associated with SOQL Injection and SOSL Injection, as detailed in Chapter 6

The choice between Dynamic Apex or an extension package should be made after careful consideration of your specific needs and circumstances. Always ensure to test for dependencies by attempting to install your package in an org where the additional feature (such as Person Accounts) is not enabled. If the installation is successful, you have succeeded in avoiding creating a package dependency on the specific feature. This decision-making process is an integral part of Salesforce ISV development that can significantly influence the compatibility and adaptability of your solution.

Dependency injection pattern – a flexible approach to customization

The **dependency injection** (**DI**) pattern is a popular software design pattern that facilitates customization and extensibility in Apex applications. This pattern allows developers to decouple different components of an application, making it easier for customers to modify specific parts of the app without affecting its core functionality.

For example, imagine you have a managed package application that integrates with an external system to fetch data. By default, your application connects to a publicly available cloud-based off-the-shelf system, but one of your customers may require integration with their in-house system. Using the DI pattern, you can create an interface that defines common methods for interacting with external systems, then develop the default class for the cloud-based system and empower your new customer to develop a new local class for their in-house system. Both classes implement the same interface, so this way, customers can choose which system they want to integrate with, without modifying the core application code.

Another example would be an app that calculates taxes for customers. Different customers may have varying tax rules and calculations. By implementing the DI pattern, you can create a tax calculation interface, and then develop separate classes for each customer's specific tax rules. This enables customers to use their custom tax logic while maintaining the integrity of the core application.

The role of interfaces, virtual base classes, and custom metadata in DI

In order to effectively implement DI in Salesforce applications, certain constructs and features, such as interfaces, virtual base classes, and custom metadata, are utilized. These elements, each carrying its unique attributes and capabilities, play an essential role in injecting customer-specific customization into the managed package. Let's delineate their roles in the following table:

Feature	Role
Interfaces	Interfaces allow the code to interact with a defined set of methods, while the actual implementation of those methods can differ from customer to customer. This allows the managed package to rely on the interface during development but doesn't have a direct dependency on the customer's specific implementation.
Virtual base classes	These classes allow developers to define a set of base methods that can be overridden by customers to customize the application's behavior. By using virtual base classes, customers can extend the core functionality of a managed package without modifying its source code.

Custom metadata	Custom metadata provides a convenient way to store configuration data for Salesforce applications. When combined with Apex reflection, custom metadata can be used to dynamically instantiate customer-specific implementations of interfaces or virtual base classes, allowing customers to inject their custom logic into the managed package without modifying the package's source code directly.
	An important aspect to consider is the distinction between subscriber-editable and developer-controlled custom metadata, as outlined here:
	• **Subscriber-editable custom metadata**: This allows subscribers (that is, customers) to modify the metadata records post-deployment. It's particularly useful when you want to grant customers the flexibility to adjust configurations based on their unique requirements without needing to redeploy.
	• **Developer-controlled custom metadata**: In contrast, this type is strictly controlled by the package developer. Once deployed, subscribers cannot modify these records. This is ideal for configurations that should remain consistent across all subscriber orgs.

Implementing tax calculations – a step-by-step example

Let's delve into our tax calculation scenario. We'll see how, using Apex DI, it's tailored to support local rules defined by our users.

1. Interface

First, we'll define a global interface for tax calculation, as follows:

```
global interface ITaxCalculator {
    Decimal calculateTax(Decimal amount);
}
```

2. Default class (part of your managed package)

Next, we'll create a default class that implements the interface. This class will be part of a managed package:

```
public class DefaultTaxCalculator implements ITaxCalculator {
    public Decimal calculateTax(Decimal amount) {
        return amount * 0.05; // 5% default tax
    }
}
```

3. Custom metadata

Within your managed package, introduce a new subscriber-editable custom metadata file named `TaxCalculatorMapping__mdt`. For the sake of simplicity in this example, we'll utilize the default fields, as follows:

- `MasterLabel` to store country codes (for example, US)

- `DeveloperName` to capture the class name (for example, `DefaultTaxCalculator`)

In a real-world scenario, it would be more appropriate to create custom fields tailored to these specific needs.

4. DI in action

Now, let's see how we can use DI to get the appropriate tax calculator for a given country:

```
global class TaxService {
    public static ITaxCalculator getTaxCalculatorForCountry(String
countryName) {
        // Fetch the tax calculator class name from Custom Metadata
        String taxCalculatorClassName = [SELECT DeveloperName FROM
TaxCalculatorMapping__mdt WHERE MasterLabel = :countryName LIMIT
1].DeveloperName;

        // Use dynamic Apex to instantiate the appropriate tax
calculator
        ITaxCalculator taxCalculator = (ITaxCalculator) Type.
forName(taxCalculatorClassName).newInstance();

        return taxCalculator;
    }

    global static Decimal calculateCountryTax(String countryName,
Decimal amount) {
        ITaxCalculator taxCalculator =
getTaxCalculatorForCountry(countryName);
        return taxCalculator.calculateTax(amount);
    }
}
```

5. Adapting to local needs

Imagine you've successfully sold your application to your first client in Poland. With the flexibility your application offers, the client can now develop their own custom tax class tailored to local tax regulations, as shown here:

```
public class PolandTaxCalculator implements ITaxCalculator {
    public Decimal calculateTax(Decimal amount) {
        // Custom tax logic for Poland
        return amount * 0.23; // 23% VAT for Poland
    }
}
```

The flexibility of this setup is that thanks to DI, their custom class seamlessly integrates with your core package, all without requiring any alterations to the original code. It's enough that they configure a new custom metadata type (set `MasterLabel` to PL and `DeveloperName` to `PolandTaxCalculator`), and your `TaxService` class is automatically going to run the local code. The following diagram illustrates the process:

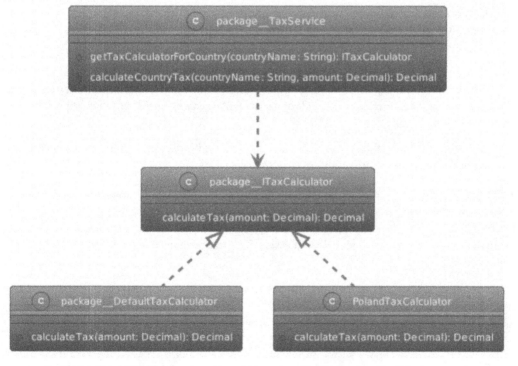

Figure 3.1: This UML diagram showcases DI in action. The TaxService, ITaxCalculator, and DefaultTaxCalculator classes are integral components of the managed package. On the other hand, PolandTaxCalculator is a bespoke class, crafted locally within the customer's organization.

You might be thinking, "Why not just incorporate the Polish tax rules directly into the package?" Well, for starters, Polish tax regulations are quite intricate. Keeping up with the tax computation logic for every country can be a hefty task. If you're not eyeing expansion in a particular region, it might not justify the investment of time and resources.

Most of all, this is just an illustrative scenario. Beyond tax computations, consider unique business processes that each of your app's users might have. It's about offering flexibility to cater to those distinct needs.

A word of caution – global means forever

When implementing DI in Salesforce managed packages, there's a crucial aspect to be aware of: the permanence of global classes.

For your interfaces or virtual base classes to be accessible outside the managed package, they must be declared as global. This ensures that they can be extended or implemented in subscriber orgs, allowing for the desired flexibility and customization. However, this accessibility comes with significant implications, as outlined here:

- **Commitment to stability**: Once you've designated a class or interface as global, it's a binding commitment. You can't later change its access to public or private. This means that any global component becomes a part of your package's public API.

- **Design finalization**: Given the irreversible nature of global, it's paramount to finalize your design before releasing it. While you can add to a global class or interface in future versions, you can't remove or alter existing methods or variables. Any change could disrupt implementations that rely on them.

- **Deletion is off the table**: Once released, a global class or interface is here to stay. It can't be deleted from subsequent versions of your managed package.

At first glance, these might seem like stringent limitations. But consider the broader picture: imagine a scenario where a subscriber has built a local class based on your global interface. If you were to alter or delete that interface, it would directly impact and potentially break the subscriber's local customizations. The rigidity of global is, in essence, a protective measure, ensuring stability and reliability for all parties involved.

In light of these considerations, treat the global keyword with the utmost respect. When planning for DI, ensure your interfaces and classes are robust and well thought out before marking them as global. It's not just about flexibility; it's a promise of consistency and reliability to your subscribers.

Ensuring seamless support for custom implementations

When allowing customers to incorporate their custom extensions, it is crucial to provide a default implementation and robust support to ensure a smooth experience. In cases where customers face issues related to performance, governor limits, or other implementation problems, support staff should be able to help them revert to a known, reliable, and supported default implementation. Quickly identifying whether an issue originates from the ISV or the customer is key to maintaining customer satisfaction.

By leveraging interfaces, virtual base classes, and custom metadata, AppExchange partners can build flexible and customizable Apex applications that cater to the unique needs of their customers. Providing strong support and a reliable default implementation ensures that customers can take full advantage of the customization options without compromising the application's overall performance and stability.

Troubleshooting with the ISV Customer Debugger

Oh, the joys of debugging! It's never a walk in the park, especially if the path takes you to a Salesforce organization that is under your customer's control and has its own unique local customizations. It's like searching for a needle in a haystack, except the haystack is made of code, and the needle is a sneaky bug that refuses to show its face.

But fear not, dear developer! The ISV Customer Debugger is here to save the day, a game-changing tool bestowed upon worthy AppExchange partners who have valiantly passed the security review process. This powerful debugger, a trusty sidekick, enables you to diagnose and debug issues within your managed packages directly in the customer's lair, all the while maintaining security and protecting your precious IP.

You may ask, "What is this magnificent ISV Customer Debugger?" Well, let me tell you! This debugger is none other than an extension of the Apex Debugger, tailored specifically for you, the extraordinary AppExchange partner. It empowers you to debug Apex code within a customer's organization without exposing the managed package's source code or compromising security.

Key benefits of the ISV Customer Debugger

For AppExchange partners who have passed the security review, the ISV Customer Debugger offers several advantages, as follows:

- **Real-time debugging**: Debug Apex code directly in a customer's organization, leading to quicker identification and resolution of issues

- **Contextual analysis**: Gain insights into how customer-specific configurations and data affect your managed package, helping you address customer-specific concerns

- **Security and IP protection**: Debug Apex code without revealing the managed package's source code or IP to the customer

- **Enhanced customer support**: Deliver faster and more effective support to your customers, improving their overall experience with your managed package

Protecting your customers' IP

It's imperative to respect and protect your customers' IP. Always be aware that debug logs may contain not only metadata but also your customers' data. When you've finished debugging, delete the entire project from the location where you stored it during the setup process. Never store your customers' data or metadata in your **version control system** (**VCS**).

ISV Customer Debugger considerations

When working with the ISV Customer Debugger, keep these additional considerations in mind:

- You can debug only sandbox orgs.

- You can debug only one customer at a time, but purchasing Apex Debugger licenses allows you to debug multiple customers simultaneously and also lets you debug in your sandboxes and scratch orgs.

- Your debugging session terminates when you click **Return to subscriber overview**. Stay logged in to your customer's org while you debug, and return to your **License Management Org** (**LMO**) only when you are done debugging.

Indeed, these considerations form the bedrock of effectively utilizing the ISV Customer Debugger. While this tool proves to be immensely helpful, its proper usage entails awareness and understanding of these pivotal points. Therefore, always keep these guidelines in mind as you navigate through your debugging sessions.

Enhancing your application with Flow

Salesforce Flow offers a powerful and flexible way for ISVs to extend the functionality of their applications and empower customers to customize business processes. In this section, we'll explore the various ways ISVs can support flows within their applications, and discuss best practices and limitations.

Flow-enabling your features and functions

As an ISV, you can make your application's features and functions available to customers within their custom flows. By flow-enabling your **Lightning Web Components** (**LWC**) and Apex methods, you can integrate them into customers' custom flows, making your app more valuable and sticky.

To achieve this, consider which features or functions customers might want to include in their custom flows. For instance, an AppExchange solution that offers a credit check function can be utilized in both interactive screen flows and headless record-triggered flows.

Providing flow templates and overridable flows

Flow templates and overridable flows allow you to deliver generic business processes that customers can use as a starting point for their custom flow logic. By packaging your industry expertise in a flow template, you can help customers bootstrap their own custom flows.

The primary difference between flow templates and overridable flows is that flow templates require customers to update all references to the template when creating a new flow, while overridable flows automatically update references when an "overriding flow" is created.

> **Best practice tip**
>
> Include references to your packaged LWCs or invocable Apex methods within flow templates or overridable flows to educate customers on how to build their own flows using your features and functions.

Offering IP-protected flows

IP-protected flows are neither overridable nor templates and are useful for preventing customers from viewing or editing a flow, protecting IP, or preventing changes to an app's behavior. Customers can still deactivate these flows, so consider using a code-based approach for logic that must always run.

Controlling the order of execution with flows – advantages of Trigger Order feature

You can utilize the **Trigger Order** feature to set the order of execution for record-triggered flows, gaining better control over your automation processes. This feature is not available for Apex triggers, which can cause issues when your package has a trigger on an object and the customer also writes a trigger on that object, as it becomes non-deterministic which order the triggers will run in.

Setting Trigger Order on flows

The **Trigger Order** option allows you to prioritize the execution of record-triggered flows for a specific object. When saving a flow, you can set the **Trigger Order** number field to determine the order of execution. You can enter a number from 1 to 2,000, which dictates the order in which flows with the same object are triggered.

For example, you can prioritize an after-save flow to run before other after-save flows on the Account object. However, you cannot prioritize an after-save flow to run before any before-save flows or before an Apex trigger.

Packaging the Trigger Order feature

The **Trigger Order** feature is fully packageable, which means it's a best practice to leave space between your flow order numbering for customers to create their own flows and slot them in between your packaged flows if they want to. This flexibility allows customers to have more control over their automation processes.

Customization with Flow Trigger Explorer

Flow Trigger Explorer is a unique feature to determine the order in which flow triggers run. If customers clone your templates or overridable flows, they can edit the Trigger Order on the clone, allowing them to further tailor the application to their specific needs.

Best practices and limitations

When packaging flows, consider the following points:

- Each flow can have only 50^2 versions in an org, affecting both customers and developers. For customers, refer them to the help page on deleting a flow version installed from a package. For ISVs, manage versions differently based on whether you use 1GP or 2GP packaging processes.

- Customers can deactivate flows in managed packages. If a new, active version of a flow is included in the next release, it will be created and executed in the customer's org, potentially causing unexpected behavior. If you have logic that must not be deactivated, consider using a code-based approach.

- If there's a possibility that a customer might decide to deactivate a flow, it's best not to set it as IP-restricted. When these flows turn back on by themselves after an upgrade, it can confuse customers. Additionally, this can complicate the process of implementing a solid release management strategy, which we will delve into in *Chapter 7*.

By offering flow templates and overridable flows, ISVs can empower customers to make their own customizations and meet their specific business needs, enhancing the value of the ISV's application.

---

2   https://help.salesforce.com/s/articleView?id=sf.flow_considerations_
limit.htm&type=5

Blending Flow and Apex

Ah, the eternal question: Apex or Flow? It's like choosing between a trusty hammer and a versatile Swiss Army knife. In the previous section, we ventured into the world of Apex, witnessing its raw power in enabling customizable Salesforce applications through DI patterns, interfaces, virtual base classes, and custom metadata. Apex, like a mighty hammer, provides a robust solution for crafting tailored applications but requires a certain level of programming expertise to wield its power effectively.

Now, let's talk about Flow, the Swiss Army knife of Salesforce customizations. Flow offers an easier way for end customers to customize business processes without having to master the art of Apex code. It's like switching from a hammer to a versatile tool that has a little bit of everything.

You know the old saying: "If all you have is a hammer, everything looks like a nail"? Well, that's true in the world of AppExchange development too. If you know only Apex or only Flow, you might find yourself making suboptimal decisions, such as using a hammer to cut a piece of wood or a knife to drive in a nail. To truly excel in the realm of Salesforce customizations, it's essential to have both Apex and Flow in your toolbox, mastering each technology and knowing when to use the right tool for the job. As with a skilled craftsman, you'll be well-equipped to tackle any customization challenge with confidence and precision.

So, dear reader, let's embark on a journey to explore the harmonious blend of Flow and Apex, where the strengths of one tool complement the weaknesses of the other. Together, these powerful tools will help you build a symphony of tailored applications, perfectly tuned to the unique needs of your customers.

Flow as an alternative to Apex for easier customizations

Flow allows end customers to clone and use flow templates and overridable flows, enabling them to easily modify business logic without writing Apex code for DI. This provides a more accessible way for customers to tailor applications to their unique requirements.

Prioritizing flows and invocable actions over Apex triggers

In the realm of automation, flows offer a significant advantage over Apex triggers, thanks to their flexibility and adaptability. Although flows can't cover every scenario that triggers handle, they empower customers by enabling them to troubleshoot, deactivate, and customize the automation packaged within their applications. This flexibility is especially crucial for automation on standard objects, where the setup of a customer's automation project is beyond their control.

It's important to recognize that your automation code may work seamlessly in one organization, but when combined with other triggers, flows, and validation rules, it could lead to errors in different orgs. The challenge with managed triggers is that their code is hidden and uneditable, making them difficult to debug and impossible to deactivate. Furthermore, trigger code can create additional headaches for organizations implementing trigger frameworks that necessitate custom boilerplate code.

With every Salesforce release, Flow becomes even more powerful, and invocable actions provide access to Apex for complex operations. When it comes to packaged automation, my initial recommendation is to lean toward flows and invocable actions as your go-to choices. However, it's crucial to bear in mind the limitations detailed in the designated section, particularly concerning deactivations and upgrade behaviors. These considerations will help determine if there are any obstacles to using this default recommendation.

In the best-case scenario, flows and invocable actions serve as a versatile toolkit for your customers' admins and a valuable resource for solution architects looking to tailor your app to their specific needs. By prioritizing flows and invocable actions over triggers, you'll enhance the adaptability and ease of use of your AppExchange application, further catering to the unique requirements of your customers.

Custom Property Editors (CPEs)

Some actions and components can be quite complex, requiring administrators to refer to the documentation for proper configuration. CPEs provide a solution for creating tailored UIs for admins working with custom Flow screen components and Apex actions. To fully understand the benefits of CPEs, we must first examine what they are and how they work.

CPEs are LWCs that can be integrated with custom Apex actions or Flow screen components. These editors can be as sophisticated as needed, depending on the requirements and design vision.

ISVs can take advantage of CPEs to create dynamic, compact, reactive, user-friendly, and visually appealing UIs for complex screen components and Apex actions. Custom validation can be enforced using CPEs, which is particularly useful for implementing input-based conditional validation. This reduces errors caused by incomplete settings and insufficient data, resulting in fewer Flow metadata errors. Configuring a component or action becomes easier for end users, primarily administrators, with the help of CPEs.

CPEs can be designed to create self-documenting UIs, eliminating the need for users to consult a separate reference document.

Building a CPE

The process of building a CPE consists of three main steps: creating an Apex action, creating the CPE itself, and connecting the Apex action to the Property Editor. Here is a brief overview of each step:

1. **Create an Apex action**: Define the logic for the custom action, including input and output variables, using Apex code.

2. **Create the CPE**: Develop an LWC that serves as the custom UI for configuring the Apex action. This involves creating an HTML file for the UI structure, a JavaScript controller for handling user interactions, and an XML file for metadata configuration.

3. **Connect the Apex action to the Property Editor**: Update the Apex action with an `@InvocableMethod` annotation that specifies the CPE's LWC. This connection allows the custom UI to override the default editor, UI, and input parameters for the Apex action.

Leveraging Platform Cache for improved performance in managed packages

Imagine you're back in the days of old personal computers, sitting in front of a clunky machine, desperately searching for that elusive turbo button. You know—the one that promised to magically boost your computer's speed and performance with a single click. But here's the thing that's going to make you smile: when it comes to Platform Cache in Salesforce, you don't need to hunt for a button or hope for some kind of ancient computer sorcery. Oh no, my dear reader—it's much simpler than that. You just add Platform Cache to your managed package, and voilà! Your application is injected with a turbo boost of improved performance. No button-clicking is required.

Platform Cache is a powerful feature offered by Salesforce that allows developers to store and access data quickly and efficiently. It provides a way to optimize the performance of Salesforce applications by reducing the time spent on data retrieval operations. As an AppExchange partner, you have the ability to include 3 MB of free Platform Cache in your managed packages, once they pass the Salesforce security review. In this section, we will discuss how to enable and utilize this free cache provisioning in your managed packages and illustrate it with a specific use case.

Platform Cache – an overview

Platform Cache is a memory layer within the Salesforce platform that stores frequently used data, allowing developers to access it more quickly than by querying the database. It operates on two levels: Org Cache and Session Cache. Org Cache stores data shared across all users within an organization, while Session Cache stores data specific to individual user sessions. By caching data at these levels, developers can significantly reduce the time and resources required to access frequently used information.

Importantly, it's worth noting that Platform Cache is accessible in Salesforce editions starting from Enterprise Edition and above. When incorporating Platform Cache into a package, it introduces an edition dependency, rendering the package unavailable for organizations utilizing the Professional Edition.

Enabling free Platform Cache in your managed packages

To leverage Platform Cache in your managed packages, define namespaced cache partitions in your package and reference them in your code. Allocate the free cache to the desired partitions and upload a new version of your application. For existing packages that have already passed the security review prior to the Spring '21 release, the cache will automatically be provisioned upon installation when the allocation is set in the managed package.

Improving managed package performance with Platform Cache

Platform Cache can be particularly beneficial for managed packages that rely heavily on data retrieval operations, as it can help to reduce latency and improve overall performance. For example, consider a managed package that frequently accesses configuration data or frequently used metadata. By storing this data in Platform Cache, the managed package can access it more quickly than by querying the database each time the data is needed. This can lead to faster response times, improved application performance, and a better UX for customers.

Case study – enhancing performance in Formula Debugger with Platform Cache

If you're still scratching your head over how to use Platform Cache, fret not! We're about to shine a light on this subject by delving into how Platform Cache was leveraged in Formula Debugger, an app we took for a spin back in *Chapter 1*. This was done to tackle performance hitches tied to scrutinizing metadata schema in sizable Salesforce orgs.

The Formula Debugger app is designed to help users identify and resolve issues with formula fields in Salesforce orgs. One of the main challenges faced by the tool is efficiently finding all formula fields within an org, which requires analyzing extensive metadata. In the case of very large Salesforce orgs, this operation can be time-consuming and may negatively impact the UX.

To overcome this challenge, the Formula Debugger app leverages Platform Cache to enhance performance and provide a seamless UX. Here's how it works:

- **Instant access**: If the platform cache is populated during the app launch, the stored values are immediately available to the user. This enables instant app usage, eliminating the wait time usually associated with heavy computations.

- **Real-time retrieval when the cache is empty**: If the platform cache is not populated, Formula Debugger attempts to retrieve all formula fields in real-time. However, with extensive metadata, timeouts may occur. If this happens, Formula Debugger will only display the initially available formula fields. Users will then see a message that reads: **Due to the large size of your organization's metadata, only the initial formula fields are immediately available for debugging. We are processing the metadata in the background. Please wait a moment and refresh the page if you need to debug fields that aren't currently listed.**

- **Asynchronous cache update**: Each time the app is launched, an asynchronous calculation process (implemented as an Apex `Queueable` class) starts in the background. This process ensures that the cache values are updated with the most recent data.

- **Storing formula fields in the platform cache**: After the formula fields are identified by the asynchronous process, they're stored in the platform cache. This method ensures faster access, as subsequent requests for formula fields are fetched directly from the cache, eliminating the need for ongoing metadata analysis. This helps to avoid hitting the Apex timeout limit in cases of large metadata sizes.

- **Seamless UX**: With the formula fields readily available in Platform Cache, users of the Formula Debugger app can enjoy a smooth, uninterrupted experience when working with the tool. The cached data allows the application to perform optimally, even in large Salesforce orgs with extensive metadata.

The following diagram illustrates the process:

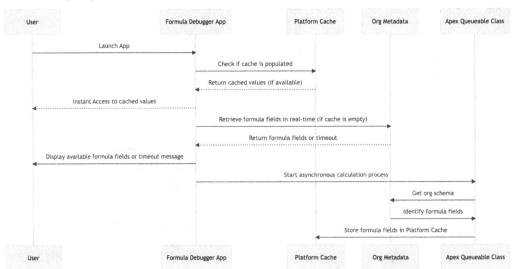

Figure 3.2: Flowchart demonstrating how Formula Debugger uses Platform Cache to improve performance

One thing to note is that the cache undergoes recalculation every time the app is launched. This means if a user adds a new formula field and wants to see it in the app immediately, they might have to wait for the cache to finish recalculating. In the context of Formula Debugger, this isn't a significant issue. If you've just created a formula field, it's likely you don't have issues with it yet, so immediate debugging might not be necessary. However, this kind of trade-off regarding cache refreshment can influence your design decisions.

In conclusion, Platform Cache is a valuable resource for ISVs looking to optimize the performance of their managed packages. By leveraging this feature, which is available for free for apps that have passed the Salesforce security review, you can significantly reduce data retrieval times and enhance the overall UX.

Crafting the UI and UX with SLDS

From the last chapter, you now know what your app should do. As we start turning this vision into reality, remember it's not just about functionality. A visually appealing and smooth UX is equally important.

Remember—a well-designed UI and an exceptional UX are the heartbeats of successful applications. They not only fulfill the users' needs and pain points; we're primed to construct our application not as a mere tool, but as a companion on our users' path to their goals.

Our focus in this section lies in crafting a UI and UX that effortlessly marries our user needs with the polished, consistent aesthetic of SLDS. This comprehensive design framework will allow our application to resonate with the familiar, user-friendly look and feel of the Salesforce ecosystem, ensuring users feel right at home as they navigate through your application.

Understanding Salesforce Lightning Design System (SLDS)

SLDS is a comprehensive design framework that provides a rich set of guidelines, components, and resources for creating consistent and engaging UIs across Salesforce applications. Developed by Salesforce, SLDS allows developers and designers to build custom applications using a set of pre-built UI components and patterns that adhere to best practices for UX and accessibility. By leveraging SLDS, you can ensure that your applications maintain a consistent look and feel with the Salesforce platform, enabling users to navigate and interact with your application more intuitively.

Key components and features of SLDS

SLDS consists of several key components and features that facilitate a smooth and efficient development process while ensuring a high-quality UX, as outlined here:

- **Design guidelines**: SLDS provides detailed design guidelines that cover various aspects of UI design, such as color, typography, layout, and iconography. These guidelines help maintain consistency across your application and align with the overall Salesforce ecosystem.

- **Pre-built components**: SLDS offers a comprehensive library of pre-built, reusable UI components that follow best practices for UX and accessibility. These components can be easily customized and integrated into your application, saving you time and effort during the development process.

- **Design tokens**: Design tokens are variables that store design-related values, such as colors, fonts, and spacing. They enable you to manage your application's design more efficiently and consistently, making it easy to update your design across multiple platforms and devices.

- **Accessibility**: SLDS is designed with accessibility in mind, ensuring that your application is usable by people with disabilities. By following SLDS guidelines and utilizing the pre-built components, you can create an inclusive application that meets accessibility standards and best practices.

Leveraging design principles for consistency and efficiency

SLDS is built on a set of core design principles that promote consistency, efficiency, and usability across all applications, as set out here:

- **Clarity**: SLDS emphasizes simplicity and clear communication through the use of straightforward layouts, concise language, and appropriate visual cues

- **Efficiency**: The system is designed to help users complete tasks quickly and efficiently by minimizing clicks, optimizing workflows, and providing relevant information in context

- **Consistency**: SLDS ensures a consistent look and feel across applications by providing a unified set of design guidelines and components, making it easy for users to understand and interact with different applications on the Salesforce platform

- **Flexibility**: SLDS is built to be flexible and adaptable, allowing you to customize and extend the design to meet your specific application requirements while maintaining consistency with the Salesforce ecosystem

By embracing these design principles, you can create a UI that not only meets your customers' needs but also delivers an exceptional UX that aligns with the Salesforce platform.

LWC standard component library

When diving into SLDS, it's crucial also to familiarize yourself with the LWC standard component library[3]. This library is a comprehensive collection of pre-built components that can be easily integrated into any LWC development.

Why prioritize LWC standard components over SLDS tags? Let's take a look at some reasons to do so:

- **Consistency and best practices**: Using standard components ensures that you're adhering to Salesforce's best practices for UI and UX. These components are designed with the end user in mind, ensuring a consistent experience across all Salesforce applications.

- **Rapid development**: With pre-built components, developers can speed up the development process. There's no need to build from scratch when a suitable component is already available.

- **Maintenance and updates**: Salesforce continuously updates and maintains the LWC standard component library. By using these components, you're ensuring that your application remains up to date with the latest features and best practices.

- **Compatibility**: Standard components are designed to work seamlessly with other Salesforce services and tools. This ensures that as you expand or integrate other services, your application remains compatible.

While the LWC standard component library should be your go-to for most development tasks, there are scenarios where SLDS tags might be more appropriate, such as the following:

- **Customization**: If you need a component that isn't available in the standard library or requires extensive customization, SLDS tags can offer more flexibility

- **Advanced features**: For features or designs that go beyond the capabilities of standard components, SLDS provides the tools to craft unique UXs

---

3   https://developer.salesforce.com/docs/component-library/overview/components

In conclusion, while SLDS offers a robust set of tools for crafting unique UIs, the LWC standard component library should be the first stop for most frontend development tasks. This approach ensures a consistent, maintainable, and user-friendly application.

Building exceptional applications

Creating an outstanding UX isn't a one-person job, nor does it end with deployment—it's a collaborative, continuous process that echoes the voice of the user from inception to implementation and beyond. UI and UX designers, along with researchers, ensure that this voice resonates throughout all stages of product development, harmonizing user needs with business goals and technical requirements.

Dr. Ralf Speth, Chief Executive Officer of Jaguar Land Rover, famously said, "If you think good design is expensive, you should look at the cost of bad design." This wisdom resonates strongly with our journey. Ignoring UX can have substantial costs, from increased customer support to additional development work (and rework), and even risks product failure. It's akin to launching a ship without checking for leaks—risky and, quite likely, disastrous.

Summary

Dear reader, as our captivating journey through the Salesforce ecosystem continues, I must emphasize that this chapter holds the key to mastering crucial Salesforce technologies. We've just concluded an exhilarating exploration of the lesser-known, yet invaluable, ISV-specific features that shape the AppExchange landscape. We shed light on the profound depths of managed packages, Apex, Flow, Platform Cache, CPEs, and crafting a UI and UX. I invite you to revisit this chapter regularly as you gain experience, ensuring these insights remain fresh and relevant. You don't have to memorize the implementation details of all technologies, but having the ability to explain how they function and the scenarios they're best suited for will enable you to make informed technical choices when mapping out your upcoming development endeavors.

You now hold in your hands the key to unlocking the full potential of these powerful technologies, often overshadowed in traditional Salesforce development yet essential for ISVs. The wisdom you've accumulated on this leg of our journey is vital for proficiently implementing your managed package. Your mastery over these distinct facets will empower you to craft innovative, tailored, and efficient applications that cater beautifully to the mosaic of your customers' needs. Embrace your newly acquired skills as stepping stones, propelling you toward the next thrilling chapter of our adventure.

In the next chapter, we're diving deep into seamless integration with external systems. We'll explore various technical architectures and a range of integration patterns. We'll journey through Salesforce APIs, Salesforce Connect, Canvas SDK, and Connected Apps. Imagine becoming an integration wizard, creating apps that satisfy customers and deliver top-notch UXs.

So, get ready, reader. The next chapter of our Salesforce journey is even more exciting as we delve further into the Salesforce universe, sharpening our skills to achieve AppExchange success!

Further reading

If you're keen on delving further into the technical nuances of managed packages, I'd suggest checking out the book *Salesforce Platform Enterprise Architecture*, authored by Andrew Fawcett. This resource can aid in cultivating a more profound comprehension of the capabilities offered by the Salesforce platform and in uncovering effective ways to leverage them for application development.

5

Seamless Integration with External Systems

Welcome, fellow trailblazers, to our next adventure: the exciting terrain of seamless integration with external systems in Salesforce! If our journey thus far has been about understanding the lay of the Salesforce land, this chapter will teach us how to build bridges that connect our creations to the world beyond.

What you're about to learn in this chapter isn't just an essential skill set; it's the cornerstone of crafting robust applications that can nimbly cross the chasms between disparate systems. In the vibrant ecosystem of Salesforce, each element you master is another tool in your adventurer's kit. So, let's review the tools we'll be adding in this chapter:

- Technical architecture: Consider this your blueprints for bridges of different types. We'll explore the two main blueprints available for ISVs and how they influence the bridges you build.

- Integration patterns: These patterns are like your trusted guidebooks. Just like cultivating a vibrant garden requires understanding the unique needs of different plants, integrating your AppExchange application with other systems requires understanding different integration patterns.

- Salesforce APIs: APIs are like the materials you'll need to build your bridges, enabling a connection between your application and external platforms.

- Salesforce Connect: Imagine this feature as a magic carpet that can fly data from distant lands (external sources) directly into your Salesforce instance.

- Canvas SDK: This toolkit is like a team of skilled artisans, helping you embed third-party web applications within the Salesforce interface.

- Connected apps: These custom-built applications are like secure passes, granting access across the borders between Salesforce and external systems.

By the time we finish this chapter, you'll be skilled at architecting bridges between your applications and external systems, using Salesforce's exceptional tools. Pack your gear, fellow adventurers, as we continue our thrilling exploration into the Salesforce wilderness! Onwards to greater understanding, integration, and, yes, adventure!

Technical architecture

Embarking on the journey of building an application in collaboration with Salesforce can feel a bit like standing at the crossroads of a grand metropolis. You have two main avenues to start from, each leading to a unique type of application.

The first avenue leads to native apps, which are primarily built within the Salesforce ecosystem and do not integrate with external systems. The second is the route to composite apps, which are designed to integrate seamlessly with other systems beyond Salesforce.

These avenues are distinguished by the amount of Salesforce technology employed in the construction of the application. However, it's worth noting that these paths aren't strictly linear. Sometimes, partners find themselves transitioning from native to composite applications and vice versa, showing that these avenues may intersect and cross over time.

Just as a city's architecture can give it a unique flavor, the choice of application type deeply influences its design. Each application is crafted to meld seamlessly into the customer's Salesforce landscape, just like a new building blending harmoniously into a city skyline. But here comes the pivotal part. This choice isn't simply about aesthetics or functionality within the Salesforce ecosystem. For composite apps, it's paramount to consider the integration with external systems, which might necessitate the use of technologies and concepts beyond what was covered in the previous chapter.

Much like a city planner considering road connections while designing a new district, your decision on the type of application influences the integration pathways with external systems. It's not merely about constructing a standalone entity but rather a connected, interactive component of a larger network. Therefore, as you start sketching your application blueprint, remember this: the type of application you're building defines not only its standalone structure but also the way it interacts and integrates with, and potentially introduces complexities into, the world beyond Salesforce.

Native applications

Native applications are built entirely on the Salesforce platform and take full advantage of Salesforce's infrastructure management, core capabilities, and innovations. This type of application benefits from the most robust features available on the market, as they are built 100% on top of the Salesforce platform.

Key aspects of native applications include the following:

- Built entirely on the Salesforce platform
- Benefit from Salesforce's infrastructure management and core capabilities
- Seamless integration into a customer's Salesforce instance
- Rapid development and innovation
- No worries about data residency – all the data is hosted right where your customer's Salesforce instance is located

Composite applications

Composite applications are the most common type of application built by ISVs. These applications are predominantly built off-platform but incorporate some functionality built on the Salesforce platform. By leveraging Salesforce technology, composite applications can fit more seamlessly into a customer's Salesforce instance, driving greater visibility and higher adoption rates.

Key aspects of composite applications include the following:

- Parts of the application are built off-platform
- Some functionality is built on the Salesforce platform
- Seamless integration into a customer's Salesforce instance
- Greater visibility and higher adoption rates

Extension packages for integrations

When integrating Salesforce with external systems, it's essential to ensure that the core functionalities of your product remain unaffected. If integration isn't a central component of your core product, consider delivering it as an extension package, a concept you might recall from *Chapter 4*.

The idea of keeping integrations outside the core package stems from the need for decoupling. This separation ensures that any potential issues or changes in the integration module don't impact the core product's performance or functionality.

Furthermore, customers often have diverse integration needs. Some might want to connect with a commonly used external system, while others might have specific requirements tailored to their operations. By employing extension packages, you can cater to these varied needs without complicating your core product.

In essence, while integrations play a crucial role in enhancing your product's capabilities, it's vital to approach them with a modular mindset. Extension packages offer a structured solution, ensuring a streamlined core product while providing the flexibility to address diverse integration requirements.

Integration patterns

Creating an AppExchange application is akin to cultivating a beautiful garden. Each integration pattern is a different plant or flower that contributes to the richness and variety of the garden. Some plants may need more water (data), others more sunlight (APIs), and still others more nutrients (user interactions). It's all about understanding their unique needs and nurturing them accordingly for your garden (application) to flourish. Salesforce has made remarkable strides in defining these integration patterns, which are covered in one of their esteemed certifications: Integration Architect[1]. The Integration Architect certification equips professionals with the knowledge and expertise needed to effectively navigate the intricacies of application integration.
For organizations heavily reliant on integrations, it is highly recommended to ensure that at least one individual in the technical team has obtained this credential. By doing so, they can leverage the insights gained from Salesforce's comprehensive integration pattern framework, thereby optimizing their integration processes and enhancing overall application performance.

Remote process invocation—request and reply

This pattern involves a client application making a request to a remote service and waiting for a response. The client is blocked until the response is received or a timeout occurs. This pattern is commonly used when the client needs to process the response before it can proceed.

For example, an ISV might use this pattern to integrate a third-party payment processing service into their AppExchange application. When a customer makes a payment, the application sends a request to the payment service and waits for a confirmation response before proceeding.

---

1   https://trailhead.salesforce.com/help?article=Salesforce-Certified-Integration-Architect-Exam-Guide

Remote process invocation—fire and forget

In this pattern, the client application sends a request to a remote service but does not wait for a response. This is useful when the client does not need to process the response immediately, or at all.

For instance, an ISV could use this pattern to send usage data from their AppExchange application to a remote analytics service. The application can continue running without waiting for a response from the analytics service.

Batch data synchronization

Batch data synchronization involves transferring large amounts of data at scheduled intervals. This pattern is useful when real-time data is not required, and it can be more efficient than transferring data in real-time for large datasets.

An example of this could be an ISV that needs to synchronize data between its AppExchange application and a remote database every night. The application collects data throughout the day, and then sends it all to the database in a single batch during off-peak hours.

Remote call-in

The remote call-in pattern involves a remote service making a request to the client application. This is the opposite of the remote process invocation patterns, where the client makes a request for the service.

An example would be an ISV integrating its AppExchange app with an external address validation service. When a user enters an address into the application, the AppExchange app sends a request to validate the accuracy and format of the address. The external address validation service then checks the address and sends back a validation result, ensuring data accuracy and consistency.

UI update based on data changes

This pattern involves updating the user interface of an application in response to changes in the underlying data hosted off-platform. This allows the application to provide real-time feedback to the user.

For instance, an ISV could use this pattern to update a cockpit in their AppExchange application whenever the underlying data hosted in their AWS instance changes. When a change is detected, the application updates the Salesforce cockpit to reflect the new data.

Data virtualization

Data virtualization is an approach to data management that allows an application to retrieve and manipulate data without requiring technical details about the data, such as how it is formatted at source, or where it is physically located. This reduces the risk of data errors and the workload of moving data around that may never be used, and it does not attempt to impose a single data model on the data.

For example, an ISV might use data virtualization to provide a unified view of data from multiple sources in its AppExchange application. The application can access and manipulate the data as if it were all in a single location, even though it is actually spread across multiple databases.

Choosing the right integration pattern

Selecting the appropriate integration pattern for your application is a key decision that can significantly impact its performance, user experience, and overall success. Before diving into the intricacies of coding, take a moment to engage in thoughtful contemplation. By asking yourself the following questions, you can streamline your development process and potentially save weeks of effort by ensuring you choose the most fitting design pattern. Remember, a little upfront planning can go a long way in creating a robust and efficient integration solution.

1. What interaction level is required?

   Consider the degree of interaction needed between your client application and the remote service. Do you require immediate responses, or can your application function independently while waiting for a response? If real-time interaction is crucial, synchronous patterns might be best. On the other hand, if your application can carry on without immediate feedback, you can explore asynchronous patterns that don't block the application's progress.

2. How vital is data consistency?

   Think about the importance of maintaining consistent data between your application and the remote service. If data accuracy is paramount, patterns that facilitate synchronous communication and immediate feedback are likely the right fit. However, if minor discrepancies in data can be tolerated, asynchronous patterns might offer more flexibility.

3. Is real-time response really necessary?

   Consider whether your client application must wait for a response from the remote service before proceeding. If not, patterns that allow for non-blocking communication, such as "Fire and Forget," could be advantageous. This approach can prevent delays in your application's workflow and responsiveness.

4. What's the data volume?

   Evaluate the volume of data that needs to be transferred. For large datasets, the Batch Data Synchronization pattern might be more efficient and practical than real-time transfers. This can help you manage network resources and maintain the application's performance.

5. Who initiates requests?

   Examine whether the remote service needs to initiate requests to your client application. Depending on the direction of communication, you may need to opt for specific invocation patterns, such as the "Remote Call-In" pattern, to accommodate these scenarios.

6. Do you require real-time UI updates?

   Think about whether your application's user interface should be updated in real-time based on external data changes. If so, patterns such as "UI Update Based on Data Changes" can help you provide a dynamic and responsive user experience.

7. Are disparate data sources involved?

   If your application needs to handle data from various sources without imposing a single data model, consider the "Data Virtualization" pattern. This approach can unify data without the need for extensive data transformation efforts.

By investing time in contemplating these questions, you lay a strong foundation for your integration solution. Remember, an hour of thoughtful planning can translate into weeks saved during development, resulting in a more efficient, effective, and successful AppExchange application. So, before you start writing a single line of code, engage in this critical phase of optimal pattern selection.

Available technologies for outbound integrations

Salesforce offers a range of tools and methods to facilitate outbound integrations with external systems. In this section, we will explore the most popular and widely used outbound integration techniques provided by the Salesforce platform.

Declarative with flows

Declarative outbound integrations in Salesforce are primarily achieved using Flow. Salesforce Flow is a powerful tool that allows users to automate business processes without writing any code. Within the realm of outbound integrations, Flow offers two main methods: outbound messages and external services.

Outbound messages are SOAP messages that Salesforce sends to external systems when specific criteria are met. They are designed to notify external systems of changes in Salesforce data. On the other hand, external services provide a way for flows to directly integrate with third-party APIs, supporting HTTP callouts with methods such as GET, POST, PUT, PATCH, and DELETE. When creating an external services package, developers can either add named credential components to the external service registration package or subscribers can establish a named credential in their org that matches the one indicated in the external service registration.

Programmatic with Lightning Web Components

Lightning Web Components (LWC), while primarily designed for building dynamic user interfaces on the Salesforce platform, is also able to perform programmatic outbound integrations.

LWC utilizes the modern Fetch API for making callouts to external services. This API provides a flexible and efficient way to fetch resources, be it over HTTP or HTTPS. The Fetch API in LWC allows developers to make asynchronous requests to external services. Developers can specify the request method (GET, POST, PUT, DELETE), headers, and body, and then process the response once it's received.

Before making a callout from LWC, it's crucial to add the base URL of the API endpoint to the Content Security Policy (CSP) trusted sites in Salesforce.

Programmatic with Apex

Apex, Salesforce's proprietary programming language, stands as a cornerstone for developers aiming for a programmatic approach to outbound integrations. It offers a comprehensive suite of tools and methods to facilitate communication with external systems.

HTTP and HTTPS callouts: Apex provides built-in classes to perform HTTP and HTTPS callouts to external services. These callouts allow Salesforce to integrate with virtually any web service, be it RESTful or SOAP-based.

HttpRequest and HttpResponse classes: At the heart of Apex callouts are the **HttpRequest** and **HttpResponse** classes. The **HttpRequest** class allows developers to set various parameters of the request, such as the endpoint URL, method (GET, POST, PUT, DELETE), headers, and the request body. Once the callout is made, the response from the external service is captured in an instance of the **HttpResponse** class, which provides methods to retrieve the status, headers, and body of the response.

Which one should you use?

Selecting the appropriate technology for outbound integrations in Salesforce hinges on several pivotal factors: the integration pattern in play, the capabilities of the external system, and the specific security prerequisites. It's imperative to juxtapose the constraints highlighted in the upcoming *Integration secrets management* section with the unique requirements of each technology, such as the necessity for named credentials. From my experience, a majority of ISVs lean toward Apex for crafting their outbound integrations. The rationale behind this preference is clear: Apex offers unmatched adaptability. It grants developers the latitude to tailor every facet of the integration, from fine-tuning request headers to devising bespoke error-handling strategies. In essence, while various paths lie ahead, the journey of integration often finds its most reliable guide in Apex.

APIs or events?

When considering the integration of Salesforce with external systems, two other technologies may come to mind: platform events and change data capture.

Platform events[2] are a part of Salesforce's event-driven architecture. They allow you to create and listen for custom notifications and events in Salesforce. These events can be published and subscribed to by both Salesforce and external systems.

Change data capture[3], on the other hand, is designed to capture changes in Salesforce data, allowing you to efficiently synchronize data changes with external systems. It's worth noting that change data capture is built on the foundation of platform events, making it a specialized type of platform event tailored for data changes.

While both of these technologies provide robust solutions for integration, I won't dive deeply into every detail. I generally lean toward using APIs for most integrations due to their versatility. However, it's worth noting that events might be particularly suitable for logging and telemetry scenarios, especially when guaranteed delivery isn't paramount. If you're interested in diving deeper into these technologies, there are an abundance of references available for a comprehensive understanding.

Challenges and limitations with platform events

Platform events come with several challenges and limitations[4]. The main consideration is that they don't offer guaranteed delivery[5], meaning that in scenarios where the infrastructure faces issues, events can get lost, making them unsuitable for transporting irreplaceable data. Additionally, there are significant restrictions on transports like CometD, which can hinder scaling your integration. Some users have also reported reliability concerns, noting that they missed around 5% of messages when integrating with external systems due to network hiccups. Additionally, in the context of outbound integration, the external system must be capable of subscribing to and processing events. This means it needs to implement the CometD protocol and be constantly listening for incoming events.

---

2   https://developer.salesforce.com/docs/atlas.en-us.platform_events.
     meta/platform_events/platform_events_intro.htm
3   https://developer.salesforce.com/docs/atlas.en-us.change_data_
     capture.meta/change_data_capture/cdc_intro.htm
4   https://developer.salesforce.com/docs/atlas.en-us.210.0.platform_
     events.meta/platform_events/platform_event_limits.htm
5   https://developer.salesforce.com/docs/atlas.en-us.platform_events.
     meta/platform_events/platform_events_considerations.htm

Keeping these limitations in mind, let's compare APIs and events in the following table:

Criteria	APIs	Events (Platform Events and Change Data Capture)
Reliability	High reliability with error handling.	Risk of lost events; no guaranteed delivery.
Scalability	Higher limits suitable for high-volume integrations.	Restrictions on transports like CometD.
Flexibility	Supports both push and pull mechanisms.	Primarily push-based.
Complexity	Straightforward request-response approach.	Potential complexity in handling missed events.
Data Integrity	Immediate feedback ensures data integrity.	Risk of data loss or out-of-order events.

In conclusion, while platform events and change data capture offer unique advantages for Salesforce customers, from an ISV perspective, APIs stand out as a more reliable, scalable, and straightforward solution for integrating Salesforce with external systems.

Integration secrets management

When creating managed packages, securing integration secrets is a priority. Different Salesforce metadata types offer ways to store and manage these secrets, including named credentials, external credentials, and protected custom metadata types. In this section, we will explore each of these options, and provide insight on why protected custom metadata types are the most secure and suitable choice for most managed packages.

Starting with named credentials, these offer a streamlined way to manage and authenticate calls to external systems. However, their use comes with substantial caveats for managed package developers. The most significant is that named credentials can be used by any code in the subscriber org. This fact inherently raises the risk of exposure and misuse of your packaged secrets. Furthermore, named credentials present practical limitations, such as the inability to include secret values in metadata due to security reasons – metadata can be accessed in plain text XML. Plus, the remote endpoint details often can't be determined at packaging time, leading to increased complexity. Therefore, I do not recommend using named credentials when shipping secrets in your managed package.

Similarly, external credentials, although designed to securely store secrets for external systems, are not without limitations. According to the Salesforce Metadata Coverage report, as of the time I wrote this book in 2023, their current lack of support for 2GP packaging is the main issue. This lack of support presents a considerable limitation when considering external credentials for managed packages. For the most up-to-date information on metadata support in Salesforce, you can check the official Salesforce Metadata Coverage report at `https://developer.salesforce.com/docs/metadata-coverage`. This resource will allow you to verify whether the aforementioned limitations have been mitigated.

This brings us to protected custom metadata types. These are highly secure options for storing secrets in Salesforce, as they can only be accessed within the same namespace. This means they are impervious to access or use any code outside of the managed package, adding an essential layer of security. Therefore, if your managed package contains secrets, I recommend using protected custom metadata types. This option also provides the flexibility to store multiple secrets for various configurations or environments.

However, storing secrets that vary between subscribers and need to be provisioned in each org requires a different approach. You could either provide instructions for creating a named credential (new or legacy) or develop a custom interface to modify protected custom metadata securely.

In conclusion, while named credentials and external credentials each have their use cases, their limitations often render them unsuitable for storing secrets in managed packages. Instead, the secure and flexible nature of protected custom metadata types generally makes them the ideal choice for this purpose.

Configuring protected custom metadata

When working with Salesforce or any similar platform, securing metadata becomes essential, especially if it contains sensitive data that could impact the security and privacy of the application or its users.

Protected custom metadata, as the name suggests, provides a layer of protection to your metadata. Once incorporated, users in the customer org cannot read or modify the information. This is highly effective in preventing unauthorized changes or potential data breaches.

However, there can be scenarios where you might want a trusted person, such as the customer's administrator, to configure certain pieces of information without providing them access to all the metadata. A common use case is when you want to allow the configuration of a consumer key and consumer secret, required for integrations.

To address such requirements, the optimal solution is to design a configuration wizard. Typically, this is a simple Lightning Web Components (LWC) interface that offers administrators an avenue to update or configure the necessary details without accessing the complete metadata. With this interface in place, the administrators provide the necessary data, and your Apex code then securely saves this information to the protected custom metadata.

Security pitfalls

While the configuration wizard offers enhanced flexibility for administrators, it's essential to remain cautious about potential security pitfalls. A key concern that developers and administrators should be aware of is the vulnerability known as "password echo." Passwords or any sensitive data should never be echoed back to the user once entered, as this is a telltale sign of insecure storage. Ideally, passwords should be stored using methods that involve hashing and salting, ensuring that even the system itself is unaware of the plaintext version, rendering a password echo practically impossible.

Additionally, fields containing sensitive data, such as **Consumer Key** and **Consumer Secret**, should remain concealed from view. Administrators might need to see these values when inputting them initially in the configuration wizard, but they should not have access to them during subsequent interactions or editing. Furthermore, always remain vigilant about where the data is logged. Ensuring that sensitive details do not inadvertently appear in debug logs, JavaScript logs, or other unintended storage points is paramount to maintaining the security integrity of the system. Such vulnerabilities can be a reason to fail a security review, a topic we will delve deeper into in the next chapter.

Utilizing Salesforce APIs for inbound integrations

You might be wondering, what exactly is an API? Well, let's break it down. You can imagine an Application Programming Interface (API) as a diligent and polite butler, always ready to deliver your messages (requests) from one room (an application) to another (a server), fetch the answer, and bring it back to you. It's all very Downton Abbey, but instead of the Dowager Countess, we're dealing with data.

APIs, in the realm of Salesforce, are like efficient bridge builders, crafting sturdy connections between your Salesforce Org and other functionalities, expanding your territory in the business ecosystem.

Types of Salesforce APIs

Okay, so Salesforce has a whole buffet of APIs – each with its own distinct flavor and purpose. It's a veritable API potluck!

SOAP and REST APIs: Consider these as the foundation of every rich API feature Salesforce provides. They're like the essential bread and butter of the API world.

Connect REST API: This is akin to a personal concierge service for mobile applications, adept at everything from delivering notifications to showcasing your Chatter feeds.

Metadata API: This gives you backstage access to the Salesforce Org. It handles the setup much like a stage manager does – managing customizations and build tools instead of stage equipment.

User Interface API: This API lets you orchestrate a unique stage performance – in this case, crafting a user interface that presents Salesforce data or metadata the way you envision it.

GraphQL API: Picture this as the maestro of the API ensemble, orchestrating harmonious interactions by allowing clients to request exactly what they need. Instead of multiple endpoints returning fixed data structures, GraphQL serves as a single endpoint, dynamically shaping the response based on the query.

Bulk API: Imagine this as a superhero sidekick, capable of handling towering volumes of data in a single stride and manipulating records in a powerful sweep.

Streaming API: This is your dedicated news broadcaster, providing a real-time stream of updates to keep you informed about every minute change in your Salesforce Org.

Tooling API: When complex metadata types require an expert hand, the Tooling API steps in, handling them with finesse.

Analytics REST API: Finally, the Analytics API serves as your dependable spy, diving into specific datasets, filters, and dashboards to fetch invaluable intelligence.

Choosing the right Salesforce API for integration

Choosing your API is a bit like a speed-dating event – you want to make sure you find the right match quickly. Do you need real-time visibility of data changes? Streaming API has a nice ring to it. Handling an avalanche of data? Bulk API could be your hero. And if you fancy opening your Salesforce Apex code to the world, the Apex SOAP and REST APIs might just steal your heart.

In the world of APIs, understanding their unique personalities and traits is key to forming a successful relationship. Choose wisely, and you'll create a powerhouse combination of tools that drive productivity and innovation while keeping user experience at the forefront.

Developing an Apex REST endpoint

The standard APIs provide a broad range of functionalities and cater to many common use cases. However, there are times when these standard offerings fall short of ISVs' need for flexibility or don't meet their specific requirements. This necessitates the crafting of custom Apex REST endpoints.

Apex REST methods empower developers to fabricate custom RESTful web services using the Apex programming language. These services, invoked externally, bridge the capability chasm where standard Salesforce APIs might not suffice. The methods offer flexibility, allowing developers to design APIs that align with bespoke requirements. Furthermore, Apex REST methods are embedded seamlessly with standard HTTP methods, facilitating CRUD operations and various other actions.

For an Apex class to stand as a beacon for external services, it needs to be adorned with the **global** annotation. This not only exposes the class as a RESTful web service but ensures accessibility from outside the Salesforce domain.

Best practices for designing your APIs

API design is a meticulous process, and adhering to industry best practices ensures they are robust, comprehensible, and secure:

- Consistency: Uniformity across naming conventions, and both request and response structures, enhances usability.

- Versioning: Inception-stage versioning facilitates change management, safeguarding against potential disruptions.

- HTTP Status Codes: Depicting the outcome of an API call using suitable HTTP status codes is paramount.

- Error Handling: Lucid and meaningful error messages aid users in troubleshooting.

- Security: Incorporate robust authentication and authorization layers. In Salesforce contexts, OAuth often emerges as a top choice. Moreover, it's vital to establish input sanitization and verification to protect against injection and XSS attacks. We'll explore these security elements in more detail in the next chapter.

- Pagination: Implement pagination for data-heavy endpoints, segmenting results into digestible sections.

- Rate Limiting: Enforce rate limits, ensuring equitable usage and mitigating potential misuse.

- Documentation: Detailed documentation, encompassing aspects such as request-response structures, errors, and illustrative examples, bolsters the user experience.

Potential pitfalls

Navigating the maze of API development and deployment, certain pitfalls can challenge the journey:

- Versioning Issues: A glaring omission of versioning can instigate considerable challenges, especially when your product evolves and modifications to the REST endpoint become inevitable. When existing users are tethered to an older version, it can lead to the cumbersome creation of near-identical REST endpoints. A remedy is the embedding of version numbers within the urlMapping, for instance, @RestResource(urlMapping='/AccountsList/v1/*'). Instituting this pattern from the inaugural version wards off future complications.

- Information Disclosure Vulnerability: A subtle leak, such as disclosing system or debugging data, can offer adversaries insights, potentially facilitating attack strategies. Such leaks typically ensue when the system or debugging data inadvertently seeps through an output stream or logging mechanism. To fortify against this, craft custom error messages, being diligent in masking intricate details such as stack traces, path information, or any debug data. It's essential to remedy any such vulnerabilities across all APIs. This vulnerability can be a reason to fail a security review, a topic we will delve deeper into in the next chapter.

API rate limit management – ensuring efficient usage

API rate limiting is Salesforce's mechanism of managing the demand on its resources. It sets a maximum limit on the number of API calls your application can make within a 24-hour period. This feature is designed to prevent an individual app from consuming resources excessively, thus ensuring equal resource distribution and optimal system performance for all apps.

The what and how of your API call limits

Salesforce lays down the law with its API call limits, varying based on the type of org, number of licenses, and extra purchased entitlements. Don't forget, the API calls counted toward these limits include not just those your AppExchange app makes directly, but also those initiated by any integrated services and automated processes within your app.

Efficient use of API calls: a strategic approach

Proper management of API calls is key to ensuring your AppExchange app's smooth operation without slamming into the rate limit. You might want to consider some tactics such as batch processing, which lets you package multiple records into a single API call. This becomes particularly important when dealing with vast data volumes. The aim is to maximize results with minimal expenditure of API calls – the essence of efficiency.

Anticipating and monitoring API usage

Instead of simply reacting to API usage, you need to be proactive. In the design phase of your managed package, calculate the expected API usage for each API your package uses. This forethought ensures that your end customers won't unexpectedly hit the limit. After your application goes live, use Salesforce's "API Usage Notifications" and the limits resource in the REST API to keep a hawk eye on your API call consumption. These measures help you spot trends and adjust your usage pattern accordingly.

Navigating "Too Many Requests" errors: a rescue plan

There may be times when your app exceeds the allocated API call limit, running into a "Too Many Requests" error. This is when you need a solid plan to handle rate-limit errors. Implementing a retry mechanism with exponential backoff is a recommended strategy to ride out this hiccup. It gives your app a timeout before trying the next API call.

In a nutshell, gaining proficiency in API rate limit management is an integral component of proficient AppExchange app development.

Salesforce Connect

Salesforce Connect is a cloud integration service that allows Salesforce users to access and manage data in external apps, right from within Salesforce. It uses the OData (Open Data Protocol) for data integration, allowing Salesforce to interact with data in external systems using RESTful APIs.

OData is an open standard protocol that allows for the creation and consumption of queryable and interoperable RESTful APIs in a simple and standard way. It enables full CRUD support (Create, Read, Update, Delete) to an external system from Salesforce.

Salesforce Connect for ISVs

For ISVs, Salesforce Connect offers a significant advantage. It is available for free as a benefit for ISV partners, with each partner receiving three licenses per customer to connect to partner-owned data sources. This means that ISVs can integrate their own external data sources into their Salesforce applications at no additional cost.

However, it's important to note that there are limitations to this benefit. The free licenses are only for connecting to partner-owned data sources, and any additional Salesforce Connect licenses for other purposes would be available as an add-on at an extra cost.

How can Salesforce Connect help reduce development costs?

Salesforce Connect can help ISVs reduce development costs in several ways:

- Simplified Integration: Salesforce Connect simplifies the process of integrating external data sources into Salesforce. This can significantly reduce the time and effort required for integration, leading to lower development costs.

- Real-Time Access: Salesforce Connect provides real-time access to external data. This eliminates the need for data replication, which can be costly and time-consuming.

- Ease of Use: Salesforce Connect uses OData, a widely used and understood protocol. This makes it easier for developers to work with, reducing the learning curve and speeding up development.

- Reduced Maintenance: By providing a seamless integration solution, Salesforce Connect reduces the need for ongoing maintenance of custom integration solutions, leading to lower long-term costs.

In conclusion, Salesforce Connect is a useful tool for ISVs. It provides a simple, cost-effective way to integrate external data sources into Salesforce, enhancing the functionality and versatility of your applications. To get access to Salesforce Connect, ISVs can log a case in the partner community under the **Log a Case for Help** type to have this added to their product catalog.

Connected apps

A connected app is essentially a bridge between an external application and Salesforce. It uses standard protocols to authenticate, authorize, and provide single sign-on (SSO) for external apps. The external apps integrated with Salesforce can run on various platforms, devices, or SaaS subscriptions.

For example, when you log in to your Salesforce mobile app and see your data from your Salesforce org, you're using a connected app. The Salesforce mobile app is a Connected App that integrates with your Salesforce org to provide you with access to your data.

Understanding Salesforce-connected apps and session IDs

In Salesforce's interconnected ecosystem, connected apps function as a key authorizing tool, allowing external systems to securely "borrow" a session ID for specific uses. It's crucial to appreciate the potent power that a session ID holds — granting a session ID to a third party is akin to handing over a loaded gun, providing them with unrestricted access and potentially extended expiration.

For in-house Salesforce development, sharing a session ID can be a practical option, but it's paramount to follow stringent security measures. In contrast, when it comes to AppExchange development, if you need to share a session ID with an external system, connected apps are not only a recommendation but a requirement due to Salesforce's security review requirements. To ensure secure integrations, ISVs must use a connected app.

Let me repeat: you can find information that connected apps aren't always essential for authorization if you check materials dedicated to Salesforce developers, not dedicated to AppExchange development. There are certain cases, especially in in-house development, where authorization is possible without a connected app. These include the following:

- An outbound message action that creates a session ID for a selected user.

- An interactive Visualforce page using its own session ID to call the REST API.

- An internal company system using a stored username, security token, or password to log in to Salesforce and obtain a session ID.

However, these alternative methods lack the advanced security measures and controlled scope of access offered by connected apps, emphasizing the value of using connected apps for secure, efficient, and controlled integrations.

Advantages of Salesforce-connected apps

Connected apps offer several key advantages. They facilitate the tracking and auditing of usage, thereby promoting transparency and control. The level of access granted can be customized, ensuring external applications only have the necessary privileges. The duration of access is also flexible, and granted access can be easily revoked without having to change your Salesforce password.

Salesforce itself utilizes connected apps in its own products, such as Workbench, Salesforce Mobile, and Environment Hub, adhering to best practices and demonstrating the importance of not directly handling raw login credentials.

Access tokens, refresh tokens, and Salesforce-connected apps

Like session IDs, access tokens and refresh tokens also provide significant access, but they're designed with an additional safety net — they're revocable and can be limited in power, thereby adding a further layer of security to data management.

Connected apps and managed packages

ISVs often wonder whether a connected app needs to be part of a package. While developers can typically perform assertions and get access tokens without an installed package, there are instances where installation becomes necessary. These include cases where administrators want to pre-authorize a connected app without user interaction, or org-specific policies such as login IP restrictions need to be relaxed for the app.

However, connected apps can be installed without the need for a managed or unmanaged package. Therefore, ISVs may not want to include the connected app in the managed package. This can be particularly relevant for hosted or off-platform integrations. Moreover, including the app in the package can complicate package development due to the need for a globally unique client ID or consumer key.

When deciding whether to incorporate a connected app into your managed package, there are several key factors to weigh. Here's a breakdown of the main considerations:

- Packaging Type Limitation: Connected apps are exclusive to 1GP (1st Generation Packaging). If you're utilizing 2GP, you'll need to create a separate package for the connected app.

- Distribution Scope: When you package a connected app, it becomes available to all your customers. This means every customer who installs your package will have access to this app.

- Consistent Authentication: One of the advantages of packaging is the uniformity it brings. By packaging your connected app, you ensure the same consumer key and secret are used across all Salesforce orgs.

- Dual-Layer Authentication: Connected apps employ a two-tier authentication system. The first set of credentials is at the user level, and the second is at the consumer or app level. This dual authentication, using both consumer key/secret and user token/secret, enhances security. In essence, it's akin to having two sets of username/password combinations. While this might seem intricate, it doesn't complicate the deployment process. Plus, if necessary, access permissions can be revoked either at the user or app level.

- App Authentication across the Platform: Upon its creation, a connected app is assigned a unique consumer key and secret. This allows the app to be authenticated across the Salesforce platform, ensuring its legitimacy.

- Flexibility with Callback URLs: A significant advantage of connected apps is their ability to support multiple callback URLs. This feature is particularly beneficial when you need to specify different environments, such as production and testing. By packaging the connected app with multiple callback URLs, customers can seamlessly switch between production and testing environments as needed.

By understanding these considerations, you can make an informed decision about whether a connected app is the right fit for your managed package.

If you decide to include a connected app in your package, one recommended way to configure a connected app for secure integration is to use the OAuth 2.0 JWT Bearer Flow. This robust and secure flow allows the application to authenticate itself to Salesforce, without the need to share sensitive information such as passwords or security tokens.

How (and why) your customer can install your connected app

Installing a connected app is more than just facilitating integration between Salesforce and external platforms. For your customer's system administrators, it's about gaining control and enhancing security. By installing and configuring a connected app, administrators can define who can use the apps, where they can access them from, and under what conditions. This encompasses setting up profiles, permission sets, IP range restrictions, and even implementing multi-factor authentication (MFA) for bolstered security.

Before diving into the installation process, it's crucial to educate your customer's system administrator on the importance and methodology of installing the connected app. This step ensures that they understand the significance of the app and can assist or take over the installation if necessary.

There are several methods for installing a connected app on your customer's Salesforce org:

- Through a Managed Package: This is one of the most straightforward methods, here, the system administrator installs a managed package that inherently contains the connected app.

- Direct Installation URL: In scenarios where the connected app isn't bundled in a package, it can be directly installed using a dedicated link. This link should be readily available in associated documentation, such as a configuration guide. Here's how to get this link:

- Sign in to the Salesforce org where you set up the connected app.

- Head to **Setup**, then select **Apps**, followed by **App Manager**. From there, locate your connected app.

- Look for the **id** URL parameter (it'll begin with OCi). Once you've found it, copy and paste it at this link: https://login.salesforce.com/identity/app/AppInstallApprovalPage.apexp?app_id=0CiXXXXXXXXXXXX

- Utilizing the Connected Apps OAuth Usage Page: This platform enlists all OAuth connected apps that are currently linked to users in your org. There will be an **Install** button next to an app if users are accessing it but haven't installed it.

- Head over to **Setup**, then pick **Apps**, followed by **Connected Apps**, and finally, choose **Connected Apps OAuth Usage**. From the list, select the app you want and hit **Install**.

No matter how you've installed the connected app, the system administrator can simply navigate to **Setup**, then choose **Apps**, followed by **Connected Apps**, and finally, select **Manage Connected Apps**. From there, you can tweak the local access permissions for the app.

Canvas SDK

Salesforce Canvas SDK is a mature and robust tool designed to integrate external web applications seamlessly with Salesforce. This technology establishes a bridge between Salesforce and other platforms, offering a diverse range of options for effective UI integrations. While canvas apps open a plethora of opportunities, understanding their strengths, limitations, and suitable use cases is key to leveraging their full potential.

Inherent challenges and benefits of Canvas SDK

Canvas SDK, despite being a powerful tool, confronts a significant challenge concerning UI and UX consistency. Since it brings the external system's user interface into Salesforce, this may not always align with Salesforce's native UI and UX conventions seamlessly. This difference can deter ISVs aiming for a consistent user interface experience across their applications. As a result, even though Canvas SDK is a mature and capable technology, its adoption rate among ISVs has not been as widespread as might be expected.

However, Canvas SDK offers several significant benefits, making it an attractive option under the right circumstances. One of the main advantages is the potential for lower development costs, especially if an interface for the external system already exists. This benefit can be a substantial advantage when compared to building a custom user interface in a managed package and integrating it via APIs.

Moreover, the Canvas SDK can simplify operations within a connected app framework, eliminating the need for maintaining two related code bases – one for the managed package and another for the external system. By reducing the number of code bases, developers can streamline their workflows and decrease the overall complexity of the system.

Aura versus Visualforce versus LWC

Developers have two main options when it comes to exposing a canvas app within Salesforce: Aura components and Visualforce, each with their unique strengths and limitations. Visualforce allows for importing the Canvas JavaScript SDK to handle Canvas events. On the other hand, Aura components can maintain the Salesforce Global Navigation Header using the `lightning:isUrlAddressable` feature. It's important to note that as of 2023, **Lightning Web Components** (**LWC**) does not support Canvas, restricting the options for using this technology within the Salesforce ecosystem.

Canvas application configurations and packaging dilemmas

Key configurations for a canvas app, such as OAuth enablement, canvas app URL, access method, and locations, are managed within the connected app. Developers also have the option to use a Canvas Lifecycle handler to manage additional aspects of the canvas app during runtime.

Canvas apps, while offering several benefits, are not frequently used due to their limitations in maintaining UI consistency and lack of support for LWC. It's also important to note that Salesforce tends to discourage ISVs from using Canvas, not due to security concerns – indeed, Canvas is safer compared to an IFrame solution – but rather because of perception. Utilizing Canvas can be perceived as a lack of serious commitment to integrating with Salesforce. When ISVs publish a Canvas-based solution for Salesforce on AppExchange, they might overlook the fact that Canvas usually implies two distinct user experiences. This can catch customers off guard and potentially lower the chances of a successful sale. There might be additional technical shortcomings with Canvas that could make partnership and app success less likely.

If you're considering using a canvas app, it's recommended to discuss your use cases with Salesforce or one of the **Product Development Outsourcer** (**PDO**) partners, described in *Chapter 12*. Their expert guidance can help ensure that your Salesforce integration aligns with best practices and is positioned for success.

Comparing integration via the REST API versus the Canvas SDK

The choice between developing a lightweight app with REST API integration and the Canvas SDK in Salesforce should be guided by several factors, each of which contributes to the ease of development, flexibility, and ultimate success of the integration. In the following table, we contrast the REST API and Canvas SDK from a range of perspectives to assist you in making an informed decision.

Factor	REST API Integration	Canvas App
Interactivity and Integration Depth	Easy to implement interactive features and deeper integration, offering a richer user experience.	Implementing interactivity and deeper integration can be challenging due to the Canvas SDK's proprietary nature.
Standard Compliance	Uses well-supported and widely understood internet standards, simplifying the development process.	Relies on proprietary SDKs and technologies that may not be universally understood, posing potential learning curves and integration challenges.
Backend and Frontend Separation	Maintains a clear separation between the backend and frontend, promoting cleaner, more maintainable code.	Often results in a mix of backend and browser scripts, complicating code management and the separation of concerns.
Requirement of Connected App	No need for a connected app, simplifying setup and reducing administrative overhead.	Requires a connected app, which adds complexity in packaging and setup.
Support for Lightning and SLDS	Fully supports Salesforce Lightning and Salesforce Lightning Design System (SLDS), ensuring a consistent UI and UX with the Salesforce environment.	Limited support for Lightning and SLDS, potentially leading to an inconsistent UI and UX compared to the standard Salesforce environment.
Starting and Scaling	Allows to start with a simple app and gradually scale up by adding features as per requirement.	The initial setup can be complicated, and scaling up by adding features might require a significant rework.

For developing a lightweight application, the REST API integration appears to offer more advantages over a Canvas app, particularly in terms of standard compliance, ease of setup, and support for Lightning and SLDS. Furthermore, the REST API's support for iterative development makes it a more flexible choice for evolving application requirements.

Summary

Well done, valiant explorers! You've successfully completed this leg of our adventure, diving deep into the world of seamless integration with external systems in Salesforce. Your valiant efforts to decipher the enigma of technical architecture and your dedication to nurturing various integration patterns, just like a dutiful gardener, have rewarded you with bountiful knowledge.

Your brave exploration led you through the realm of Salesforce APIs, akin to unearthing hidden treasures. You've uncovered the magic of Salesforce Connect, your personal teleportation device, ready to whisk data from distant lands into your Salesforce kingdom. The Canvas SDK revealed itself as your loyal craftsman, embedding third-party applications seamlessly into Salesforce, and connected apps stood as vigilant gatekeepers, ensuring safe passage between Salesforce and external systems.

As we bid adieu to this chapter, remember the insights you've gathered are invaluable in building robust applications that integrate effortlessly with external systems. But hold on to your explorer's hat, because our next adventure beckons us into the security review process. We'll decipher the cryptic scrolls of Apex and LWC code requirements, and learn how to survey external systems and endpoints for potential threats. You'll master the tools of the trade, Salesforce Code Analyzer and Checkmarx, to ensure your code's security and compliance. We'll also prepare documentation and identify false positives, essential to successfully navigating the security review. So, tighten your grip on the adventurer's compass as we continue our thrilling journey toward AppExchange success!

Security Review

Greetings, bold adventurers of the digital realm! As we traverse the ever-evolving landscape of Salesforce, we face a crucial challenge—the fierce dragon known as "security review." Aye, 'tis a formidable beast, but fear not! Our noble quest, armed with the right knowledge and tools, is to tame this dragon, win its trust, and ultimately ensure the security of our precious treasure—customer data.

Prepare for a journey through the following territories:

• The significance of the security review process and its role in maintaining high-security standards in Salesforce applications

• Ensuring compliance with Salesforce security requirements and avoiding common pitfalls

• Tools and techniques for scanning external systems and endpoints

• Preparing false positive documentation for a smoother security review process

• Embracing the journey of continuous security improvement as an AppExchange partner

By the end of this chapter, you will be a seasoned navigator of the security review process, equipped to build trust with your Salesforce subjects and ensure the flourishing of your application within the grand kingdom of AppExchange.

Tighten your boots, fellow explorers! Our journey continues, driven by the famous words of Salesforce CTO, Parker Harris, "Nothing is more important to our company than the privacy of our customers' data." Thus we march, toward a future of secure Salesforce adventures!

Understanding the security review process

Welcome to the exhilarating marathon of developing your first AppExchange application! You're tying up your laces at the starting line of a course where the sprint of innovation links arms with the endurance of security. Salesforce, the world-class race organizer in the marathon of **customer relationship management (CRM)** platforms, has staked its reputation on one thing above all—trust. And a significant water station on this trust marathon? The security review process— an exhaustive vetting that each application must clear, akin to our marathon's rigorous checkpoints, before making it to the finish line at the Salesforce AppExchange marketplace.

Think of the security review process as your personal marathon trainer, diving into the granularities of your application's design, architecture, and data handling practices. Its mission? To uncover those sneaky, potential security cramps and ensure your application is fit enough to run Salesforce's marathon of high-security standards. It's the thorough pat-down at the starting line, scanning everything from your application's running gear (source code) and energy gels (data storage) to its hydration strategy (transmission methods).

As committed marathoners in this AppExchange race, understanding the security review process and its race rules is not a "nice-to-have"—it's your race-day strategy. It's not just a daunting hill to conquer but a pacing guide, helping you avoid those brutal wall-hitting moments. Its job? To help you spot potential security side-stitches early enough in the training cycle, giving you ample time to tweak your stride, hydrate, or whatever it takes to keep those issues from slowing you down. This strategic approach to security is not only your ticket to a safe and successful race day (read: application) but also your personal PR in the trust-building race with your users.

Training with security at the forefront is like diligently following a well-planned marathon training program—it's tough and requires dedication, but boy does it pay off! It steers you clear from those nasty, time-guzzling injuries (read: revisions) later in the race and boosts your odds of breezing through the security review checkpoint at the very first attempt. Plus, it shows your users that their security isn't an eleventh-hour, carb-loading attempt for you, but a well-thought-out part of your training regimen. And who knows, this could be the secret sauce that nudges them to cheer for your application on the big day!

Fees and timeline

The security review process involves several key steps, as follows:

1. You submit your application for security review via the Partner Community.
2. The security review Operations team verifies your submission, a process that typically takes 1-2 days.
3. Your submission is then added to the Product Security queue.
4. The Product Security team performs tests on your application and validates the results.
5. Finally, the security review Operations team notifies you of the results.

The timeline for *steps 3-5* typically spans 4-6 weeks. However, it's worth noting that most ISVs don't pass the security review on their first attempt. While some applications might get approved on their first or second try, others might need a third attempt or even more. As a result, you can optimistically anticipate your application to be live on the AppExchange marketplace within a minimum of 4 weeks from your initial submission. Yet, it's also possible for the entire process to stretch to 3 months or longer. Oh, and just a heads-up! If you're aiming to drop your app during a peak time, such as around *Dreamforce* (you know—that massive annual Salesforce event), there might be some extra submission deadlines you'll want to keep an eye on to get your results in time.

Figure 6.1: Security review timeline

In terms of fees, for freemium, paid, or solutions requiring a paid add-on, the security review fee is $999 for each of the following scenarios: initial security review, resubmission after addressing detected issues from a previous security review, periodic re-review of an earlier approved solution, and when a partner requests an audit of a new version of their solution. You can submit up to four packages with the same namespace in a single submission, with a single payment of $999 per attempt.

Given that submissions typically require two attempts to pass, the average total cost for getting your application through the security review process is $1,998.

However, it's important to note that security review fees are waived for free solutions. This means that whether it's an initial security review, a resubmission after addressing detected issues in a previous security review, listing a new version of a solution that was previously approved, or a periodic re-review of a solution that was previously approved, there is no charge.

The fees may be subject to change, and the figures given are current as of 2023. You can check the most recent fees at `https://developer.salesforce.com/docs/atlas.en-us.packagingGuide.meta/packagingGuide/security_review_fees.htm`.

Testing your application

Ensuring the security of your application is paramount before submitting it for the Salesforce security review. This process involves not just a review of your application's architecture and components, but also its potential vulnerabilities. In the following subsections, you'll learn some key practices to guide you in testing your application.

Pre-assessment

Before submitting your application for a security review, perform an internal assessment of your solution to confirm its architecture is secure. Evaluate all aspects, such as object permissions, included components, custom code, web services, and third-party services being used. The aim is to secure all possible entry points and vulnerabilities that could be exploited to access data.

Your application should be robust, adhering to Salesforce best practices such as bulkifying your Apex code when dealing with records in triggers and avoiding code injection in **Salesforce Object Query Language** (**SOQL**), Apex, or cross-scripting.

Adversarial testing

After you've addressed all known security issues, try to find more! Encourage your testing team to think like hackers and attack your product to try to steal its data. This adversarial testing approach, coordinated with your team's security advocate, could reveal vulnerabilities that have been overlooked. The *OWASP Web Security Testing Guide* is an excellent resource to help you devise a plan for adversarial testing. You can find it on the **Open Worldwide Application Security Project** (**OWASP**) web page: `https://owasp.org/www-project-web-security-testing-guide/`.

By following these strategies, you can submit your application for the security review with confidence, knowing you've done everything possible to secure your application. Your meticulous attention to potential vulnerabilities will not only ensure a smoother security review process but will also lead to a safer, more reliable product for your users.

Components required for the AppExchange security review process

Running a successful security review process on AppExchange is like preparing for a big city marathon—it requires the right gear, a solid understanding of the race route, and, of course, the tenacity to see it through. This chapter is your personal fitness trainer, mapping out the must-have components for this marathon while also explaining why you need to tie your laces tight, wear breathable fabric, and carry energy bars. Or, in AppExchange terms, why you need a reliable test environment, well-organized documentation, effective static code analysis results, and clear false positive documentation.

Preparing the test environment with an installed and configured managed package

Your test environment is like your running shoes in this marathon. Just as a seasoned runner needs the right shoes that provide support and prevent injuries, a good test environment forms a solid base for your application, helping identify any bugs or vulnerabilities..

A well-prepared test environment is essential for the security review process. Use the Environment Hub, described in *Chapter 2*, to create a test environment, and then install your managed package and configure it. This environment should be a fully configured and authenticated demo org, complete with sample data to help the reviewer understand how your app works. Having a proper test environment ensures that the reviewer can effectively assess the security and functionality of your app.

Salesforce's Environment Hub offers a streamlined solution for creating and configuring a new Salesforce org, which you can utilize as a security review test environment.

You can create a preconfigured security review test org using Salesforce Trialforce template ID 0TT3t000002nvUr[1]. After setting it up, install and configure the latest version of the package in the test org.

Alternatively, you can utilize the Environment Hub to create an empty org and configure it manually. For seamless access and operations, it's crucial to safelist Salesforce's IP ranges. While you have the option to set these login ranges at the profile level, doing so at the network level can restrict the size of the IP range you're allowed to set. To ensure your org's security and accessibility, please safelist the Salesforce IP ranges provided in its official documentation[2]. Additionally, to let Salesforce employees log in to your org seamlessly, include the following specific IPs and ranges:

- 13.108.0.0 - 13.111.255.255
- 62.17.146.0 - 62.17.146.255
- 85.222.134.0 - 85.222.134.255
- 104.161.246.0 - 104.161.246.255
- 122.15.249.154, 59.144.126.115
- 182.71.125.154 - 182.71.125.155
- 182.72.29.238 and 136.232.119.246

---

1   https://salesforce.quip.com/pfqeA8kRTraY
2   https://salesforce.quip.com/XaCHAb5Yo15Y

If **two-factor authentication (2FA)** is enabled in your test org, you should additionally disable it for the review process.

Remember—the package you install must match the version you're submitting for the security review and should not be in a beta state. If an extra org setup is needed to use your app, make sure to do that as well.

If your test org is not configured correctly, the security review Operations team is going to notify you about it via email and specify the next steps:

Dear Partner,

Thank you for your recent Security Review submission for Formula Debugger. Before we can begin the review however, there are some issues with your submission which must be resolved:

Regarding your submission:

- **Identity challenge is enabled on your org.**
-
  - you'll need to safe-list Salesforce IP ranges. you can set login ranges at the profile level (or you can also do it at the network level, but it limits the size of the IP range you can set.
  - Please safe-list the following Salesforce IPs ranges (https://help.salesforce.com/articleView?id=000321501&language=en_US&type=1&mode=1) and also the following:
  - 182.72.29.238, 182.71.125.154, 182.71.125.155, **136.232.119.246, 13.110.78.8**
  - **ranges: 1>13.108.0.0 - 13.111.255.255**
        2> 62.17.146.0 - 62.17.146.255
        3>85.222.134.0 -85.222.134.255

Figure 6.2: A screenshot of an email notifying you about issues encountered within the test environment, emphasizing the need for attention and resolution

Documentation

Next up, documentation. This is the equivalent of your hydration strategy. You wouldn't run a marathon without a water bottle, would you? A well-documented application ensures you're quenching the thirst of reviewers with vital information, helping them understand your application better. Prepare the following documents:

- **Description of the app**: Write a comprehensive description of your app to help the reviewer understand its purpose and functionality.

- **Solution architecture**: Provide an overview of your application, including any relevant information about your solution and architecture that the Salesforce review team should know.

- **Use-case document**: Outline the primary use cases of your app, focusing on how users interact with it. This document should guide the reviewer through the app's functionality and help them understand how it works.

Salesforce doesn't provide specific templates or requirements for these document formats. Instead, you're encouraged to adhere to industry standards. Your Salesforce Architect should guide you through this process. If you find it challenging to document your architecture, it might indicate a gap in your design capabilities. In such situations, it's advisable to collaborate with a **Product Development Outsourcer (PDO)** Partner to avoid potentially costly mistakes during the app development phase. We'll explore this option in more detail in *Chapter 12*.

Having well-prepared documentation enables the reviewer to gain a thorough understanding of your app and its architecture, ensuring an efficient review process.

Static code analysis results

Think of static code analysis results as your energy gel packs. Just like how these gel packs offer instant energy boosts, your static code analysis results give immediate insight into the performance of your application's code and its security posture. Conduct your own review using scanners to identify potential vulnerabilities and improve your app's security. Salesforce recommends four scanners, as follows:

- **Salesforce Code Analyzer**[3]: Uses multiple rule engines to scan your code, including Apex, Visualforce, JavaScript, and TypeScript. It can be integrated into your **continuous integration (CI)** process to regularly monitor code health. Powered by the Salesforce CLI, this plugin is mandatory for the security review process. Any findings from the **Security** category should either be resolved or documented as false positives.

---

3 https://developer.salesforce.com/docs/atlas.en-us.packagingGuide.meta/packagingGuide/security_review_code_analyzer_scan.htm

- **Checkmarx**: Scans solutions hosted on the platform, including Apex code, Visualforce elements, and Lightning components. As of 2023, when I'm penning this book, it's a compulsory component of the security review process. Hence, any findings should either be addressed or noted as false positives. Looking ahead, it's conceivable that Salesforce Code Analyzer might fully take over its role in the future.

- **Chimera**: Integrates the best open-source scanning technology in one service, powered by Heroku. Use if your solution has parts that reside on another platform that you control. Use Burp Suite or **OWASP Zed Attack Proxy (OWASP ZAP)** instead of Chimera if your solution connects to external endpoints that you do not control.

- **ZAP**: A free online scanner created by OWASP that requires installation on a local system. Use if part of your solution is deployed on a domain that you don't control.

These scanners help you identify and address potential vulnerabilities, ensuring a more secure app and a smoother security review process.

Force.com Source Scanner Results

Job Type: Portal	Preset: PortalAll	Scan Id:
Description: N/A		Email Address:user@email.com
Security Issues: 43	Service Version: v3.2	Scan Start: 2021-07-21 01:46:56
Quality Issues: 76	CxEngine: 8.9.0.210 HF7	Scan End: 2021-07-21 03:22:53

For any questions about this service, please consult our scanner help page at
https://security.secure.force.com/security/tools/forcecom/scannerhelp

Query	Group	Issues
SOQL SOSL Injection	Apex Critical Security Risk	11
Sharing	Apex Serious Security Risk	28
URL Redirection Attack	Apex Serious Security Risk	3
FLS Create	Apex Serious Security Risk	1
Bulkify Apex Methods Using Collections In Methods	Apex Code Quality	25
Multiple Forms In Visualforce Page	Apex Code Quality	14
Queries With No Where Or Limit Clause	Apex Code Quality	2
Async Future Method Inside Loops	Apex Code Quality	3
Test Methods With No Assert	Apex Code Quality	29
SOSL SOQL Statments Inside Loops	Apex Code Quality	1
Hardcoding Ids	Apex Code Quality	1
DML Statements Inside Loops	Apex Code Quality	1

Figure 6.3: A snapshot of the Checkmarx scan results revealing numerous vulnerabilities in a package, highlighting the extensive effort required to address and resolve these issues

False positive documentation

Finally, false positive documentation is your race-day bib. Just as your bib identifies you in the marathon, false positive documentation distinguishes genuine security threats from false alarms. It's like the bib that says, "No, I'm not just a spectator who wandered onto the course. I'm running this race!"

If the static code analysis results identify any false positives—issues flagged as potential vulnerabilities that are not actual risks—prepare documentation explaining why these issues are not genuine vulnerabilities. This document should address issues from all scanners relevant to your submission. Additionally, document any intentionally implemented use cases that may not seem secure to the reviewer. This documentation should clarify the context and reasoning behind the flagged issues, demonstrating that they do not pose a risk to your app's security.

False Positives

CRUD Create

Logger.cls (line 67)

A helper class called Logger.cls makes it possible to create and retrieve the Log__c entities used to store application logs. CRUD/FLS enforcement was omitted because application logs should be created in the system context.

CRUD Read

Util.cls (lines 377)

This query should retrieve and cache RecordTypes in the system context.

Env.cls (lines 41-44)

With the help of that query, you can obtain basic org configurations like IsSandbox, LanguageLocalKey, etc. The system context should be used for this.

Bulkify Apex Methods Using Collections In Methods

TestDataFactory.cls

Methods are not used outside of the context of a test; they are only used for automatically instantiating test data for unit tests.

Test Methods With No Assert

Path 1 (Test_HttpSvc.cls)

The method in question makes use of the HttpCalloutMock class, which has an assert in the response method.

Figure 6.4: A partial excerpt from the false positive documents providing responses to specific findings in the Checkmarx report, encompassing details such as the type of finding, precise location, and clarifications regarding each identified issue

Now that you're familiar with the process of preparing false positive documentation, let's dive right into the submission process.

The submission process

After all your hard work in planning and preparing, you're now equipped to submit your app! Make your way to the Salesforce Partner Community, log in, and navigate to the **Security Review Wizard**. You'll spot the wizard in a new tab (aptly named **Security Review**) in the **Listing** section of the Partner Community.

If you're submitting your app for review for the first time, you'll have to connect your uploaded package to a listing, which occurs on the **App** tab. Here, you'll also answer a few fundamental questions; then, you can initiate your submission.

Here are the necessary steps to complete in the wizard:

1. **Contact Information**: This is where you'll specify who will be reached out to for more information or for a failure or pass notification. Ensure one of your contact options is a distribution list.

2. **Compliance**: In this section, you'll provide information regarding your company's security readiness. If your app interacts with the **payment card industry** (**PCI**), credit card information (if you integrate with a credit card gateway), the **Health Insurance Portability and Accountability Act** (**HIPAA**), and so on, this is where you'll provide this information. If none of these aspects applies to your app, simply check **N/A** and proceed.

3. **Questionnaire**: Here, you'll detail your packaged solution's architecture and any third-party services it integrates with. Essentially, you're describing the general architecture environment required by your packaged application.

4. **Docs**: This is where you'll upload code scans, false positives, solution architecture, and use-case documentation you've prepared.

5. **Test Environments**: Here, you'll submit credentials for your demo environment and any integrated off-platform service, client, mobile, or desktop app. You're required to submit a fully configured representative demo environment of your packaged solution.

Security review operations verification

The security review operations verification phase is a crucial step in Salesforce's security review process. This phase entails checking for the presence and correctness of related packages in the demo organization, ensuring the submitted version is accurate, verifying the completeness of use-case documentation, and assessing the validity of scans and false positive documentation. Any discrepancies in these areas can cause delays in the review process. Once the verification is complete, you'll receive an email either confirming your application's placement in the security review queue or detailing any issues that need resolution:

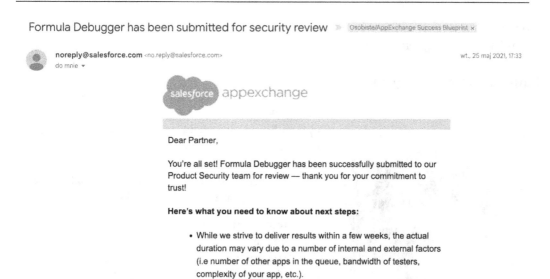

Figure 6.5: A screenshot depicting an email confirmation indicating that your application has successfully entered the security review queue

Submitting an application for a security review with a trial PBO

For Salesforce partners who intend to submit a **second-generation package** (**2GP**) for security review and are still operating on a trial PBO, there are certain guidelines and practices to follow. This is to ensure a smooth security review process and prevent potential delays or operational issues.

In the context of the **Partner Application Development Agreement** (**PADA**) and **Salesforce Partner Program Agreement** (**SPPA**) described in *Chapter 2*, it's important to note that the completion of the PADA is a key requirement for activating a PBO from trial mode. However, the new security review procedure allows for the submission of an app without having to complete the PADA first.

To avoid problems that may arise from using a trial Dev Hub org for the security review, the security review team has implemented a default policy of blocking 2GPs built on trial Dev Hub orgs from entering the security review. This policy is intended to prevent complications that can occur if a 2GP becomes orphaned due to the expiration and purging of a trial Dev Hub org.

For partners facing this block, there is an option to book a remediation meeting with Salesforce experts to review their submissions. In these sessions, the risks associated with using a non-active Dev Hub org are explained, and clear guidance is provided to rectify any issues identified. If it is confirmed during the remediation meeting that the partner is planning to activate their PBO after executing the PADA, an exception to the "no trial Dev Hub org" policy may be granted. This allows the partner to progress through the security review process while concurrently finalizing the contract with the Salesforce ISV Sales team.

To optimize the security review process, partners without a PADA in place may proactively schedule a remediation meeting before submitting for a security review.

Failing the security review

Alright, dear reader, take a deep breath and let's have a heart-to-heart chat. Imagine you're walking the red carpet of AppExchange stardom, and then...you trip. In more professional terms, your application has failed the security review. But before you start seeing that as a tabloid scandal, I want you to repeat after me: "It's not the end of the world."

Sure—resubmitting your application means you have to cough up the fee ($999, to be precise) and you'll have to wait a few more weeks but think of it as your entrance being delayed for a grander reveal. The point is, that this hiccup in your journey to AppExchange fame might affect your **go-to-market (GTM)** timeline, but it's far from a showstopper.

Now, about the "failure". That word sounds quite dramatic, doesn't it? Conjures up images of doom and gloom. But hold on—let's toss that mindset out the window. Let's not think of it as failing, but rather as...learning. Salesforce, the benevolent godparent of AppExchange, truly wants you to flourish. However, it also has to keep the interests of its customers in mind, who are the potential audience for your showstopping app.

So, what if it takes a few iterations of your package before you finally pass? Don't think of Salesforce as a stern judge on a talent show, giving a verdict on your performance. It's more like a friendly mentor who gives you constructive criticism, wanting you to improve and shine. If you struggle, they're ready to sit down with you during office hours to give you the helping hand you need.

The security review process? Well, let's call it what it really is: a security-hardening sprint. The feedback you get from Salesforce is basically your personal trainer, helping you sculpt your app into the perfect shape. So, dust yourself off and get ready for another round—every hurdle is a step toward a more secure app.

Why doesn't the security review spot all vulnerabilities in the first round? Well, each review is like an episode of a TV show—time-boxed and structured. The advantage? It keeps costs manageable for you and reduces review queue times. But as with any good series, there can be a few cliffhangers. Not every issue is spotted or fully resolved in a single episode.

Why might your app pass the initial scan and fail the deeper review? Think of the initial scan as a general health checkup, while the deeper review is more like a full medical examination. The latter requires more detailed assessment and human expertise, catching more subtle issues.

What if you've fixed all the findings but still fail the security review? Imagine you've baked a cake and the recipe asks you to remove the lumps in the batter. You find and remove some, but not all. The security review report points out the lumps (security issues), but it may not highlight every single one. After all, creating a smooth batter (secure code) is part of your recipe (development process).

Remember—this journey isn't about ticking boxes. Security isn't a task you check off your to-do list. It's a mindset, a philosophy—a lifestyle, if you will. So, prepare to embrace it wholeheartedly, and before you know it, you'll be making your grand entrance.

The email shown in the following screenshot contains a report that includes descriptions of vulnerabilities that were found in a failed security review:

Formula Debugger: Security Review - Your App Did Not Pass   Osobiste/AppExchange Success Blueprint ×

noreply@salesforce.com <no.reply@salesforce.com>   śr., 9 cze 2021, 20:51
do mnie, appxsecurityreview@salesforce.com ▾

salesforce appexchange

Dear Partner,

We have completed the security review of your application . Unfortunately, we have found some issues which concern us, and thus, at this time we cannot approve your application for final listing.

Trust and security are core values at Salesforce, and we are committed to working with you to resolve those issues. The following vulnerabilities need to be resolved:

-Lightning: CSP-Incompatible Javascript

In order to list Formula Debugger publicly on the AppExchange, the vulnerabilities from the report must be fixed.

Figure 6.6: A sample email notification illustrating a failed security review, showcasing a list of vulnerabilities alongside an accompanying detailed report

You can view the details in the following screenshot:

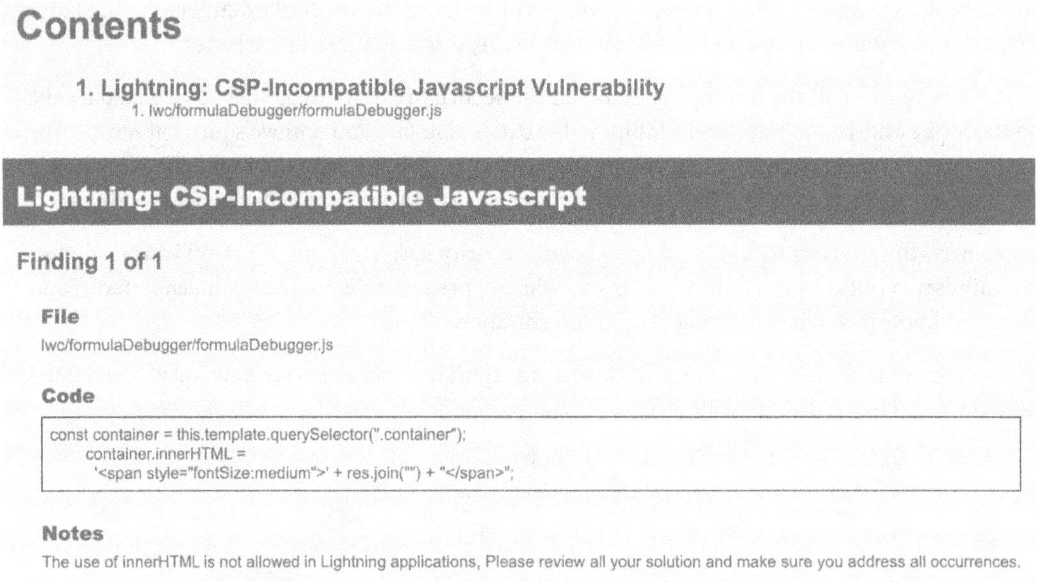

Contents

1. Lightning: CSP-Incompatible Javascript Vulnerability
  1. lwc/formulaDebugger/formulaDebugger.js

Lightning: CSP-Incompatible Javascript

Finding 1 of 1

File

lwc/formulaDebugger/formulaDebugger.js

Code

```
const container = this.template.querySelector(".container");
    container.innerHTML =
      '<span style="fontSize:medium">' + res.join("") + "</span>";
```

Notes

The use of innerHTML is not allowed in Lightning applications, Please review all your solution and make sure you address all occurrences.

Figure 6.7: An exemplar report revealing vulnerabilities identified by
Salesforce during a comprehensive security review

Addressing challenges and advancing development

A first-time security review failure is not uncommon and shouldn't be considered a disaster. Instead, developers should embrace this as a learning experience, taking the feedback from the security review team to heart to make necessary enhancements to the application. Quick triage of identified issues, clear delegation of tasks among team members, and swift remediation of problems are crucial steps following a failed review. It's important to keep the lines of communication open with management to ensure everyone understands the plan and actions needed to rectify the issues. To avoid potential hiccups and to maintain a smooth process, I suggest keeping any new code separate from the main branch until the security review gets the green light. This separation ensures a neat, clear passage through the packaging organization and fosters an efficient, orderly resolution of security issues.

Partner office hours

Partner office hours are a useful opportunity that Salesforce offers for free to help AppExchange partners comprehend and navigate the security review process. Available in two formats, Operations and Technical, these sessions offer direct access to Salesforce's security review team members, providing guidance on everything from submission logistics to the resolution of specific technical issues. Let's take a closer look:

- **Operations office hours**: These sessions are dedicated to answering questions about the logistics and requirements of the security review. They can be especially helpful if you're unsure about which components of your solution fall under the scope of the review, what kinds of reports and scan results are expected from you, or what happens if your solution doesn't pass the review.

- **Technical office hours**: These are meant to provide specific security-related technical assistance. They are invaluable when you need help navigating AppExchange security requirements, implementing secure design elements in your solution, understanding and handling issues detected by automated security scanning tools, interpreting findings in your security review report, distinguishing between genuine issues and false positives, and figuring out how to resolve flagged issues in your security review report.

Given their popularity, it's recommended to schedule your office hours as early as possible. You can book these sessions via the Partner Security Portal. Providing detailed information about your questions or concerns in the intake form will allow for a more productive and focused session.

Security requirements

When you set off on the exciting journey as a part of the AppExchange Partner Program, there's an essential road map that you must follow—the security requirements. These obligations are not just for all AppExchange Partners and their applications but also are tailored for those applications that are closely associated with certain technologies or industry-specific uses.

Each time you make or modify an AppExchange listing, it's like signing a virtual pact that you've complied with these requirements. Although this document attempts to be comprehensive, it doesn't cover every possible security scenario. Hence, Partners are always urged to adhere to the industry security norms applicable to them.

Before your solution graces the AppExchange marketplace, there's a checklist to tick off. It comprises the following items:

1. **Designate a security expert**: Security is not an afterthought but an integral part of the development life cycle. Having a dedicated security expert in your team not only ensures compliance with security guidelines but also prevents unnecessary security breaches during coding.

2. **Implement a security policy**: Create a robust security policy that clarifies how your company safeguards customer data. Also, inform customers about their part in securing the solution.

3. **Inventory third-party libraries**: Maintain a list of all third-party libraries and their versions necessary for your solution to function properly.

4. **Create architecture diagrams**: Provide diagrams that portray data touchpoints, information flows, authentication, authorizations, and other security controls.

5. **List certifications**: Share all relevant certifications, such as HIPAA, the **PCI Data Security Standard (PCI DSS)**, **System and Organization Controls 2 (SOC 2)**, and **International Organization for Standardization (ISO)** 27001.

6. **Document security-assurance activities**: Note down activities, including software development life-cycle methodology, vulnerability management, remediation **service-level agreements (SLAs)**, supplier and dependency security program, security awareness training, and security breach response procedures.

7. **List sensitive data**: Provide a comprehensive list of sensitive data that your solution processes or stores.

8. **Disclose data storage locations and providers**: If you deal with regulated data, disclose the data storage locations, mentioning countries and providers such as **Amazon Web Services (AWS)**, Azure, and **Google Cloud Platform (GCP)**.

9. **Identify third-party data sharing**: List all third-party suppliers that you share customer data with.

10. **Share contact info**: Publish contact information for seamless customer support and incident reporting.

As you fulfill these requirements, remember that they serve as your trust-building arsenal for your AppExchange journey.

Developing secure applications

Building secure applications is a crucial responsibility for every developer. This section provides a high-level overview of secure application development practices, drawing on Salesforce's *Secure Coding Guide* and resources provided by OWASP. However, these guidelines only scratch the surface of application security. For in-depth information and detailed guidance, developers should delve into the resources provided by OWASP and Salesforce's comprehensive *Secure Coding Guide*.

Overview of security controls

Salesforce provides robust built-in security controls such as object-level (**Create, Read, Update, Delete—CRUD**), **field-level security** (**FLS**), and sharing rules. Developers should familiarize themselves with these controls and leverage them to enforce access restrictions and protect data at different levels.

Using HTTPS for secure communication

All connections to external endpoints from your Salesforce application should use HTTPS. This ensures that all data exchanged between your application and the endpoint is encrypted, providing a basic level of security against data interception and tampering.

Implementing secure JavaScript and CSS

Using JavaScript and CSS securely is paramount to protect against common web vulnerabilities. It's recommended to use modern frameworks such as Salesforce's Lightning for JavaScript and avoid inline styles in CSS to comply with Salesforce's **Content Security Policy** (**CSP**).

Understanding CSP

Salesforce employs CSP in the Lightning Framework to mitigate **cross-site scripting** (**XSS**) and other code injection attacks. Developers should learn about CSP and adhere to its guidelines for secure application development.

Avoiding common web vulnerabilities

Developers need to be vigilant against common web vulnerabilities such as XSS, **cross-site request forgery** (**CSRF**), and insecure session cookie handling. A deep understanding of these vulnerabilities and techniques to prevent them is essential for developing secure applications.

Embracing secure coding practices

Salesforce recommends secure coding practices such as using `WITH USER_MODE` in Apex and avoiding SOQL queries within `FOR` loops. Incorporating these practices into your development process can help prevent security vulnerabilities.

Handling sensitive data

Extra caution should be exercised when handling sensitive data. Never store sensitive information in clear text; output it to debug logs, write it to the platform cache, or store it in cookies. Always use the secure storage mechanisms provided by Salesforce

XSS

XSS is a widespread vulnerability wherein an attacker injects unauthorized JavaScript, VBScript, HTML, or other active content into a web page, thereby affecting other users viewing it. These unauthorized scripts can hijack user sessions, submit unauthorized transactions, steal confidential information, or deface the web page. Developers can combat XSS attacks by validating input data, encoding output data, and leveraging security libraries and frameworks.

SOQL/SOSL Injection

Salesforce Object Query Language (SOQL)/Salesforce Object Search Language (SOSL) Injection is a form of attack where malicious SOQL or SOSL statements are inserted into an entry field that is then executed by the database. This can expose sensitive data or modify database contents. SOQL/SOSL Injection attacks often succeed due to insufficient input data validation and the use of dynamic SOQL/SOSL statements by developers. To mitigate this, developers should use parameterized queries or stored procedures instead of dynamic SOQL/SOSL statements.

Cross-Site Request Forgery (CSRF)

CSRF is an attack type where an attacker deceives a user into performing an action on a website without their consent. This allows the attacker to perform actions such as changing passwords or making unauthorized purchases. CSRF attacks are often successful because developers do not adequately validate requests or use anti-CSRF tokens. To counter CSRF attacks, developers should implement anti-CSRF tokens and ensure all requests are validated before processing them.

Arbitrary redirect

Arbitrary redirect is a vulnerability that enables an attacker to redirect users to a malicious website without their knowledge or consent. This could lead to sensitive information theft, such as login credentials, or malware installation on the user's computer. Arbitrary redirect attacks often succeed due to insufficient input data validation or non-usage of URL whitelists by developers. To avoid arbitrary redirect attacks, developers should use URL whitelists and validate all input data.

Insecure communications

Insecure communication is a vulnerability where sensitive information is transmitted over an unencrypted channel. This opens a window for attackers to intercept and read the data, leading to the theft of sensitive information such as login credentials or credit card numbers. Such attacks are often successful because developers either do not use encryption or employ weak encryption algorithms. To prevent insecure communication attacks, developers should employ strong encryption algorithms such as **Secure Sockets Layer/Transport Layer Security (SSL/TLS)** and ensure all sensitive data is transmitted over secure channels.

Avoiding common pitfalls

Throughout the development process, certain pitfalls can arise. Awareness of these issues can help prevent them from occurring and strengthen the security of your application. In the following subsections, we'll explore how to navigate through potential pitfalls that may arise during the development process. By being aware of these issues, you can effectively prevent them and enhance the overall security of your application.

Using sample code in production

Sample code available on the internet can be an excellent learning tool but should never be directly included in production packages. Reusing such code can propagate vulnerabilities throughout packages, even if unintentionally by the sample code author. Therefore, always write your own code for production.

Storing sensitive data insecurely

Insecure storage of sensitive data, such as API keys, cryptographic keys, passwords, and so on, can expose your application to potential threats. Adhere to enterprise security standards when exporting customer data from the Salesforce platform and storing sensitive data within the platform. Any data breach or loss resulting from a vulnerability in your solution could jeopardize your relationship with Salesforce.

Notifying the user if a package installation accesses an org's metadata

There might be instances where your package needs to fetch or modify metadata during its installation or an update. The `Metadata` namespace in Apex is equipped with classes that symbolize metadata types. Additionally, it offers classes that facilitate the retrieval and deployment of metadata components directly to the subscriber org. Here are some key considerations regarding metadata in Apex:

- Metadata components can be created, retrieved, and updated using Apex code. However, the deletion of these components is not supported.

- At present, records of custom metadata types and page layouts are accessible in Apex.

- Managed packages that haven't received Salesforce's approval are restricted from accessing metadata in the subscriber org. An exception to this is when the subscriber org activates the **Allow metadata deploy by Apex from non-certified Apex package version** org setting. This setting is beneficial during the testing phase or beta releases of your managed packages.

It is mandatory to notify the user if your package interacts with metadata during installation or update or if it incorporates a custom setup interface that taps into metadata. For installations that engage with metadata, users should be informed in the package description. The notification should transparently convey to customers that your package possesses the capability to modify the subscriber org's metadata.

For those seeking a template for the notice, Salesforce provides an example[4]:

```
This package can access and change metadata outside its namespace
in the Salesforce org where it's installed.
```

Including unminified source files

Include unminified source files corresponding to all minified files in static resources to facilitate the review of custom JavaScript. Ensure that these files have the same name (except .min) for scanning purposes. Additionally, provide source files for all languages that transpile to JavaScript, such as JSX.

Ensuring static resources are free of known vulnerabilities

Ensure that all libraries included in static resources are free of known vulnerabilities. This can be achieved by searching **Common Vulnerabilities and Exposures** (**CVE**) databases or using security tools such as Snyk or RetireJS.

Versioning

When submitting your application for security review, submit a point release (for example, 8.5→9.0, and so on), not a patch release. The Security Review system is designed to work with major and minor releases; patch releases are not supported.

Disclosing sensitive information in debug statements and URLs

Avoid disclosing sensitive information in debug statements and URLs. Sensitive information, such as **personally identifiable information** (**PII**), passwords, keys, and stack traces, can expose potential attack vectors. URLs can inadvertently store sensitive information in server logs, browser history, or search engine indexes.

TLS/SSL configuration

Ensure your server supports and is configured to use secure cryptographic options. Weak ciphers such as SSLv2/SSLv3/TLSv1.0 should not be supported. At the time of writing, versions less than TLSv1.2 should be disabled.

---

4   https://developer.salesforce.com/docs/atlas.en-us.packagingGuide.
     meta/packagingGuide/packaging_metadata_in_apex.htm?q=metadata

Commented code

While small snippets and samples are allowed in comments, full functions and classes that are commented out should be removed.

Password echo

Avoid storing sensitive information in your application's source code. This information can be easily accessed in clear text by anyone who has access to the source code.

By being aware of these pitfalls and taking the necessary measures to avoid them, you can significantly increase the security and integrity of your Salesforce applications.

Scanning external systems and endpoints

If you thought the marathon of Salesforce solution building was just about the Salesforce track, prepare to embrace the detours. Picture this—your application, mid-race, takes a side route to an external application or integrates with a third-party service. Exciting? Definitely. Challenging? Absolutely. That's where the external application scan comes into play. It's like your trusty map, ensuring your application stays on a secure path even when it ventures off the main course.

So, you've integrated with an external application or employed a third-party service. All endpoints involved need to be as secure as a top-grade running shoe. And every connection has to be authenticated, like verifying a marathon bib on race day. Storing Salesforce credentials such as a refresh token and an access token? They must be secured in an encrypted database like your most cherished marathon medal safely tucked away.

Taking it a step further, suppose your application links arms with a website, maybe redirecting to another site in the middle of the race. Just as you'd have to know every twist, turn, and incline of your marathon route, you need to scan all the website's pages. Found a pothole or a sharp turn? You're responsible for fixing it. After all, no one likes unexpected surprises on race day!

These external application scans are akin to those grueling hill training sessions in preparation for the big race—they're tough, but they go a long way in fortifying your application's stamina and endurance, resulting in a safer UX. Much as in a marathon, the tougher the training, the stronger you become and the better you perform on race day. So, let's gear up and embrace these detours—they're not just part of the journey; they're what makes the race worthwhile.

Tools for scanning external systems and endpoints

Salesforce encourages you to use specific tools to scan your application. The Chimera scanner is one of the tools available directly on the Partner Security Portal[5]. Others are independent tools you may need to use in certain scenarios. Here's a quick overview.

Chimera

Chimera checks for security vulnerabilities in external endpoints of your solution. It scans solutions from a Salesforce IP address and doesn't require a download. If you're using endpoints on domains that you don't own, you need to use OWASP ZAP or Burp Suite because Chimera requires the upload of a token to the root of the external server.

12/10/2022, 11:38   Chimera Scanner Consolidated Security Report

CHIMERA CONSOLIDATED REPORT

https://appexchange.successblueprint.sh/

The below report outlines vulnerability and informational findings that were discovered via automated scanning. It is possible that there are other vulnerabilities that were not discovered during automated scanning and are therefore not included on this report. You should always supplement automated scanning with manual security testing. It is also possible that some or all of these findings are false positives. All reported items should therefore be verified manually.

The attack vector and evidence of vulnerability associated with each item is listed with a description of the vulnerability. Suggested remediation steps and additional educational resources for each class of vulnerability are also provided.

Please note that this is not a comprehensive list of vulnerabilities in your application. Similiar and additional vulnerabilites outside of this report may exist. Please look through your entire codebase for additional security issues.

Contents

1. Incomplete or No Cache-control Header Set
  1. https://appexchange.successblueprint.sh.sh/dashboard.html
  2. https://appexchange.successblueprint.sh.sh/robots.txt
2. CSP: Wildcard Directive
  1. https://appexchange.successblueprint.sh.sh/dashboard.html
  2. https://appexchange.successblueprint.sh.sh/assets/vendor-4f0d2d94506a73a18dec5d6f7d38151d.js
  3. https://appexchange.successblueprint.sh.sh/assets/vendor-4f0d2d94506a73a18dec5d6f7d38151d.js

Figure 6.8: A sample security report generated by the Chimera scanner, highlighting identified vulnerabilities and potential security risks within a system or application

OWASP ZAP

ZAP is a free, community-driven proxy for web app security testing. It's used to scan external endpoints and requires a download. ZAP can be used with endpoints on domains that you don't own because it requires the upload of a token to the root of the external server.

---

5 https://security.my.salesforce-sites.com/sourcescanner/

Burp Suite

Burp Suite is another tool used for scanning external endpoints. It requires a download, and Salesforce doesn't provision Burp Suite licenses for security review. If you need to use it, you will need to purchase a license independently.

However, bear in mind that different tools might assign different severity levels to identified vulnerabilities. Any vulnerability marked with a severity level of **High+** should be addressed or documented, explaining why it won't be fixed as part of the false positive document.

The challenge with commercial APIs

When preparing a managed package for security review, it's customary to evaluate external systems using tools such as Chimera, ZAP, or Burp. This process, however, presents several challenges if you don't own the external system but use one of the commercial APIs. Firstly, embedding Chimera tokens or obtaining explicit permission for a scan is often not feasible. Secondly, many commercial API providers are presumed to have stringent security measures already in place. Lastly, expecting these providers to address security concerns highlighted by individual developers can be impractical, especially when these APIs are integral to enhancing the functionality of Salesforce apps.

As per Salesforce's *Security Review Overview*[6], even if ISVs don't directly own the external endpoints or services their app integrates with, they remain within the purview of the security review. Salesforce adopts a holistic approach, ensuring every component of an offering is tested to safeguard customers and their data. This encompasses any third-party web applications or services linked with the app. Moreover, ISVs must secure written consent from third parties, authorizing Salesforce to test their endpoints.

For situations where this approach seems overly stringent, it's advisable for partners to reach out to Salesforce directly, perhaps through an office hours call. This can facilitate discussions on potentially excluding certain external systems from the review scope and instead providing a declaration in the submission.

Salesforce's trusted list

Salesforce maintains an unofficial roster of public APIs deemed secure based on previous evaluations. If an app integrates with one of these APIs, there's no need to provide Chimera/ZAP scan evidence during the security review. API providers such as Stripe and Google are examples of those included in this list. For instance, if your app leverages the Google API for address validation, you won't need to perform security scans on Google's endpoints. However, this list isn't publicly accessible. ISVs are encouraged to engage with their technology solutions team members, **Partner Account Manager (PAM)**, or **Technical Advisor (TA)**, to ascertain if a particular API is on this roster. Alternatively, initiating a security review support case can also provide clarity.

---

6 https://partners.salesforce.com/pdx/s/learn/article/isv-security-review-overview-MC4QVWO6S2FVFD5MNRMLIEF3UBGQ?language=en_US#media

Preparing false positive documentation

In the process of conducting security scans for your application, you may encounter what are known as "false positives." These are instances where the security tool reports a potential vulnerability, but upon further investigation, it turns out that the identified issue does not pose an actual security risk within the context of your application.

It's essential to document these false positives thoroughly. The documentation should provide a detailed explanation for each reported vulnerability that you have classified as a false positive. Your explanation should provide clear reasons why the identified issue does not represent a security risk for your application. It should also include any mitigating factors or security measures that are in place that prevent the reported vulnerability from being exploited.

The false positive documentation serves as a reference during the security review process. It provides the Salesforce security team with your perspective and helps them understand your reasoning behind classifying certain reported vulnerabilities as false positives.

Here are some steps to follow when preparing your false positive documentation:

1. **Identify potential false positives**: Start by identifying potential false positives in the security scan reports. Not all reported vulnerabilities are actual security risks in your specific context.

2. **Analyze and confirm**: Analyze each potential false positive thoroughly. Confirm that the reported issue does not pose a security risk for your application in its real-world use.

3. **Document your findings**: For each confirmed false positive, provide a detailed explanation in your documentation. Include information on the reported issue, your analysis, and why it's not a security risk.

4. **Include mitigating factors**: If there are mitigating factors or security measures in place that prevent the reported issue from being exploited, include these in your documentation.

5. **Review and validate**: Review your false positive documentation to ensure it's clear, concise, and accurate. Have it validated by a security expert or a knowledgeable team member.

By providing detailed and accurate false positive documentation, you can help speed up the security review process and increase your chances of passing the security review on your first attempt.

Chimera findings

Risk Level	Scanner	Status
Incomplete or No Cache-control Header Set	Chimera	False positive
Timestamp Disclosure - Unix	Chimera	False positive

Detailed Investigation of Chimera Security Alerts

Incomplete or No Cache-control Header Set

The cache-control header is being set correctly across the board by the platform. The Cache-Control header is used by the two files that were found during the scan, allowing them to be cached for only 1 hour (or 3600 seconds). If 'robots.txt' is cached for an hour, it has no bearing whatsoever. The other file, "dashboard.html," is a static resource that can be cached for up to an hour without harm. Additionally, we stipulate that clients must re-validate their resources after 1 hour, causing them to continually check for updated versions.

Timestamp Disclosure - Unix

Because ChimeraReport.html displays the results of a CSS z-index value of 99999999, which is not a Unix timestamp, this is a false positive.

The other findings consist solely of mathematical calculations, such as 1?NaN:e>94906265.62425156? Math.log(e)+ Math.LN2. The Salesforce Chimaera scanner is flagging the second decimal place of the number 62425156 as potentially revealing a Unix time stamp. This is not a Unix timestamp.

Figure 6.9: An example of a false positive document accompanying Chimera's consolidated security report, aimed at addressing and clarifying any inaccurately identified vulnerabilities or risks

Making sure you haven't forgotten anything

After reading this chapter, you understand what it takes to prepare for the security review. Before you proceed with your submission, you can additionally verify that every detail has been addressed. Overlooking even a minor aspect can lead to potential delays in the review process. Consider using the Security Review Submission Requirements Checklist Builder to ensure nothing is missed. Based on your app's technical architecture, this tool will generate a comprehensive checklist of all the necessary steps you need to prepare before your submission.

You can find the checklist builder here:

```
https://checklistbuilder.herokuapp.com/
```

Security Review Submission Requirements Checklist Builder

Tell Us About Your App

Select All That Apply

- On Salesforce Platform -

Managed Package

Quip App

Marketing Cloud App

- External to Salesforce Platform -

Website   API Endpoints

Mobile App

Browser Extension

Desktop/Client App

(?)

Compile Checklist

Your Checklist

1. Force.com Source Code (Checkmarx) Scanner Results
   - You can access the scanner via the Partner Security Portal
   - Please also add an accompanying false positive document for any issues above 'Code Quality' severity.
   - If any issues need to be fixed, please resolve them and re-run the scan to show clean results.
   - Note: if your package does not contain any scannable code, you do not need to run this scan. Instead, on your submission, upload a document that confirms your offering contains no custom code.

2. Code Analyzer Results:
   - We are now asking partners to run Salesforce Code Analyzer in addition to Checkmarx. This is because we want to encourage you to use the same tools as are used by our Security Review Team, who heavily prefer Code Analyzer over Checkmarx due to its ability to catch more issues (particularly CRUD/FLS violations, the most common reason for failure).
   - Follow these easy steps to run a scan.
   - Note: We are not currently blocking submissions for lack of Code Analyzer results, since we know the tool is new to many of you, but you can really maximize your chances of passing the review by using it.

3. Salesforce test environment:
   - Follow this quick guide to create a 2FA-disabled security review test org using our trial template.
   - Alternatively, you can create a Developer Edition org (via this link) and then follow these instructions to disable 2FA.
   - Install your managed package in the org (make sure it is the same version as the one submitted for security review)
   - Provide login credentials for an admin-level user.

4. Ensure your Dev Hub org is not a Trial Org

Figure 6.10: A screenshot of the Security Review Submission Requirements Checklist Builder interface, a tool designed to streamline the preparation process for security review submissions

Crossing the security review finish line.

And you did it! You crossed that security review finish line like a seasoned marathoner! Let's take a moment to soak in the applause and bask in the glory of the finisher's medal hanging around your app. This is your well-deserved moment in the Salesforce sun—your app has just passed the rigorous security review and is ready to take its victory lap on the AppExchange marketplace

The fact that you're here means you didn't just sprint through the starting miles; you paced yourself, hydrated, persevered through the cramps, and kept your eyes on the finish line. Passing the Salesforce security review isn't just another race day bib to your collection; it's a testament to the rigorous training regimen and hard work you've put in. So, go ahead and indulge in a celebratory carb-loaded meal or a post-race ice bath. You've earned it!

But let's not forget, even after the euphoria of race day, a true marathoner knows that the race doesn't end at the finish line. It's a lifestyle. Similarly, this is just the beginning of your app's journey. With your app now on track, it's crucial to keep up the pace and continue the hard work, ensuring that it stays fit, secure, and ready to tackle the next race—whether that's an update or an upgrade.

So, as you bask in the glory, remember to keep your running shoes ready. Let's continue to train, stay hydrated, and keep those energy bars handy because maintaining and enhancing the security of your app is a marathon, not a sprint. After all, the most rewarding part of the marathon is the journey, not just the finish line. And remember—the crowd users will always cheer for an app that runs the race of security with endurance and dedication!

 noreply@salesforce.com <no.reply@salesforce.com>   pon., 28 cze 2021, 19:24
do mnie, appxsecurityreview@salesforce.com ▼

Dear Partner:

Congratulations! Your application has passed our Security Review process.

Now that your application has been approved, you can make your listing public on the AppExchange for the world to see. Please follow the steps outlined below to make your application available for test, purchase or download on the AppExchange. We've provided some sponsorship details below as an option to market your product.

Thank you for joining our Partner Program. We are committed to your continued success!

All the Best,

Security Review Operations

Figure 6.11: A screenshot of an email announcing the successful completion of a security review, conveying a positive outcome and ensuring compliance with the required security standards

Periodic security re-reviews

In the world of Salesforce AppExchange, life's not all calm seas and clear skies. Occasionally, you'll be invited for a security re-review. Think of it as a routine check-up for your application to ensure it remains fit and secure.

When you upgrade a managed package that has already passed the security review, you're in luck. There's no need for another full-fledged review. Simply link the new version to your AppExchange listing, and you're good to go.

Salesforce keeps a keen eye on the AppExchange landscape. It assesses potential risks and time elapsed since your solution was listed to determine if a re-review is required. No need to panic, though. It's just standard procedure to ensure continuous security.

To determine which listed solutions are due for a re-review, Salesforce assesses potential risk and considers the length of time since the solution was listed. Risk-factor reports are generated to evaluate potential threats. If your solution shows significant change, it is more likely to undergo a re-review. However, if the risk factor is low, your solution might not be flagged for a re-review. From my experience, most applications are not flagged for a re-review within the first 2 years following the initial security review, but officially, it can happen anywhere between 6 months and 2 years.

Is your solution due for a re-review? Simply check the **Listing Readiness** area in the Salesforce Partner Console. If it says **Security Review Required**, then it's time for a revisit. If **Ready to List** is displayed, a re-review is not mandatory, but feel free to request one if you like.

If your solution falls short of Salesforce's security standards, Salesforce will reach out. You will typically be given 60 days to resolve the issues. In extreme cases, your AppExchange listing might be temporarily removed. Fix the security issues, pass the follow-up review, and you'll be back on the public stage in no time.

To submit for a periodic security re-review, just follow the same steps as before in the Salesforce Partner Console.

Summary

Congratulations, intrepid Salesforce explorers! You've wrestled with the security review dragon and emerged victorious, having mastered the intricacies of its lair. From understanding its significance to dodging the traps of common pitfalls, you've valiantly ensured your Salesforce applications meet the highest security standards.

You've become proficient in using scanning tools for external systems and endpoints and skillfully mastered the delicate art of documenting false positives, smoothing out the rocky terrain of the security review process. By embracing the ethos of continuous security improvement, you've proven your mettle and dedication as a responsible AppExchange partner.

Yet the journey is far from over, dear trailblazers. While the echo of your triumphant roars against the security review beast still reverberates through the Salesforce realm, a new horizon beckons us—the world of release management. This next phase of our journey is about mastering the art of deployment and release, learning about package versions, patch releases, and the majesty of the push upgrade API. Our goal? The golden rule of ensuring that all our customers always have the latest and most secure version of our app. A fresh challenge awaits, promising deeper knowledge, exciting revelations, and greater AppExchange glory. So, fasten your seat belts and hold onto your hats, because the adventure continues!

Further reading

- Salesforce's *Secure Coding Guide*: https://resources.docs.salesforce.com/244/latest/en-us/sfdc/pdf/secure_coding.pdf

- OWASP's *Web Security Testing Guide*: https://owasp.org/www-project-web-security-testing-guide/

Part 3: Delivering Value

Pop the champagne! You've cooked up a brilliant app, and now it's time for the grand unveiling. But here's the twist – in the virtual restaurant of tech, it's not just about the dish you've prepared; it's about the dining experience. Remember, even the finest of meals can be spoiled by a messy presentation or a delay in serving.

You see, in the grand kitchen of businesses – whether it's a fiery start-up, a simmering established enterprise, or a zesty service-oriented buffet – it's all about garnishing your offering with value. Not just any value, but the melt-in-your-mouth, *"I'll have what she's having!"* kind.

By the time you've digested this part (pun absolutely intended), you'll be the master chef of app delivery, ensuring every course, from app release to customer onboarding, is a Michelin-star-worthy experience.

Today's menu features include the following:

- *Chapter 7, Release Management*
- *Chapter 8, Onboarding New Customers*
- *Chapter 9, Operational Excellence*

7

Release Management

Salutations, brave Salesforce wanderers! Ready to lace up your explorer boots once more? Fantastic, because it's time to delve into the deep, mystical forests of release management. This isn't a fairytale forest, mind you, but a crucial landscape in the grand scheme of software applications, ensuring your hard work and creativity reach their rightful destination—the end-user kingdom.

Now, think of release management as your trusty guide leading you safely across the perilous bridge between the development mountains and the bustling end-user city. Without it, we risk falling into a swirling vortex of software inconsistencies and chaos. Doesn't sound like a nice picnic spot, does it?

As we navigate this forest, here are the landmarks we'll explore:

- **The towering redwoods of release management**: Understand why they stand tall and mighty in this landscape
- **The mysterious version types**: Much as with different tree species, we'll learn to identify them by their unique characteristics
- **The thunderous waterfall of push upgrades**: Harness their power to ensure your application updates flow smoothly toward your users
- **The rare flora of the latest package version**: Learn how to keep your users in this ever-blooming part of the forest, steering clear of the wilted branches of outdated versions
- Last but not least, we are going to answer a fundamental question: How often should you release and deploy?

By the end of our hike through this chapter, you'll emerge as an adept ranger of release management, proficient in guiding your software applications from the serene tranquility of development to the lively hubbub of end users. So, grab your metaphorical map and compass, and let's venture into the release management forest together!

Unveiling release management

Now, if you've ever had the pleasure of experiencing the intricate dance of a pizza delivery, you'll understand that there's more to it than just tossing dough and spreading sauce. Release management, in essence, is the pizza delivery of the tech world. It's the art of carefully crafting your pizza (or software) and skillfully navigating it from the fiery furnace of your development environment to the eager taste buds of your end users, making sure it arrives hot, fresh, and delectably irresistible.

It's about precision and timing—ensuring that your Marinara (your core software) is well cooked and your toppings (features) are added in the perfect order, without being too heavy-handed with the pineapple (bugs). Heaven forbid! And it doesn't end when the pizza leaves the oven. In fact, the real challenge begins then. Picture this: Your delivery driver (deployer) must weave through traffic (the live environment), taking care not to jostle the pizza (maintain integrity) and ensuring it arrives with the cheese still molten and the crust still crisp (consistent UX).

So, what exactly is release management? It's the process of managing, planning, scheduling, and controlling a software build through different stages and environments, including testing and deploying software releases. In simpler terms, it's the art of smoothly delivering your application from your development environment into the hands of your end users. The process extends beyond mere code deployment to consider how your application will be received and used, encompassing elements such as user adoption, training, and documentation.

Release management is pivotal in minimizing the risks associated with the deployment of new functionalities and maintaining the integrity of live environments while offering a consistent UX. It is the confluence of project management, software development, and IT service management principles. Its importance can't be overstated, as it helps ensure the smooth transition of software from concept to customer.

In the Salesforce ISV context, release management is especially important as you juggle package versions, patch releases, push upgrades, and more while making sure that your customers are using the most updated and secure version of your application.

On our thrilling journey to mastering release management, we'll not only explore these aspects in depth but also understand the nuances between deployment and release. These are often used interchangeably but are indeed different facets of the process. The distinction becomes crucial as we climb further up the mountain.

The role of DevOps in Salesforce release management

DevOps, a philosophy that combines software **development (Dev)** and IT **operations (Ops)**, plays a crucial role in Salesforce release management. DevOps is all about promoting better communication, collaboration, and integration between developers and operations teams, ultimately leading to more reliable, frequent, and efficient software releases.

DevOps in the Salesforce ecosystem

In the Salesforce ecosystem, DevOps is integral to effectively managing releases, particularly for AppExchange applications. With multiple environments, configurations, and users to consider, having a robust DevOps practice can streamline the process and ensure quality and consistency.

Continuous Integration and Continuous Delivery (CI/CD)

A cornerstone of DevOps is the principle of **Continuous Integration and Continuous Delivery (CI/CD)**. CI/CD involves automating the steps in the application delivery process, from initial code commit to final release. In the context of Salesforce, this could mean automating code deployments, running tests, and managing environments.

CI/CD offers several benefits, such as faster identification of bugs or issues, quicker deployments, and the ability to release more frequently and reliably.

Collaborative culture

DevOps is not just about tools and automation; it's also about culture. A DevOps culture encourages collaboration and communication between development and operations teams, breaking down silos and promoting shared ownership of the release process. This can lead to better understanding and visibility across teams, improved problem-solving, and higher-quality releases.

Adopting a DevOps approach can greatly enhance Salesforce release management. It can help organizations deliver more reliable AppExchange applications more frequently and with fewer errors. By leveraging DevOps tools, principles, and culture, you can create a more effective and efficient release process, ultimately leading to better outcomes for your customers.

The difference between deployment and release

In the intriguing world of Salesforce and AppExchange, understanding the distinctions between deployment and release is pivotal to successful application management. Let's delve into these two facets of release management.

Deployment

Okay, my pizza-loving friends, let's talk deployment, the unsung hero of the pizza (read: software) world. Imagine deployment as the careful act of transferring your painstakingly prepared pizza from the pizza peel to the roaring oven—from staging to production, if you will. It's all about precision, dexterity, and a dash of flair, just to keep things interesting.

Now, the act of deployment is about more than just shuffling our metaphorical pizza from point A to point B. It's about ensuring that our Marinara masterpiece lands in the oven without folding in on itself or losing any of its carefully placed toppings (features), much like ensuring our code not only transfers to the live environment but also performs beautifully, without triggering a system-wide tomato sauce (code) catastrophe.

The deployment process is generally focused on the technical aspects of getting the new code or features into the live environment, ensuring it functions as expected and doesn't disrupt existing systems.

In the context of Salesforce AppExchange, deployment involves the addition of new metadata components (such as Apex classes, custom objects, or Lightning components) to your managed package and the subsequent installation of this updated package into a target Salesforce org. This target org could be your customer's production org or a sandbox org.

Release

Release, on the other hand, is a broader concept. It encompasses not just the technical deployment of new software or features, but also everything else that goes with it to ensure the update is successfully received and adopted by end users. This includes elements such as user training, documentation updates, communications, and any necessary data migration.

In Salesforce, a release often involves coordinating the deployment of multiple related changes, executing post-deployment steps, managing permissions and feature visibility, and driving user adoption through communication and training.

So, why does this distinction matter? Often, in the rush of project completion, these two terms are used interchangeably. However, understanding and maintaining the distinction between deployment and release is essential for effective release management. A successful deployment does not guarantee a successful release. You might technically deploy new code without any errors, but if the end users are not prepared for the changes or if the new features aren't properly documented, your release might face difficulties.

In the end, the distinction boils down to this: deployment is about the technology; release is about people. As we navigate through the world of release management, balancing both these aspects is critical for success.

Driving consistency and cost efficiency in releases

Stepping into the early stages of any start-up adventure, releases are often intricate puzzles, demanding both time and financial investment. We find this true, especially within the Salesforce AppExchange ecosystem.

Setting a goal for consistency and reduced costs

One observation that stands out prominently is the trajectory of successful partners whose deployment efficiency stagnated once they breached the 20+ customer threshold. I've seen ISVs with staggering 6-month deployment cycles. This sluggish pace might be acceptable when your target audience is confined to large enterprises with an appetite for complexity, but it turns into a formidable roadblock when mid-sized companies become part of your market scope.

The primary goal, therefore, should be to gradually decrease release time and cost while driving consistency. It is an art and science that requires deliberate attention from the outset.

Building a professional services team or partnering with System Integrators

To bring this goal to fruition, one approach is to consider building a professional services team internally. Such a team, specializing in your application, can work wonders to streamline the deployment process.

Alternatively, creating alliances with **System Integrators** (**SIs**) can be equally rewarding. These organizations come with an extensive experience portfolio and can provide you with insights to refine your release process. We are going to explore this option in *Chapter 12*.

Continuous improvement in the release process – an internal feedback loop

But whether you choose to build internally or partner externally, remember to inculcate a culture of continuous improvement. Post-release, make it a point to gather feedback, measure time and cost, and identify gaps.

Reflect on questions such as these: *How did the last release go? How can we reduce costs and improve the process? Are there any areas that need more attention or resources?*

The aim should be to draw lessons from each release, utilizing these insights to enhance the next. This commitment to improvement and cost reduction will eventually allow you to extend your services to a broader market segment in an efficient and effective manner.

Effective communication in release management

Consider transparency and clarity as our metaphorical GPS and phone number combo. They're the tools that allow our delivery person to navigate the winding streets, avoid traffic jams, and reach the customer promptly. Equally, they give the customer the ability to track the pizza's progress and know exactly when to set the table.

In the realm of release management, it's the same story. You might be sitting on the most well-crafted release in the history of software development. But without clear and transparent communication, our end users might find themselves wandering around in confusion. It's like knowing you ordered a pizza but not knowing when it'll arrive. Frustrating, right?

The role of communication in release management

Communication in release management isn't merely about announcing changes. It is a strategic effort to ensure new features or changes are understood, appreciated, and ultimately used effectively by the end users. Communicating the "why" behind the updates, along with the "what," can significantly aid user adoption and satisfaction. Moreover, communication aids in setting clear expectations, enabling users to plan their activities around the release schedule.

Creating and sharing release notes

Release notes are an indispensable part of this communication process. They provide a detailed summary of updates, bug fixes, new features, or improvements included in the release. They should clearly state the benefits of the new changes, allowing users to understand the value they bring.

Well-written release notes serve as a documentation resource, letting users revisit them for clarification if needed. Sharing these notes well ahead of the release allows users time to understand the upcoming changes and ask questions or voice concerns, if any.

Scheduling releases and communicating the schedule

It's not just the "what" and "why" that's important, but also the "when." A well-planned release schedule, communicated effectively, can do wonders in ensuring smooth transitions. It enables users to plan for the release and minimize disruptions to their day-to-day operations.

Make sure to communicate not just the release date, but also any important timelines related to the release, such as periods of expected downtime, deadlines for any necessary user action, or dates for training sessions on the new features. Regular reminders as the release date approaches can also be beneficial.

In summary, effective communication in release management is all about transparency, clarity, and timeliness. By considering your users as partners in the release process and keeping them informed every step of the way, you can navigate the waters of release management smoothly, ensuring a better experience for all.

Release naming convention

In the vast sea of release management, setting sail without a proper naming convention is akin to venturing forth without a compass. A well-defined naming convention helps guide your journey, enabling you and your users to keep track of the different releases and understand the changes they bring.

Understanding Salesforce AppExchange managed package versioning

Salesforce AppExchange managed packages follow a three-part versioning model consisting of a major version, a minor version, and a patch version. This model, often referred to as **Semantic versioning (SemVer)**, is widely used in software development and provides a clear, standardized approach to version naming. Let's look at this in more detail:

- **Major version**: The first number in the version denotes the major version. This is incremented when you make incompatible API changes or significant functional changes that may impact the UX or require substantial user adjustments.

- **Minor version**: The second number represents the minor version. This typically reflects backward-compatible functionality enhancements. Think of new features that add value but do not disrupt existing functionalities.

- **Patch version**: The third number stands for patch versions. This is increased when you make backward-compatible bug fixes or minor changes that do not add new functionalities or disrupt existing ones.

By embracing a well-defined naming convention and understanding Salesforce AppExchange managed package versioning, you can effectively navigate the ever-changing landscape of release management, ensuring seamless communication and a comprehensive understanding of release changes for both users and developers.

Understanding version types

As a partner navigating the vast terrain of Salesforce's AppExchange marketplace, understanding the different types of package releases available is a fundamental part of effective release management. In this section, we will explore full releases, patch releases, and beta releases, each with their unique purposes, limitations, and ideal usage scenarios.

Full releases

Full releases represent a significant progression of your application, encompassing either minor or major changes in functionality and often involving the addition of new metadata. Each full release is identified by an incremented major or minor version number.

A full release allows developers to add new components, delete obsolete ones, and modify existing metadata, facilitating large-scale enhancements to the application. An example might be introducing a new module or substantial functionality to your AppExchange application that would warrant a full release.

Patch releases

Patch releases, on the other hand, are a subtler type of update, focused primarily on bug fixes and minor adjustments that do not alter the app's existing functionality. These updates are often vital for resolving vulnerabilities or issues identified post-release.

However, patch releases in Salesforce are bound by certain limitations. They do not permit the inclusion of new metadata, nor changes to the application's API or global classes. Their purpose is purely to deliver backward-compatible fixes. For instance, if an existing feature of your application has a bug affecting performance, deploying a patch release to address the issue would be the appropriate step.

Beta releases

Finally, beta releases serve as testing grounds for new features and functionalities before they're included in a final full release. These packages allow for comprehensive testing and feedback gathering, which is useful for identifying potential issues early in the development process.

Beta releases can be installed in scratch orgs, sandboxes, and Developer Edition orgs, providing an environment that closely resembles the impending production setting. However, a significant limitation accompanies these advantages: beta releases cannot be updated. Consequently, a prerequisite for installing the ultimate full-release version involves uninstalling the beta release. This may necessitate additional steps, such as manual uninstallation of the previous version or a sandbox refresh, integrated into the deployment process.

Moreover, the transition from beta to final release might also entail challenges regarding the preservation of test data across various testing cycles. The inherent restrictions of beta packages might preclude the seamless continuity of test data, potentially necessitating reconfiguration or re-population in each iteration of testing.

It's important to note that deploying beta packages in long-standing customer sandboxes may not be the most suitable approach. The limitations discussed earlier might render beta packages less feasible within these enduring environments.

Considering these factors, the most suitable environment for making the best use of beta packages is within scratch orgs. In this scenario, incorporating automated scripts to rapidly generate relevant test data and systematically establish new scratch orgs emerges as an indispensable investment. Through the implementation of this approach, complications linked to uninstallation, data retention, and limitations inherent in beta releases can be adeptly managed. This not only streamlines the process but also amplifies the effectiveness of beta testing. It's important to note that, with this strategy, a new scratch org is generated each time a new beta package is released, ensuring a fresh and controlled testing environment for every iteration.

Applying a naming convention

Imagine you're releasing version 2.8.4 of your application. Here, "2" is the major version, indicating the main iteration of your application, "8" represents the minor version, pointing to specific added features, and "4" marks the patch version, accounting for any bug fixes or minor improvements.

By following this versioning system, you provide a snapshot of changes included in the release, right in the version name itself. It also allows users to understand the impact and nature of updates quickly.

But remember—while the numbers are informative, they are not descriptive. Therefore, it's essential to complement your versioning with detailed release notes, providing context and insights into what each version brings to the table.

Publishing your latest release on AppExchange

Successfully navigating the currents of release management doesn't just end with creating a new version of your application. A significant step that often requires conscious attention is updating your listing on AppExchange. It's important to understand that simply releasing a new version does not automatically make it visible on AppExchange. The listing needs to be manually updated, allowing customers to see and access the newest iteration of your application.

The specifics of managing your AppExchange listing, including how to effectively market your new release, will be covered in more detail in *Chapter 8*. We'll take a deeper dive into strategies for making your application stand out on the crowded shelves of the AppExchange marketplace, from crafting compelling descriptions to utilizing screenshots and customer reviews effectively.

Discovering the power of push upgrades

Enter the realm of push upgrades—the high-tech drone of application development. In this whirlwind landscape of ever-changing code and feature enhancements, keeping your customers up to speed can feel like trying to deliver a pizza during rush hour. But thanks to Salesforce's customer-centered ethos, we have push upgrades in our delivery arsenal.

Picture this: instead of a delivery person stuck in traffic or having to navigate a confusing neighborhood, we have a drone. This marvelous machine flies high above the chaos, directly delivering a piping hot pizza to the customer, quickly and efficiently. That's your push upgrade—a futuristic courier ensuring that the freshest version of your managed packages is delivered and installed across your customers' orgs, without as much as a bump in the road.

What's more, this drone delivers whether or not the customer is home. It simply leaves the pizza in a safe, predetermined location (okay—we might still need to figure out how to prevent the neighborhood dog from claiming it as a free lunch). It's the same with push upgrades. They seamlessly install the latest and greatest functionalities, regardless of whether the customer is actively using their org or not. It's the upgrade method of the future, today!

Salesforce itself releases its own applications three times a year using push upgrades, and many ISVs have also successfully adopted this approach.

Push upgrades – a brief overview

Push upgrades are a unique feature of Salesforce AppExchange, designed to provide managed package developers with an automated mechanism to roll out updates or enhancements to their customers. This not only ensures that all customers are using the most up-to-date version of your application but also saves them from the hassle of manually installing new package versions.

Push Upgrade API

The **Push Upgrade** API is the enabler behind this convenient process. It is the technology that brings the entire operation to life, allowing developers to schedule and manage push upgrades programmatically.

The API offers various features that help control and streamline the push process, including the following:

- **Scheduling push upgrades**: You can use the API to schedule a push upgrade job for a particular date and time, ensuring your customers receive updates as per your release timeline.

- **Batch control**: The API allows you to set batch sizes, determining how many subscriber orgs will receive the upgrade in each batch. This is beneficial when managing large customer bases, enabling a smoother transition and reducing the risk of overwhelming your resources or your customers' orgs.

- **Status checks**: The API provides options to monitor the status of your push jobs, providing insights into how many orgs have been upgraded, which are in progress, and if any have encountered issues.

- **Version selection**: The Push Upgrade API lets you select a specific version of your package to push. This means you can control the exact updates each customer receives.

- **Selective targeting**: The Push Upgrade API goes even further by introducing advanced targeting options. You can customize upgrades based on specific organizational needs, including directing upgrades to sandboxes, production orgs, or particular versions. Plus, upgrades can be selectively pushed to specific orgs, enabling highly personalized deployment.

Now, you may be wondering how you can access this valuable Push Upgrade API. Fear not! You can wield its power directly from the command line, or you can navigate its features through the familiar terrain of Package Visualizer, which we previously explored in *Chapter 2*. Armed with this knowledge, you can confidently navigate the realm of release management, knowing you have the power to deliver seamless upgrades to your users.

Embracing push upgrades safely and effectively

It's common for ISVs to hesitate when considering the utilization of push upgrades. The notion of automatically transmitting updates to customers often evokes a sense of uncertainty, primarily due to concerns about potential disruptions or incompatibilities that may arise.

Despite their vast potential benefits, push upgrades often remain unexplored territory in the release process. It's not uncommon for many customers to operate on legacy versions of applications, requiring manual updates to their orgs. This practice not only constrains the effectiveness of the release process but also increases operational overhead.

One viable solution to this predicament is the incorporation of customer-editable custom settings, such as an Opt-out for Push Upgrade setting. By default, this would allow customers to be upgraded to the latest version of the package automatically. However, it also empowers the customer's administrator to disable the auto-upgrade feature should they prefer to maintain manual control. An example of how to implement this in a post-installation Apex script is provided here:

```
global class PostInstall implements InstallHandler {
    global void onInstall (InstallContext context) {
        Config__c config = Config.getConfig();
        if(config?.Opt_out_from_Push_Upgrade__c) {
            System.assert(false,
            'Update blocked by Custom Settings->Config->
            Opt out from Push Upgrade');
        }
    }
}
```

With this solution, you can readily update all customer orgs that permit automatic upgrades. Another solution is to utilize the **Feature Management App** (**FMA**) discussed in *Chapter 2*. You can either employ the LMO-to-Subscriber feature parameters to disable push upgrades for certain customers or you can construct a configuration panel that enables your customer's administrator to utilize the Subscriber-to-LMO feature parameters to opt out, much like the approach used with custom settings.

This approach significantly reduces **time to value** (**TTV**) and decreases delivery costs by streamlining the upgrade process. It's a win-win scenario, offering enhanced efficiency for ISVs while granting customers autonomy and control over their upgrade process. With prudent planning and execution, push upgrades can indeed be a powerful tool in the Salesforce ISV's arsenal.

Understanding push upgrade failures and monitoring results

Push upgrades are a fantastic tool for ensuring that your users are up to date with the latest features and improvements of your app. However, even the most robust systems are not without their occasional pitfalls. To effectively manage push upgrades, you need to understand why they might fail and how to monitor their results.

Common causes of push upgrade failures

In my experience with conducting weekly push upgrades to over 100 production orgs, I've noticed a few common reasons why push upgrades may fail. These are set out here:

- **Timeouts**: Push upgrades can occasionally fail due to timeouts. This happens when Salesforce's server takes too long to process a request. It's a common issue that can occur due to high server load or complex processes that take a long time to execute. Often, merely retrying the push upgrade can resolve this issue.

- **Salesforce performance issues**: At times, Salesforce's performance can be impacted by maintenance, updates, or high usage. These performance issues can cause push upgrades to fail. Again, often, a simple retry, once performance has improved, can lead to a successful upgrade.

- **Subscriber org configuration**: Sometimes, push upgrades can fail due to configuration issues in the subscriber's org. For example, a subscriber might have certain settings, permissions, or customizations that conflict with the components of the upgrade.

- **Salesforce limits**: Salesforce has certain limits in place to maintain performance and integrity. If a push upgrade causes an org to exceed these limits, the upgrade will fail. For instance, Salesforce allows only one lookup field from Activity to any standard object. Suppose your package includes a new custom lookup from Task to Opportunity. In this case, your package has used up 100% of this limit. If one of your customers had a local custom lookup, the installation would fail due to this limit.

Monitoring push upgrade results

To effectively manage push upgrades, it's crucial to monitor their results. There are a few ways to do this, as follows:

- **Push Upgrade API**: This is a programmatic way to retrieve information about your push jobs, and it's an effective method for large-scale or automated operations.

- **Package Visualizer**: This is a comprehensive tool designed to provide ISVs with the ability to manage their applications more efficiently. Package Visualizer contains a feature that allows you to monitor push upgrade results, along with other crucial information about your packages.

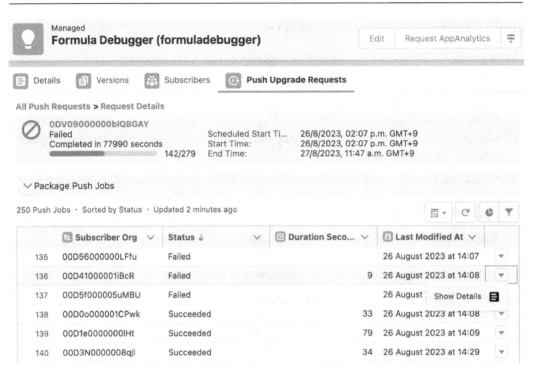

Figure 7.1 – Package Visualizer provides a clear view of push upgrade results

When an upgrade fails, you can view the error message to understand the reason for the failure. While some error messages are common and well-documented, others may require a more detailed investigation. By leveraging these tools, you can quickly diagnose and address any issues, ensuring a smooth upgrade process for your customers.

Leveraging early releases in customer sandboxes

Salesforce's sandbox environments, combined with tools such as Push Upgrade, offer ISVs valuable opportunities to refine their AppExchange releases. Adopting early releases in customer sandboxes allows for a streamlined release process, ensuring your AppExchange products are of top quality and free from bugs. This strategy not only ensures the highest-quality releases but also gives customers ample time to familiarize themselves with updates before they go into production. Salesforce's sandbox, push upgrades, and comprehensive release notes form an ideal framework for this.

An early release strategy means introducing your new AppExchange version in a controlled setting prior to the production release. The benefits include the following:

- **Gathering valuable feedback**: Customer sandboxes serve as platforms to gather firsthand feedback on your app's enhancements

- **Training customers**: Before the official release, customers gain practical experience with the new version

- **Mitigating risks**: Highlight and address issues that might have been overlooked during in-house testing

To optimize early releases in customer sandboxes, adhere to these guidelines:

- **Test in your own environment first**: Always test the new version in your sandbox or scratch org to ensure functionality and performance.

- **Provide detailed release notes**: Offer customers a clear overview of new features, bug fixes, and other alterations.

- **Communicate sandbox upgrade dates in advance**: Notify customers about upcoming sandbox upgrades well in advance, providing them with the opportunity to plan accordingly and ensuring a seamless transition. Additionally, consider an opt-out option for those who require more time.

- **Supply training resources**: Equip customers with video tutorials, documentation, or webinars to navigate the new version.

- **Foster open communication**: Maintain avenues for customers to voice concerns or feedback, reinforcing app quality and customer trust.

While customer sandboxes are a great place to get early feedback, they shouldn't be treated as a replacement for your internal **Quality Assurance** (**QA**) processes. Alright—don't throw tomatoes at me for stating the obvious, but I just gotta get this off my chest: Your customers aren't free QAs. They trust your brand and expect a certain level of quality. Ensure you've done your due diligence in testing before pushing anything to their environments.

Looking for practical ways to put this into action? Your partner, Salesforce, sets an excellent example with its robust sandbox environments, comprehensive release notes, and other innovative tools—it truly exemplifies how this process should be executed.

Ensuring customers use the latest package version

In the realm of Salesforce AppExchange application development and release management, there exists a golden rule: "Always ensure your customers are using the latest version of your application." This is not merely a recommendation but a crucial aspect of maintaining app integrity, delivering a consistent UX, and minimizing security risks.

Push upgrades, as previously discussed, are an invaluable tool to effortlessly implement this rule. By automating the process of delivering updates directly to your customers' orgs, push upgrades relieve customers of the responsibility of manually installing new package versions. Not only does this ensure all customers are using the most current and secure version of your application, but it also enhances the overall customer experience by eliminating the hassle of manual updates.

The importance of the latest version

But why is it so important for customers to use the latest version of your application? The reasons are manifold, as we can see here:

- **Enhanced security**: Each new version of your application should ideally include the latest security patches and fixes. By using the most recent version, customers are assured of the highest level of security.

- **New features and improvements**: The latest version of your app will have all the new features, enhancements, and performance improvements that you've worked hard to develop. Ensuring customers use the most recent version allows them to benefit from these updates and enhancements.

- **Reduced support complexity**: By having all your customers on the same version, you simplify the task of providing support. This uniformity eliminates the need to maintain documentation for multiple versions and allows your support team to focus on current issues rather than dealing with problems tied to outdated versions.

- **Compliance**: For industries and applications where compliance with regulations is essential, using the latest version can be critical. Updated versions will be compliant with the most recent regulatory changes, protecting both you and your customers.

Hence, the golden rule is not just a best practice, but an essential strategy for maintaining app integrity, offering a superior UX, and fostering trust among your customers. The use of push upgrades and other release management strategies is instrumental in your app's successful implementation.

Potential pitfalls and their remedies

You've turned your oven up to full blast and you're cranking out hot, delicious pizzas—your application's newest release. But here's the thing: not everyone is biting into the latest, tastiest version of your culinary masterpiece.

This situation in the pizza-filled world of AppExchange application development and release management can be like delivering a piping hot pizza to someone who's still working on their cold leftovers from last week. It's not exactly the most appealing dining experience, and it could turn into a kitchen nightmare if you don't catch it early on.

This troublemaker is one of the pepperoni-sized challenges that organizations often face: managing customers using legacy versions of their applications. It's like trying to convince someone that the pizza they ordered and have been eating is not as good as the one you just pulled out of the oven. Ignoring this issue is like leaving a pizza in the oven too long—it could potentially snowball into a burnt mess that's not only heartbreaking to look at but also expensive and painful to clean up.

Customers using different legacy versions

Maintenance of numerous versions of an application is highly time-consuming and costly. A single critical bug could necessitate building multiple patches, maintaining various branches in the repository, and orchestrating complex customer communication. Moreover, customers often resist push upgrades due to apprehensions about breaking changes and a desire to control the upgrade timeline—often to train their end users. This issue can be bifurcated into two categories—technical and behavioral.

Technical solution – separating deployments from releases

The key is to distinguish between deployments and releases. Deploying involves moving code and configuration from one environment to another while releasing means making that code and configuration accessible to users. Though release depends on deployment, it is entirely feasible to deploy without releasing, by "hiding" those features from users until they are ready to use them.

This separation forces teams to ponder about deploying features without impacting the system, hence promoting good design, reversibility, and controlled impact of changes. In essence, it's about "reducing the blast radius" of each alteration, a crucial capability to foster DevOps within your team.

Additionally, consider enhancing the **License Management App** (**LMA**) with the FMA, described in *Chapter 2*. Feature parameters are represented as Metadata API types in your packaging org and as records of custom objects in your subscriber's org. You can reference these values in your code, similar to how you reference any other value in a customer's org.

Behavioral solution – proactively managing expectations

A part of onboarding new customers should involve managing their expectations about the fully automated release process. This challenge is akin to the adoption of new systems and technologies. If we can alleviate the fear of releasing new versions automatically by demonstrating the stability and predictability of the software, the advantages of using the latest version should push customers in the right direction.

Bear in mind that this is not a temporary fix but a strategic transition that should be planned in advance and communicated to all customers with a realistic timeline. From my consulting experience, a mid-size ISV affected by this issue, depending on the number of customers using legacy versions, needs on average a 2–4-year timeline to solve this issue. It's best to do it right from the start.

Benefits of addressing this issue

By tackling this problem head-on, you substantially limit the scope of what needs to be maintained by the engineering team and supported by the customer service team. Ideally, there should only be two versions of any app to maintain: a stable one (currently used by all customers) and a newly built one (awaiting approval). This is a significant step toward increasing the release frequency.

This strategy would also improve several DevOps **key performance indicators** (**KPIs**) such as lead time (from code committed to code deployed), deployment frequency (to production), **Mean-Time-to-Restore** or **MTTR** (from a production failure), and release manager's workload.

In conclusion, preemptively addressing potential pitfalls in release management, especially when dealing with legacy versions, not only streamlines your operations but also fosters a sense of trust among your customers, boosting their confidence in your ability to deliver seamless updates and maintain application integrity.

Contractual clauses and support fees

An important factor to consider when aiming to keep your customers on the latest version of your software is to manage expectations from the beginning, and this can be facilitated by terms and conditions in the contract you form with them.

Including upgrade terms in the contract

When onboarding new customers, it is advisable to include a clause in the agreement stating that customers consent to automatic push upgrades. This clause ensures that your customers are aware they will receive the latest versions of your application as soon as they are available.

This kind of clause can serve two primary purposes, as follows:

- It sets a clear expectation that the customer's installed software will stay up to date with the latest features and security patches.

- It allows you to maintain only the latest versions of the software, reducing the overhead and cost of supporting multiple older versions.

Applying extra support fees for legacy versions

Even with contractual clauses, there may be cases where customers are hesitant or outrightly decline to move to the latest version of the software. They may prefer to stick to an older, familiar version. In such cases, to compensate for the additional support and maintenance costs associated with supporting multiple legacy versions, you can apply an extra fee for support of these older versions.

The rationale behind this approach is to cover the extra costs associated with maintaining and supporting multiple older versions of your software. While it is crucial to respect the customer's choice, it is equally important to ensure that your organization's resources are utilized optimally.

By having these provisions in place from the start, it is much easier to manage expectations and ensure that customers are utilizing the latest, most secure, and feature-rich version of your app. Not only does this strategy help in providing a better service to your customers, but it also significantly reduces the complexity and cost associated with supporting and maintaining multiple older versions.

Justifying support costs – the financial calculations

When facing additional support costs tied to maintaining a dedicated version for a specific customer, it's crucial to have a clear picture of what that financial burden looks like. It's like being on a tightrope, and balance is the key. You want to provide the best service to your customer, but not at the cost of sinking your own ship.

In most mid-sized organizations, the task of running these numbers falls within the purview of your **Chief Technology Officer (CTO)** and **Chief Financial Officer (CFO)**. They should be able to jointly crunch these numbers, balancing the technical implications with the financial realities.

For those of you in smaller start-ups, where your "CTO" might just be in reality your lead developer with an impressive title on the business card, don't worry. There's always the option of bringing in an external expert to help with these calculations. They'll be able to offer an unbiased perspective based on your costs of development and the typical life cycle of software development. I'm going to show you some options in *Chapter 12*.

Regardless of how you come up with the figure, the aim remains the same. This number will serve as the backbone of your business offering. It will give you a solid ground to stand on when explaining to your customers why it's in their best interest (and yours) to use the latest version of your app. It's like saying, "Trust me, I've done the math!". And who can argue with that?

Monitoring your package versions with the LMA

As you have already learned in *Chapter 2*, the LMA is an incredibly powerful Salesforce tool that allows ISVs to manage leads, licenses, and usage for their AppExchange packages. In this section, we will revisit the LMA and focus on its use for monitoring different versions of your package in use by customers.

Delving deeper into the LMA

The LMA doesn't just allow you to manage licenses; it also provides crucial real-time insights regarding the deployment and usage of your AppExchange packages. This data includes the package version installed, the type of Salesforce org it's installed in (production or sandbox), and the status of the license.

These insights can be instrumental in determining how many customers are using specific legacy versions of your package. This knowledge is precious when you need to make decisions regarding feature enhancements, deprecations, or fixing bugs specific to particular versions.

Keeping track of package versions

By default, Salesforce populates the LMA records in your **Partner Business Org** (**PBO**) every time a customer installs or upgrades your package. This automated process allows you to accurately monitor which versions of your package are in use across your customer base.

You can create custom reports in the LMA housed within your PBO, using standard Salesforce reporting tools. By adding details such as Lead or Account to your report, you can pinpoint the version of a package a customer has installed, be it in a trial org or a production one.

To gain comprehensive insights, consider creating different reports for each of your packages by filtering on the `sfLma__Package__c` field. You can then compile these reports into a unified dashboard, giving you a combined view of usage across all your packages:

Figure 7.2 – Example of the "Orgs by Major Release" report from the LMA

Figure 7.2 clearly shows the distribution of our customers across various versions of our application. Most of our customers are up to date, using the latest stable version (0.39). However, there is a small subset of users still operating on legacy versions (0.5, 0.13, and 0.18).

How often should you release and deploy?

Now that you understand the differences between releases and deployments, as well as the power of push upgrades, the question arises: How often should you release and deploy?

The frequency of releases largely depends on several factors such as your development team's speed, your customers' adaptability to new changes, and your organization's strategic goals. Many ISVs choose to release new features three times a year, aligning with Salesforce's release cycle. This cadence allows ample time for development, testing, and ensuring compatibility with the Salesforce platform's updates.

On the other hand, deployments can be performed as frequently as you want. They can serve as an excellent tool for delivering updates, bug fixes, and enhancements promptly. For example, during my tenure as a release manager at IPfolio (a substantial OEM), I introduced a weekly cycle of deployments. This approach ensured swift delivery of minor bug fixes and new feature-related code to all customers. However, since these features were not officially announced and were undocumented, only a select group of pilot customers had access to them.

This strategy enabled us to adhere to DevOps principles and maintain agility without the burden of maintaining multiple versions of our package. Yet, we still officially released new features only three times a year.

And remember—a release is not just about the technical aspects. It's also about the human aspect, such as communication, providing release notes, offering training to your customers, and so forth.

By now, you should have a solid understanding of not only *why* but also *how* to design your release management process to best fit your organization's needs. Balancing the frequency of releases and deployments effectively will ensure that your team can deliver continuous value to your customers while also managing change and maintaining stability.

Why don't you just release weekly?

"But can't we just release new features every week?" I hear you ask. The answer is yes, you technically could. But should you? That's a whole other kettle of fish.

Your end users, believe it or not, aren't always thrilled by surprises. Sure—in a **Business-to-Customer (B2C)** scenario, rapid updates and changes might be acceptable, even exciting. But in the **Business-to-Business (B2B)** world, that's not always the case. Imagine showing up for work on a Monday morning, coffee in hand, only to find that the tools you were using just last week have changed overnight. Yikes.

And it's not just about managing the shock value. Do you have the bandwidth to offer adequate training, documentation, and support for these new features every week? Updating your product is one thing, but getting your users up to speed is a whole other challenge.

Frequent updates without proper communication and support can lead to a slew of issues. We're talking about poor adoption of new features, skyrocketing support costs, and overall user dissatisfaction. Think of it this way—change management is an art form in and of itself. It exists because, generally speaking, people don't really enjoy surprises at work.

So, yes—you should deploy your latest code frequently, but releases? Not so much. Just look at Salesforce for a real-world example: it deploys updates frequently but only has three major releases per year. So, while it's tempting to show out your shiny new features as soon as they're ready, remember that patience is a virtue, especially when it comes to software release management.

Summary

Great job, trailblazers! We've mastered release management, armed with our knowledge of version types and push upgrades. We've ensured our customers always have the latest tools, and we've learned to choose the perfect times to release and deploy. The result? A seamless software transition from design to end user, without disrupting live environments.

The practical skills you've gained are crucial for stability, risk minimization, and successful change management in your Salesforce ISV journey. It's as important as starting a fire in the wilderness.

But we're not done yet! Our next adventure is onboarding new customers. We'll learn to create an attractive AppExchange listing, optimize trial experiences, speed up installations and upgrades, design automated onboarding processes, and manage local changes made by our customers. So, pack your bags, trailblazers. Our next adventure awaits! Let's conquer customer onboarding together!

Further reading

After navigating through the thrilling waters of release management, you may feel the call to deepen your knowledge and refine your skills further. To guide you on this quest, I have a compelling recommendation: *Mastering Salesforce DevOps* by Andrew Davis.

8

Onboarding New Customers

Ahoy, Salesforce explorers! As we dawn upon a new day in our software safari, we find ourselves facing another enthralling challenge—onboarding new customers! Picture it as inviting newly made friends to a house you've constructed. The grand tour should be captivating enough to make them want to move in and be long-term roommates, shouldn't it? This chapter will provide you with the master blueprints to do just that.

In this part of our expedition, we will be discovering the following topics along the way:

- **Crafting a winning AppExchange listing**: Let's start with the crucial part—a journey full of creativity, strategy, and the chance to make your app shine brighter than a disco ball at a '70s party.

- **The art of onboarding**: Welcome new users and show them around your digital house. We'll learn how to keep the tour engaging and downright fun because, let's face it, no one remembers a dull party!

- **Instructions for installation**: Not all of us are as handy as *Bob the Builder*. We'll discuss how to provide crystal clear instructions that even a caveman could follow to install your application.

- **Supporting local changes by your customers**: It's like allowing your roommates to redecorate their rooms. We'll delve into embracing customer customization and supporting local changes, without turning your application into a Picasso painting.

- **Crafting cinematic demos**: Imagine being a film director for a moment, where your application is the star of the show. We'll uncover the secrets of creating demo videos that could win an *Oscar* for "Best App Introduction"!

- **Providing an interactive trial experience**: Ever wanted to test drive a spaceship? Well, with Test Drive and Trialforce, we'll learn how to give your users the thrill of steering your app around their problem galaxy.

By the end of this chapter, you'll be armed with navigational charts to create an effective onboarding process that encourages potential users to become full-time, happy dwellers in the house of your software.

Buckle up, brave explorers! Let's plunge into the engaging world of onboarding new customers and inspire them to become permanent members of your Salesforce neighborhood!

Crafting an effective AppExchange listing

Much like the thrill of setting up a '70s disco party, the art of crafting an effective AppExchange listing is a whirlwind adventure of creativity, strategy, and making your app stand out. Think of it as your chance to put your app in the spotlight, shining brighter than the glitziest disco ball, catching the eye of every passerby on the AppExchange dance floor. Just as with the disco ball, your AppExchange listing is not just there to look pretty—it plays a pivotal role in reflecting your app's unique features in myriad dazzling ways to attract potential customers. It's where your app puts on its platform shoes and flares, struts its stuff, and says, "Yes—I am the answer to all your business needs!"

Successfully passing the security review is like getting an invite to the most happening party of the year (congrats, by the way!). Now, we need to make sure you're dressed to impress. Your AppExchange listing is the trendy outfit your app wears to this party, designed to catch the eye and spark conversations. It's your stage, your spotlight, your opportunity to show your audience how you can move (or, in less disco terminology, how your app can solve their problems).

In this section, we'll be your personal stylists, guiding you through creating a compelling ensemble—an effective AppExchange listing. We'll delve into key elements that will make your app stand out on the competitive Salesforce dance floor. You'll learn how to twirl your **unique selling proposition (USP)** under the limelight and how to optimize your listing for maximum visibility.

So, don your platform shoes, and let's get groovy with crafting an effective AppExchange listing that's sure to make your app the life of the Salesforce party!

Creating a clear and compelling app name and headline

The name and headline of your app are often the first things potential customers encounter, so it's essential to choose a name that is clear, memorable, and reflects your app's core functionality. A well-chosen name and headline should accurately describe your app's primary function, be easy for customers to understand, and stand out from other apps in the marketplace. Additionally, avoid industry-specific jargon or acronyms that may confuse potential customers. Before finalizing your app name and headline, test them with your target audience to ensure they resonate with them and accurately convey your app's value proposition.

Writing an engaging app description and the first slide

An engaging app description and first slide are critical components of your AppExchange listing as they provide potential customers with an overview of your app's features, benefits, and use cases. To craft an engaging app description and first slide, focus on the value your app provides to customers, highlighting the problems it solves and the benefits it delivers. Use simple, straightforward language that is easy for potential customers to understand, and incorporate keywords related to your app's functionality and target market to improve search visibility and help customers find your app more easily. Also, showcase real-world examples of how your app can be used to address specific customer pain points or achieve desired outcomes. In the first slide, consider including an ungated demo or a clear and concise slide on the problems you solve, the value of your solution, and why you and why now. Viewers may bounce immediately if they don't understand your solution.

Designing eye-catching app images, videos, and slides

Visual elements such as images, videos, and slides can significantly enhance your AppExchange listing by providing potential customers with a more engaging and informative experience. Invest in high-resolution images that showcase your app's UI, key features, and benefits. You should test the slide format and resolution early, as AppExchange has strict requirements regarding size, dimensions, and format.

Produce a short, professional video that demonstrates your app in action, highlights its **unique selling points** (**USPs**), and showcases customer testimonials. Ensure that your images, videos, and slides are optimized for viewing on mobile devices, as many customers will access the AppExchange marketplace from their smartphones or tablets. When designing slides, focus on the problems you solve, why it's important, and why now. Your slides should not be just a feature/function list. If no one understands the problems you are solving and why it's important to them, screenshots alone won't help.

Showcasing customer testimonials, reviews, and trust-building

Customer testimonials and reviews play a significant role in influencing potential customers' decision-making process and helping build trust in your app. Encourage your satisfied customers to leave reviews on your AppExchange listing and consider showcasing standout testimonials in your app description or other marketing materials. Actively reach out to your existing customers and ask them to share their experiences with your app on the AppExchange marketplace. Engage with customers who leave reviews, thanking them for their feedback and addressing any concerns they may have. Highlight customer success stories on your AppExchange listing, demonstrating how your app has helped customers achieve their goals. Reviews are a strong factor in determining the order of search results on AppExchange, so building trust through reviews, case studies, and customer videos is crucial.

The importance of trusted reviews on AppExchange

Trusted reviews on AppExchange enable customers to understand which reviews are written by select Trailblazers, making them more impactful. They allow customers to easily identify feedback from the community's most active, knowledgeable, and helpful members, making it easier for them to make informed decisions for their business.

Having a healthy collection of reviews on your AppExchange listing is crucial for not only the success of your customers but also the success of your business as a partner. Trusted reviews can influence and potentially drive even greater demand for your app, and having more recent positive reviews can positively impact your performance in the AppExchange Partner Program.

Top strategies to increase positive listing reviews

To build up your reviews, it's essential to approach this process in a fair and transparent way. Collaboration between marketing and customer-facing roles, such as sales and customer success, is key to creating formal responsibilities for each role, including rewards for success. By setting specific goals, such as targeting a certain number of reviews, you can make review generation one of your formal employee measurements. Keep in mind that only reviews with a rating of 4.0 or higher should count toward your goal.

Don't hesitate to ask your customers—especially special groups of Trailblazers such as Trailhead Rangers, Salesforce MVPs, and top reviewers—for reviews. If your salesperson or customer success manager is having a positive interaction with a customer, use that opportunity to generate a review together in real time. This can be done by asking the customer to log in, walking them through the process, and completing the review in under 3 minutes.

Keeping your reviews fresh is important in influencing the Customer Success pillar of your Partner Trailblazer Score. Ensure that your most recent review is not outdated. Encourage customers to post reviews that share their honest opinion of your app and—specifically—how they are using it, as generic reviews are neither helpful nor encouraged.

Finally, engage with reviewers by responding to reviews, especially negative ones, to address concerns and show appreciation for positive feedback. This demonstrates that real people are providing great customer success for your app. By following these strategies, you can build up a collection of trusted reviews on your AppExchange listing, empowering customers to make informed decisions and enhancing your Partner Program performance. This will ultimately contribute to the success of your app in the competitive Salesforce AppExchange ecosystem.

Providing clear pricing, support information, and justifying your value

Transparent pricing and support information are essential components of an effective AppExchange listing, as they help potential customers understand the costs and resources associated with using your app. Include detailed pricing information on your AppExchange listing, outlining any pricing tiers, bundles, or discounts you may offer. Clearly communicate the support resources available to customers, such as documentation, training materials, or customer support channels. Your listing should also explain why you are the preferred vendor, especially if you're competing with other apps on the AppExchange marketplace.

Optimizing your listing with keywords and searchability

Make sure you understand how people would search for your solution or solutions in your category and ensure these keywords are reflected in your listing. The **Top AppExchange Searches** feature on the partner Analytics dashboard can help you with this task. It shows what customers searched before finding your listing, helping you determine which keywords to focus on. Incorporating relevant keywords in your app name, description, and other content will improve search visibility and help customers find your app more easily in the crowded AppExchange marketplace.

By following these guidelines and incorporating the additional tips provided, you can craft an effective AppExchange listing that showcases your app's **unique value proposition** (UVP), engages potential customers, and ultimately drives sales. With a compelling listing in place, your app will be well positioned to succeed in the competitive Salesforce AppExchange ecosystem.

The importance of updating your AppExchange listing for new managed package versions

As a Salesforce ISV Partner, keeping your AppExchange listing up to date is essential for maintaining customer trust and showcasing the latest features and improvements of your app. When you publish a new version of your managed package, it's crucial to update your listing accordingly. In this section, we will discuss the importance of updating your AppExchange listing when you release a new version of your managed package and provide guidance on how to do so effectively.

The significance of updating your AppExchange listing

Regularly updating your AppExchange listing with the latest version of your managed package is vital for several reasons. First and foremost, it demonstrates your commitment to continuous improvement and customer success, which helps build trust and confidence in your solution. It also allows you to showcase new features, enhancements, or bug fixes, ensuring that potential customers are aware of the full capabilities of your app. Staying competitive in the Salesforce AppExchange ecosystem is critical, and keeping your listing updated signals that your app is evolving and staying ahead of the competition. Lastly, an up-to-date listing can positively impact your search ranking on the AppExchange marketplace, as it may be considered more relevant and valuable to potential customers.

Effectively updating your AppExchange listing

When updating your AppExchange listing for a new managed package version, start by ensuring that your listing displays the correct version number and release date. Next, revise your app description and feature list to reflect any new features, enhancements, or bug fixes introduced in the latest version of your managed package. Be sure to use clear and concise language that is easy for potential customers to understand.

Additionally, replace outdated images, videos, or documentation with updated versions that showcase the latest features and improvements of your app. This includes updating screenshots, demo videos, and user guides to reflect the most recent version of your managed package. Finally, encourage customers who have experienced success with the latest version of your managed package to leave reviews on your AppExchange listing or share their success stories. This not only adds credibility to your app but also helps potential customers understand the benefits of using the most recent version.

Public or private

Upon launching an app on the AppExchange marketplace, one critical decision that every partner needs to make is whether to set their listing as public or private. This choice not only affects your product's visibility but also plays a significant role in determining your sales strategy.

A listing on AppExchange represents an entry that customers can search for and install the managed package directly by clicking on the given URL. With SEO compliance, these listings provide ease of search and customer ratings and serve as a strong marketing presence. Each listing has a 1:1 relationship with a package, implying that one listing points to a single package. However, this package can be interchanged. For instance, if you have a *Listing A* tied to *Package A*, it's entirely possible to switch and have *Listing A* pointing to a different package—say, *Package B*.

Public listings are searchable entries on the AppExchange marketplace. They allow your product to have broad visibility, letting potential customers find it independently. By using this feature, you may increase the likelihood that new users browsing the AppExchange marketplace will find your app.

In contrast, private listings are not searchable on the AppExchange marketplace. However, they can be shared via a unique URL with selected customers. This type of listing allows for a more focused and tailored distribution strategy, allowing you to directly reach out to targeted customers and share the link to your app.

The decision between a public and private listing depends heavily on your sales and distribution strategies. If you aim to broaden your reach and allow customers to discover your product organically, a public listing would be more advantageous. However, if you want a more targeted approach, directly reaching out to potential customers and offering them a unique URL, then a private listing would be more suitable.

The art of customer onboarding

Have you ever bought a car without taking it for a test drive? Or adopted a pet without meeting them first? Likely not. The same principle applies when customers consider purchasing an application on the AppExchange marketplace. They need a taste, a glimpse, a "test drive" of your product before making a decision. Think of it this way—our journey has been akin to baking the most delicious pastry, and now, we're at the point of letting our customers take that first mouthwatering bite.

Our first stepping stone? Recording an engaging demo video. The demo video is the equivalent of a movie trailer for your app. It's your opportunity to create a compelling narrative around your application, highlighting its features and demonstrating its value. Remember—a well-crafted demo video can create a sense of intrigue, curiosity, and even excitement about your app. Moreover, with a well-set AppExchange listing, as your potential users engage with the demo, leads are seamlessly populated in the **License Management App** (**LMA**).

Next, we have our "test drive." The test drive is akin to taking a brief spin in a car on a designated track, supervised by the owner sitting beside you, where you can't explore all its features, but you get a feel for it. In a like manner, the **Test Drive** feature also populates leads in the LMA.

Then, we move to Trialforce, the extended hands-on experience. Imagine letting the customers take that new car for a spin for the weekend. Trialforce allows customers to provision a free trial of your offering, quickly and easily. It's a chance for them to interact with your app, experience it in their own environment, and see how it feels. And while they're testing the waters, Trialforce is also quietly working in the background, creating leads for you. This means while your customers are contemplating, you're gaining valuable insights to track usage and convert prospects into paying customers.

So, as we delve deeper into this chapter, keep in mind that onboarding new customers is a delicate dance. It requires a blend of strategy and creativity to keep things interesting. Let's put on our dancing shoes and take to the floor.

Recording an engaging demo video

Crafting an engaging demo video is like scripting a captivating story. You're essentially taking the viewer on a tour of your application, showing them its unique features, highlighting its advantages, and—most importantly—demonstrating how it can solve their problems.

Start by identifying the key features you want to showcase. Remember—you're not just demonstrating what your app does but also how it brings value to the customer. Think about your customers' pain points and how your app addresses them. Make sure these aspects form the core of your video narrative.

Next, plan your script. An unplanned video is like a rudderless ship—it may have a lot of energy, but it lacks direction. Your script should provide a clear and concise overview of your application, its benefits, and how it works. Avoid jargon and overly complex language; instead, aim for a conversational tone that's easy to understand. Remember to conclude with a strong **call to action** (CTA), inviting viewers to take the next step, whether that's starting a free trial or reaching out to your team for more information.

When it comes to the actual recording, quality matters. Use a good screen recording tool and invest in decent audio equipment—your viewers will appreciate clear visuals and crisp sound. Consider using software such as `demoboost.com` or `guidde.com`. These tools not only facilitate high-quality recording but also offer features that help you highlight important parts of your application, guide viewer attention, and create a more interactive experience.

Keep your video concise and engaging. Long, drawn-out videos risk losing viewer attention, so aim for a runtime of about 1-3 minutes. However, if your application has a lot of complex features that need more time to demonstrate, consider creating a series of shorter videos instead of one long one.

Finally, remember that your demo video is not a one-time thing. As your app evolves, so should your demo video. Regularly update your video to reflect new features, improvements, and changes in the UI.

A well-crafted demo video can significantly boost your app's visibility and appeal. It's your chance to make a powerful first impression, so take the time to plan, record, and perfect your demo video. Remember—the best demo videos tell a story: the story of how your app can make your customers' lives easier and better. Happy recording!

Rolling out a test drive in the AppExchange cosmos

Test Drive is a signature feature of the Salesforce AppExchange marketplace, acting as your launch pad to give prospective astronauts (I mean, customers) a taste of what it's like to commandeer your spaceship—uh, application! It comes equipped with a fully loaded sample data module, making it as ready as a spaceship prepped for lift-off.

Just imagine the AppExchange marketplace as a high-tech, spaceport showroom, where your slick and shiny spaceship (your app) is ready for a quick journey around the nearest nebula. Except here, the shiny spaceship isn't just for admiring from afar—it's for them to hop in and pilot through the cosmos of their specific needs!

Essentially, a test drive org is a read-only org you set up. This org is a shared playground for your prospects to explore your application without altering any records. Given its nature, your app should be optimized to showcase results within these boundaries. Let's see how to set up this experience:

1. **Enable test drives**: Begin by logging in to the Partner Community, find the listing where you want to offer a test drive, click on it to open the AppExchange publishing console, select the **Trials** tab, and check **Offer a Test Drive**.

2. **Create a test drive org**: Click **Create Test Drive** and fill in the details, making sure to associate the package containing your app. Salesforce will create an org and send you login credentials for both administrator and evaluation users.

3. **Configure the test drive org**: Log in as the administrator to add sample data and perform other setup tasks. Then, log in as the evaluation user to define a password.

4. **Connect the test drive org to your AppExchange listing**: Return to the **Trials** tab in the publishing console, click **Connect Organization**, enter the login credentials for the evaluation user, click **Submit**, and then finally, **Save**.

There you have it! Your test drive is set to go. Prospects can select the **Test Drive** button on your AppExchange listing and access the test drive org as read-only participants. This feature is particularly beneficial for apps that effectively convey their value without a need to insert or update records.

For a successful test drive, it's vital that your sample data and scenarios resonate with typical applications and enable your prospects to see your app's full range, even in a non-editable context. The aim is to craft a rich, engaging experience that captivates your potential clients, leaving them keen for more.

In-App Guidance for a more interactive test drive

In-App Guidance is a Salesforce feature that can enrich the Test Drive experience for your customers. This feature acts as an interactive guide within the application, helping users navigate through the app and understand its features and functionalities.

To configure **In-App Guidance**, you simply need to access the setup page in the test drive org, navigate to **In-App Guidance**, and click on **Add Prompt**. From there, you can select the type of guidance you wish to provide (such as floating prompts or docked prompts), the pages it will appear on, the duration it will display, and the frequency of its appearance.

Utilizing **In-App Guidance** can provide potential customers with a walkthrough of your app. This tool can be especially handy to highlight key features, explain complex functionalities, and guide users through specific workflows. It's like having a virtual tour guide that helps your customers explore the nooks and crannies of your app.

Unleashing the force of Trialforce

Remember how exciting it was to test-drive that spaceship? Now, imagine handing over the spaceship controls to your customers. Yes—we are talking about Trialforce, the quintessential warp-speed experience for your AppExchange solution. Think of it as the "Galactic Superpower" for a full-on, immersive "take-the-helm" moment for your customers.

So, why embrace the cosmos of Trialforce?

Well, Trialforce is like the constellation of tools at your disposal, not just allowing you to zip through the universe, but also helping you navigate it with finesse. As you provision trials, you're creating leads in the LMA. Imagine this as creating a map of potential new planets (customers) ready for exploration.

Here's why Trialforce is like the "hyperdrive" for your app's success:

- It's your marketing campaign's best friend, enabling you to broaden your customer reach and adoption
- It allows you to make a personalized impression, customizing everything from branding to functionality, data, and trial experience
- It's your one-stop shop for managing trials for different offerings, versions, and editions
- It lets your customers, even those without administrator access, sample your app without having to log in to their production environment

A few main components underpin Trialforce—the **Trialforce Management Organization (TMO)**, the **Trialforce Source Organization (TSO)**, and Trialforce templates. Here's how they fit together:

- **TMO**: Your starting block for Trialforce, the TMO is where you'll manage everything post-setup. Here, you can whip up TSOs and carve out templates for custom branding.

- **TSO**: TSOs act as the mold for the trial orgs that your customers receive. You can install your offering, add sample data, and configure your TSO to deliver an optimal customer experience. Branding can also be personalized, picking from templates set up in the TMO.

- **Trialforce template**: Think of this as a snapshot of your TSO at a specific point in time. Once your offering is installed and your configurations are done, you can create a template. This template is what defines the trial org provisioned each time a customer signs up for a trial.

Setting sail with Trialforce

To get Trialforce up and running, there are a series of steps that you need to follow, as set out here:

- Develop a managed package

- Pass the security review

- Set up a **License Management Organization (LMO)** to supervise customer access

- Link a version with the LMO and determine the license defaults

- Request a TMO

- Optionally, craft customized branded login pages and emails in the TMO

- Generate a TSO from the TMO

- Install the managed package in the TSO and customize it as desired

- Create a new Trialforce template from the TSO

- Associate the Trialforce template with the AppExchange marketplace

Revving up the spaceship for a journey through the cosmos isn't an overnight endeavor —it involves careful preparation and a series of meticulous steps. Much as with our space metaphor, setting up Trialforce also requires time and precision. It might take a few days before you can embark on your journey, but once you've cleared all checkpoints and everything is in place, you'll be ready to set your very own "Trialforce spaceship" soaring.

Rolling out free trials

You have a few options for dishing out free trials to prospective customers, as presented here:

- **From Salesforce, through AppExchange**: Customers can kick off a trial directly from an AppExchange listing.

- **Using HTML forms on your external website**: Upon a prospect submitting a form, Salesforce provisions a trial based on the Trialforce template. You can employ the `SignupRequest` API when using such a form.

- **Employing the SignupRequest API independently**: This is for those who seek more refined customization. Trials can be activated programmatically.

And there you have it, fellow space travelers! With these routes on your stellar map, you're now ready to send your app into orbit, connecting with prospective customers in ways that are as varied and dynamic as the stars in our galaxy.

Please keep in mind that as your product evolves, so should your trial templates. Any updates or branding changes need to be reflected in your trials.

Integrating trials on your web page

One effective method of extending your AppExchange solution's reach is to feature free trials directly on your website. Utilizing HTML forms in conjunction with the `SignupRequest` API not only drives engagement toward your business but also presents a comprehensive showcase of your solutions to potential customers. Upon form submission, Salesforce allocates a trial that aligns with your predefined Trialforce template.

Understanding the SignupRequest API

The `SignupRequest` API serves as a tool when it comes to activating free trials on your website. Executing API calls to the `SignupRequest` object enables you to generate sign-ups for potential customers, collect in-depth sign-up data, analyze this information, and synchronize sign-up data with your pre-existing business operations.

Implementing trials on your website

To implement trials on your website, perform the following steps:

1. **Activation of SignupRequest API**: To activate the `SignupRequest` API, open a support case in the Salesforce Partner Community using your **Partner Business Org** (**PBO**) credentials. This will get the API operational in your organization.

2. **Selection of a sign-up form hosting option**: Evaluate and opt for a suitable hosting solution for your sign-up form. This could range from a Node.js and React app hosted on Heroku to a Lightning component hosted on an Experience Cloud site, a Visualforce page hosted on Sites, or a Web-to-Lead form.

3. **Creating sign-ups through the API**: Implement API calls to the `SignupRequest` object for the creation of sign-ups aimed at potential customers, allowing you to customize the sign-up journey.

4. **Generating proxy sign-ups for OAuth and API access**: The `SignupRequest` object lets you programmatically create an organization without dispatching any system-generated emails to the user. Consequently, you can acquire an OAuth access token to log in to the organization and perform API requests from it, all without requiring any user action.

5. **Provisioning trial orgs**: Leverage Trialforce to provision a no-cost trial of your solution for potential customers.

Adhering to these steps enables you to integrate free trials of your AppExchange solution smoothly into your website, thus enhancing prospective customer experience and amplifying the visibility and adoption of your product offering.

Facilitating app trials through direct installation from AppExchange

At times, the most effective trial experience for a potential customer may simply be permitting them to get your application directly from your AppExchange listing. This immediate hands-on experience allows customers to evaluate your application in their Salesforce environment, providing a realistic understanding of how your solution would fit into their workflows.

The key to this process lies in the LMA. When a customer installs your app from the AppExchange marketplace, a license is automatically created in your LMA. By default, this license is set to expire after a predetermined trial period, which you can define according to your business needs.

To specify the default trial period, follow the next steps:

1. Navigate to your LMA.

2. Click on the **Packages** tab.

3. Select the relevant managed package.

4. In the **Package Detail** page, edit the **Default Trial Length (Days)** field.

5. Save the changes.

This setting allows you to define the standard duration of the trial period (typically, it is set to 30 days). The moment a potential customer installs your app, their trial period commences, and upon reaching the end of this period, the license automatically expires unless they purchase a full license.

The direct installation strategy works optimally when the configuration process of your application is streamlined and automated. Customers typically appreciate a smooth, hassle-free setup process that lets them start using your app without needing extensive technical assistance or going through complex setup manuals.

However, creating a seamless installation process often requires a fair bit of planning, design, and testing on your part. In the following section, we will delve deeper into strategies and techniques to optimize the installation experience, making it as smooth and customer-friendly as possible. These improvements to the installation process can significantly impact your customers' initial impression of your app, influencing their decision to transition from a trial user to a paying customer.

Converting trials into paying customers

The key to converting these trials into real customers lies in the effective management of the trial period and strategic interaction with the potential customer. During the trial period, maintaining close contact with potential customers is crucial. A recommended practice is to reach out to them a day after the trial begins to address any questions they might have. It's also essential to make contact just before the trial ends, enabling your sales team to guide them toward becoming paying customers effectively.

In *Chapter 2*, we explored the use of your PBO to implement automated processes. This knowledge is particularly useful when designing your trial processes. One key consideration is the duration of the trial period. By default, it is set to 30 days, but based on my experience, a 14-day trial period is usually sufficient for customers to form an opinion about your product. Furthermore, a shorter trial period can help maintain a more efficient sales cycle.

A caveman's guide to installing your application

Picturing the Salesforce ecosystem as an international home improvement store, your application is one nifty toolkit waiting to be picked up by customers. Now, imagine your customer is more of a *Fred Flintstone* than a *Bob the Builder*. Yabba dabba doo! This section is all about making that toolkit so easy to assemble that even our beloved caveman won't break a sweat.

Especially if your application is developed in the ISVforce program, chances are a significant portion of your customers will swing by the AppExchange marketplace and pick up your app. The first impression counts, and the initial installation process is your app's handshake. It's crucial that we get this right because, let's be honest, no one wants a wobbly, awkward handshake.

In this section, we will stress the importance of a smooth and speedy installation and upgrade processes, plus the provision of an installation guide that's as easy to follow as a connect-the-dots puzzle. The aim? To ensure your customers, whether they're Bob or Fred, have a seamless experience, right from the word go.

System administrator – the key persona

The installation process is typically handled by the system administrator in most organizations. This individual plays a key role in the decision to adopt or uninstall your app. Therefore, it's crucial to consider their experience when designing your installation process.

Design your app's installation to be intuitive, and ensure the instructions are clear, easy to understand, and cater to various technical skill levels. By providing user-friendly guides, tooltips, and walkthroughs, you help the system administrators, thereby positively influencing their impression of your app.

Swift installation and upgrades – a must

Speed and simplicity are key when it comes to the installation process. A prolonged or complex installation can frustrate customers and leave them with the impression that your application is flawed. Therefore, optimizing your installation process to be as quick and straightforward as possible is a necessary step toward making a great first impression.

The same principle applies to your app's upgrade process. Regular upgrades are part and parcel of the customer's journey with your app. Ensuring these upgrades are smooth and don't disrupt existing functionalities will help you maintain customer satisfaction.

High-quality installation guides

Crafting high-quality installation guides is as crucial as the development of the app itself. This documentation should provide a detailed description of all manual steps involved in the installation and configuration process. Keep in mind that writing effective documentation is a skill in its own right.

To ensure the quality and usability of your guide, it should be thoroughly tested. This means having someone unfamiliar with the installation and configuration of your app follow the guide. By doing so, you can uncover any potential ambiguities or complexities in your documentation, and refine it for better clarity and simplicity.

Enhancing installation with post-installation scripts

For developers aiming to streamline the installation or upgrade process of their managed package, post-installation scripts offer a useful tool. These scripts, which are specified Apex classes, run automatically after a subscriber installs or upgrades a managed package. They allow developers to customize the installation or upgrade process based on the specifics of the subscriber's organization, enhancing the UX.

Post-installation scripts can perform various functions such as populating custom settings, generating sample data, notifying an external system, or initiating a batch operation to populate a new field across a large set of data. It's important to remember that the script is executed as a special system user representing your package, meaning all operations performed appear to be done by your package.

These scripts have the power to initiate batch, scheduled, and future jobs. However, they cannot access Session IDs and can only perform callouts using an asynchronous operation. The callout occurs after the script has run and the install is complete and committed. To avoid installation issues, the script must not call another Apex class in the package using the `with sharing` keyword.

The post-installation script is an Apex class implementing the `InstallHandler` interface, which has a single method, `onInstall`. This method specifies actions to be executed upon installation. It receives a `context` object as its argument, which provides information such as the organization ID where the installation is happening, the ID of the user initiating the installation, the version number of the previously installed package, and whether the installation is an upgrade or a push.

Note that if the script fails, the installation or upgrade process is halted. Any errors in the script are emailed to the user specified in the **Notify on Apex Error** field of your package. Therefore, the script must be designed carefully and tested thoroughly.

You can test a post-installation script using the `testInstall` method of the Apex `Test` class. After creating and testing the script, it can be specified in the **Post Install Script** lookup field on the **Package Detail** page.

Post-installation scripts are vital for facilitating a smooth setup process. When effectively implemented and tested, they can contribute to a successful adoption of your app, as the seamless setup process leaves a positive impression on users. However, they must be handled with care, with detailed documentation and extensive testing, to ensure they function as intended without causing unintended changes in the users' environment.

Implementing automated onboarding – toward scalable installations

The installation of the AppExchange app can sometimes be a complex procedure, particularly when the app requires comprehensive configuration or integration with external systems. Despite the utility of post-installation scripts, they might not always be sufficient to ensure a seamless setup. In such situations, a practical solution is to design an automatic onboarding process that guides the system administrator through the necessary steps.

One way to create an engaging and intuitive onboarding process is by developing a custom **Lightning Web Components** (**LWC**) interface, often referred to as a "Configuration Wizard." This tool can guide system administrators through all the steps needed to configure the application, grant permissions, and more.

But why invest time and resources in building a custom interface when all these configuration steps can be performed directly in Salesforce Setup?

The answer lies in the UX. The system administrator, being a key persona in the decision-making process of purchasing an app, should have the most streamlined and straightforward experience possible. A well-constructed onboarding process not only simplifies setup but also helps educate administrators about your app's features and how they can leverage them to derive maximum value.

Remember—every interaction your customer has with your product influences their perception of it. An efficient, user-friendly onboarding process that makes the installation and configuration of your application easy can significantly boost customer satisfaction and, ultimately, increase the likelihood of a purchase.

In this context, designing an automated onboarding process for scalability becomes more than just a technical challenge—it's an essential aspect of your customer engagement strategy. Always prioritize your customers' needs and consider how you can make their journey easier and more productive. This attention to detail will pay dividends in terms of customer loyalty and your app's overall success.

Staying cool when your customers make local customizations

Consider the Salesforce platform as an architecturally diverse neighborhood, with your application being one of the modern, appealing houses. Your customers move in, captivated by the design. But as they get comfortable, they start to move the furniture around. They might even knock down a wall or paint the ceiling a bright color. Essentially, they are making changes, just as any occupant would in a real house, to make it their own.

This is the very essence of the Salesforce platform, a neighborhood designed for customization and adaptability. As your customers get familiar with their new surroundings, they will inevitably seek to extend and modify the installed applications, including your managed package. This section will take you on a walkthrough of this sometimes chaotic, but always exciting, interior design process. We will discuss how to manage these changes and support your customers' creative endeavors, all while maintaining the integrity of your "house."

Embracing customer customization

Your customers' motivation to extend your application can actually be beneficial for your business. If customers build additional customizations on top of your managed packages, it creates a deeper integration of your solution into their business processes, making it harder for them to discontinue using your app.

Defining support levels for local changes

Providing support for customers who have made local changes that disrupt the core features of your app can be challenging and costly. It is crucial to define what type of support you can provide and to consider different support levels. For example, you can create **Silver**, **Gold**, and **Platinum** support levels that offer varying degrees of assistance for local changes.

Providing documentation

Supply detailed documentation that includes examples of local changes that are officially supported. This documentation will not only guide customers through the customization process but also help them avoid potential pitfalls that could cause issues in the future.

Building a knowledge base

As issues occur due to local changes, start building an internal knowledge base about known patterns of customer customizations and effective strategies to support them. This will not only streamline your support process but also provide valuable insights into how customers are using and extending your app.

To facilitate this, you can leverage your PBO. Furthermore, consider utilizing standard Salesforce features such as knowledge articles and Communities. Knowledge articles allow you to document and share solutions to common issues, making it easier for both your team and customers to find answers to their queries. Communities, on the other hand, provides a platform for users to share experiences, ask questions, and interact with each other. This not only fosters a sense of community but can also lead to the discovery of novel uses and extensions for your app.

By integrating these resources into your strategy, you can build a comprehensive knowledge base that enhances your support process and provides valuable customer insights.

Regularly reviewing and learning

Regularly review the knowledge base. If you notice that many customers are developing similar local customizations, it might be a signal that a particular feature or functionality is in demand. You could consider incorporating these popular customizations into your app as new features, thereby productizing customer demand and enhancing the overall value proposition of your solution.

Remember—it's about finding the right balance. You want to encourage your customers to get the most out of your app and the Salesforce platform, but you also need to manage and support these customizations effectively. With the right approach, you can turn this challenge into an opportunity for enhancing customer satisfaction and strengthening your product's market position.

Voyage to product adoption

Fasten your seatbelts, dear astronauts of app development, as we prepare to embark on an incredible journey from planet "Awareness" to the star-studded realm of "Integration." This isn't merely a round trip to "Installation." No—we're aiming for the farthest reaches of the "Continuous Use and Payment" nebula. This section of our cosmic journey offers you a star chart to guide your expedition, curated from the brightest insights of in-depth research and practical application. So, set your app coordinates, keep your eyes on the constellation of customer satisfaction, and let's set sail to deep-space "Product Adoption"!

Understanding product adoption

Product adoption strategies help identify potential barriers and create effective tactics to encourage users to adopt new technologies. These strategies are particularly pertinent in the digital product landscape, as they assist in anticipating user behavior, even in the absence of a dedicated research team or resources to conduct comprehensive user research.

Key factors of product adoption

Several elements influence product adoption, with five of the most crucial ones being the following:

- **Relative advantage**: Does your product offer advantages over competitors?
- **Compatibility**: Does your product align with the users' existing systems and workflows?
- **Simplicity**: Is your product user-friendly and easy to navigate?
- **Trialability**: Can users easily experiment with your product before making a commitment?
- **Observability**: Are the benefits of using your product clear and tangible?

Effectively measuring and understanding these factors can significantly increase the likelihood of product adoption.

Adopter categories – different stages, different needs

In the context of AppExchange applications, adoption typically happens at different stages. There are typically three main personas involved: the manager who approves or purchases the product, the administrator who installs it, and the end user who works with it daily. Each of these roles has different needs and interacts with the product differently, thus impacting their adoption journey.

To design effective product adoption strategies, it's essential to understand the specific needs of each adopter category. This table should help us do that:

Adoption factors	Managers	Administrators	End users
Relative advantage	Interested in the product's ability to solve business issues and drive efficiencies	Looking for products that are simple to configure	Want a tool that lightens their workload
Compatibility	Assess if the product aligns with business needs and existing systems	Evaluate how seamlessly it integrates with other systems	Keen on products that operate as expected
Simplicity	Look at the product's impact on the team's workload	Prefer easy-to-implement solutions	Opt for products that are straightforward to use
Trialability	Need to test the product before fully committing	Concerned about setup time	Prefer risk-free trials
Observability	Focus on the product's impact on revenue and efficiency	Require tracking tools to monitor performance	Need to see immediate benefits

By applying the diverse perspectives outlined in the preceding table, you can tailor adoption strategies to meet the distinct needs of managers, administrators, and end users effectively.

Crafting a product adoption framework

With an understanding of the different user needs and the factors affecting adoption, you can create a set of guidelines or heuristics. These may vary according to the context but will serve as a foundation to guide your approach toward product adoption.

For example, under *Relative advantage*, an end user may examine the product's ability to solve frequent problems (stickiness) and provide improved functionality. Under *Compatibility*, they may assess software compatibility and customizability. The heuristics for each factor can be defined similarly.

While this framework won't universally apply to all contexts, it provides a solid foundation to construct a product adoption strategy that caters to your unique users' needs. By understanding and enhancing product adoption, your AppExchange application can flourish in the competitive digital marketplace.

Integrating product-led growth strategies in onboarding new customers

Product-led growth (**PLG**) is a business methodology where the product itself serves as the primary driver of customer acquisition, conversion, and expansion. By focusing on UX, the product becomes the centerpiece of the company's growth strategy, resulting in satisfied customers who not only stay longer but also promote the product to their networks. Here are some strategies Salesforce AppExchange Partners can employ to drive PLG.

Focusing on UX

At the heart of a PLG strategy is the UX. To drive adoption and usage, your product must be intuitive, easy to use, and provide value from the first interaction. Strive to eliminate friction points and make onboarding as seamless as possible. The more users engage with your product, the more likely they are to see its value and become paying customers.

Implementing a freemium or free trial model

Allowing users to try your product before committing to a purchase reduces the perceived risk and can drive adoption. The freemium model offers a basic version of your product for free while reserving premium features for paying customers. Free trials allow users to experience the full product for a limited time. Either way, ensure your free offering is compelling enough to hook users and encourage them to upgrade.

Prioritizing customer success

With PLG, every user could potentially become a paying customer. Therefore, it's crucial to prioritize customer success from the outset. This might involve creating comprehensive self-service resources, having responsive customer support, and proactively reaching out to users who might be having difficulties. Happy users are not only more likely to convert but also to become advocates for your product.

Leveraging analytics

Understand how users interact with your product by tracking key metrics such as daily active users, session length, and feature usage. These insights can help you identify which aspects of your product are most valuable to users and where there might be opportunities for improvement. Use this information to guide your product development and focus on features that drive user satisfaction and retention. We are going to cover this aspect in detail in *Chapter 10*.

Encouraging virality

Word-of-mouth referrals are an incredibly powerful growth driver. Encourage users to invite others to use your product by building sharing features directly into your product. For B2B products, this could be as simple as allowing users to collaborate with their colleagues within the app. Incentives, such as additional features or storage space, can also encourage users to make referrals.

Onboarding new customers with Professional Editions

The Salesforce CRM offers a few different editions: **Professional Edition (PE)**, **Enterprise Edition (EE)**, and **Unlimited Edition (UE)**. While the latter two editions are equipped with robust functionalities, the focus of this section is on PE, which is often used by smaller businesses. It's important to note that the functionalities and features discussed prior in this context apply by default to EE and UE.

Understanding the differences between these editions is crucial when selling your app to existing Salesforce customers, as it influences the design and functionality of your app. Salesforce editions can be grouped into two clusters for ease of understanding: PE and EE/UE. The editions within each cluster share similar functionalities.

For those using scratch orgs for development, the "edition" attribute in the scratch org definition file is your tool to determine the Salesforce edition of that scratch org. By crafting diverse scratch org definition blueprints, you can seamlessly conjure scratch orgs of varying setups for examination. Always consider bookmarking this file in your initiative and synchronizing it with your version system. Remember—PE lacks certain functionalities present in the other editions. Hence, an app molded on your primary development scratch org definition file may clash with a PE org. Designing for PE? It's essential to recognize these distinctions and evaluate them using PE orgs.

To understand which features and objects are available in a particular edition, review the edition comparison table[1] or the online help. Testing your app by installing it in PE test organizations is recommended to ensure everything functions as expected. You can create PE test orgs using the Environment Hub, as described in *Chapter 2*.

All Salesforce editions have limits that restrict the number of apps, objects, and tabs that can be used. However, luckily for ISV partners, any managed package publicly posted on the AppExchange marketplace no longer counts against these limits.

In terms of API access, it's not normally supported in PE organizations. However, after passing the security review, you are eligible to use some APIs for building composite applications.

Supporting multiple editions of Salesforce provides the opportunity to offer richer versions of your app. This can be achieved either by using extension packages or leveraging Dynamic Apex, as described in *Chapter 4*.

---

1   https://www.salesforce.com/editions-pricing/sales-cloud/

Summary

We've journeyed through creating an engaging AppExchange listing and onboarding new customers, like seasoned explorers. We've crafted a vibrant listing, hosted welcoming parties, created exciting demo videos, and offered thrilling trial experiences. We've also handled installations and supported local changes with expertise, all key steps in converting new users into loyal customers. The knowledge gained is not just a bonus, but the key to a thriving Salesforce community.

But there's no time for resting, fellow explorers. As we pack up our camp at onboarding, the sunrise of operational excellence calls us to our next expedition. In the next chapter, we'll embark on a journey of efficiency, performance optimization, and delivering high-quality customer support. We'll learn how to build efficient workflows, maximize revenue, manage channel orders efficiently, and ensure top-notch customer support. These next pages are your roadmap to honing your processes, sharpening your service, and polishing your product to a brilliant shine. So, strap on your explorer's gear, and let's set forth into the land of operational excellence!

Operational Excellence

Welcome back, brave explorers of the Salesforce wilderness! Today, we're setting our sights on the thrilling land of operational excellence. As with the mythical city of El Dorado, it promises riches beyond belief—customer satisfaction, revenue growth, and, if we're lucky, a little less hair-pulling during our workday.

Our journey through the rugged terrains of operational excellence will involve traversing through some very intriguing landscapes, as follows:

- **The forest of efficient processes and workflows**: In this dense jungle, we'll learn how to cut through the clutter, establish clear paths, and ensure our journeys (read: business operations) are as smooth as a well-oiled machine. Don't worry—we've got some handy machetes (process tools) to help us on this one.

- **The river of high-quality customer support**: Next, we'll cross this mighty river, uncovering the secrets of keeping our passengers (customers) happy during the voyage. It's all about navigating the rough waters (customer queries) with the finesse of an expert oarsman (support executive).

- **The AppExchange Checkout valley**: Here, we'll explore this beautiful valley filled with automated cash registers (**Checkout**), making the buying process as seamless as a gentle breeze. Think of it as setting up an open-air market that customers simply love to visit!

- **The Channel Order App (COA) mountain range**: Then, we'll scale these mighty mountains to get a bird's-eye view of our operations, using the COA as our trusted climbing gear. This is where orders come to life, much like the peaks rising majestically to meet the sky.

- **The crossroads of decision—Checkout Management App (CMA) or COA**: Finally, we arrive at the all-important crossroads. It's a choice between the CMA and the COA, two paths promising to lead us to the treasure of operational excellence. Don't fret; we've got a detailed map (this guide) to help you choose wisely.

As we prepare to embark on this exciting expedition, remember, fellow explorers, the journey might be tough, but the view from the top is worth every step. So, let's lace up our boots, fasten our backpacks, and venture into the thrilling journey toward operational excellence!

Building efficient processes and workflows

Like seasoned explorers making their first steps into an untouched forest, ISVs embarking on their Salesforce AppExchange journey must chart out a clear path ahead. These paths aren't just directions scribbled on an old piece of parchment—they represent your structured processes and workflows, the vital veins that keep the lifeblood of your operations flowing smoothly. When properly set up, they ensure every task and responsibility fits neatly into your ecosystem, just like puzzle pieces snapping into place.

Without these paths, your jungle expedition might turn into a chaotic scramble, with everybody scrambling around like monkeys on a caffeine high. The tasks can become a jumbled mess, the underbrush (roles and responsibilities) can trip you up, and before you know it, you're face-first in a mud pit of confusion and inefficiency. A mud facial might be great for your skin, but it's certainly not great for your business health!

To ensure our operations are as sleek as a jungle cat on the prowl and not as clumsy as a baby elephant taking its first steps, we need to dive into the undergrowth of operational processes with our trusty machetes (process tools) at hand.

The thrilling aspect of creating a new product is often the novelty of the experience. Doing something for the first time is not only an opportunity for innovation but also a chance to establish a functional process around it. If an approach proves successful, documenting it as a formal process allows you to create a replicable framework. This documentation then becomes the initial version of your process, upon which you can continually iterate and improve. To delve deeper into implementing efficient workflows and processes, let's explore key strategies and techniques in the upcoming section.

Process implementation

In the process of designing and executing efficient workflows, certain principles from management essentials courses can be invaluable. Here's how you can employ them in your ISV journey:

- **Process mapping**: This technique involves outlining each step involved in executing a task or achieving a specific outcome. By creating a visual representation of the sequence of events, you can better comprehend the workflow, identify potential inefficiencies, and highlight opportunities for enhancement.

- **Leverage automation**: With Salesforce's suite of automation tools, such as Flow Builder, you can automate repetitive tasks. This not only increases operational efficiency but also allows your team to focus on strategic and complex issues.

- **Standardization and documentation**: Create a uniform approach to executing tasks by standardizing your processes. Documentation ensures that these standardized processes are understood and accessible to all, ensuring consistency and providing a reference point during personnel changes.

- **Continuous improvement**: Cultivate a mindset of continuous improvement. Review and refine your processes and workflows regularly in response to feedback, evolving business needs, and advancements in Salesforce technologies.

- **Performance metrics**: Define key performance metrics to gauge the effectiveness of your processes. Regular assessment using these metrics can pinpoint areas that require attention and track the success of implemented changes.

- **Inclusive decision-making**: Involve your team in the process of designing and refining workflows. Their unique insights and collective buy-in can result in more robust, effective, and sustainable processes.

Creating efficient processes and workflows is an ongoing endeavor. It necessitates constant analysis and adaptability to ensure alignment with changing business needs and industry trends. As an ISV, the foundation of your operational success within the Salesforce AppExchange ecosystem lies in effective, agile, and resilient processes and workflows.

Example – customer trial conclusions

Let's say that you utilize Trialforce to offer potential customers a trial period for their products. This trial phase is a pivotal time for potential customers to experience the product and evaluate its value. Thus, having effective processes in place to manage this period is crucial for an ISV. A common process utilized by ISVs includes managing communications as the trial period comes to a close, extending the trial if necessary, and updating the status of Opportunity records in the **Partner Business Org** (**PBO**).

Process overview

For example, as an ISV, you could create an automated process using Salesforce's Flow. This process can trigger a notification to the Account Manager associated with a customer's trial a certain number of days before the trial's end. This reminder can prompt the Account Manager to reach out to the customer, answer any pending queries, and help them transition to a paid subscription if they decide to continue using the product.

Another crucial part of this process can be the extension of the trial period if required. Sometimes, a customer may need more time to explore the product before they can make a purchasing decision.

Requesting a trial organization extension

Salesforce provides a mechanism for partners to request an extension for their **Trialforce Source Organization (TSO)**, Demo or Test, or Customer Trial Organization. Here's the process:

1. Log in to **Help & Training**.
2. Select **Create a Case**.
3. Fill out the **Subject** and **Description** fields.
4. After waiting a few seconds, select **Pick a Different Product/Topic**.
5. Choose **Partner Programs & Benefits > Trial Org Extension**.
6. Enter the required information in the specified fields and submit. The extension will be applied automatically to the organization.

A Customer Trial organization can be extended for up to 90 days per request. Make sure to submit only one request per organization ID.

Lastly, the final step of your process could be updating the status of the associated Opportunity record in your PBO. This way, your sales team can keep track of the customer's journey, from the trial phase to a possible conversion to a paid customer.

By implementing this systematic approach, you can manage the end of trial periods more efficiently. This enhances customer experience during the critical trial phase and improves your chances of transitioning them into long-term, paid customers.

In addition to managing trial periods efficiently, establishing robust processes for customer support is crucial. In the next section, we will explore strategies and best practices for ensuring high-quality customer support, which plays a vital role in customer satisfaction and business growth.

Ensuring high-quality customer support

In our Salesforce AppExchange expedition, consider technical support as the trusty riverboat ferrying us across the swirling currents of customer queries. It's more than just a humble vessel for troubleshooting—it's a strategic compass guiding us toward the shores of business success. Especially when you're paddling in the waters of subscription software, where the journey isn't a one-off cruise but a series of renewals, the happiness of your passengers (read: customers) is what keeps the riverboat afloat.

Imagine each customer query as a turbulent wave hitting our boat. Handled poorly, it might just capsize, sending our precious cargo (customer satisfaction) sinking to the depths.

But in the hands of an expert oarsman (our skilled support executive), each wave can be navigated with finesse and assurance, keeping our passengers dry and our boat on course.

The role of tech support is especially crucial during the initial stages of a customer's journey. A negative experience can create a lasting impression and may affect AppExchange reviews. These reviews provide a public perception of your company and its offerings, shaping how your brand is perceived in the marketplace.

Technical issues within the Salesforce ecosystem can arise from a variety of places, including the intricacies of your application, the Salesforce platform itself, or individual customer orgs. Unearthing the root cause of a problem can be a challenge given the complexity of these areas. Therefore, having a capable team and the right tools to analyze and resolve issues is crucial.

With the Salesforce platform regularly introducing updates and new features, ISVs must stay current to avoid accumulating technical debt. Overlooking these changes can lead to increased challenges for your tech support team. Regular activities such as regression testing, security scans, and API interactions can help maintain the health of your application and lessen support challenges.

The leading ISVs integrate their product development, customer success, and tech support teams at the executive level. They carefully monitor AppExchange reviews and respond promptly. The assessment of their team's technical acumen and ensuring the availability of necessary tools for problem resolution are also given priority.

Let's not forget that the role of tech support extends beyond solving technical issues. It's about ensuring customer success and driving business growth. A well-structured and effective tech support team is a key ingredient for a successful business recipe in the Salesforce AppExchange ecosystem.

Support RACI matrix

Applying a **Responsible, Accountable, Consulted, Informed** (**RACI**) matrix to your tech support processes can be transformative. This clarity of roles and responsibilities allows for efficient decision-making and resource utilization.

Let's break it down with some examples:

- **Responsible**: These are the individuals or teams who perform an activity or make a decision. For instance, an application engineer might be responsible for resolving a technical issue reported by a customer. They are the ones in the trenches, getting their hands dirty to ensure that problems are promptly addressed.

- **Accountable**: These are the people who own the outcomes of a decision or an activity. For example, the Head of Support could be accountable for the overall performance of the support team, ensuring issues are resolved within agreed **service-level agreements** (**SLAs**) and to the satisfaction of the customers.

- **Consulted**: Those whose opinions are sought and with whom there is two-way communication. For example, the product development team might be consulted about a persistent bug reported by multiple customers. Their expertise is crucial in devising a solution or a workaround.

- **Informed**: Those who are kept up to date on progress, often only on completion of the task or decision. They do not typically need to be consulted, nor do they contribute directly to the task or decision. In the context of an ISV, the sales team could be kept informed about major issues that could impact their customer relationships or potential deals.

To illustrate how this could work in a real-world scenario, consider a customer who reports a critical issue with your app. The application engineer (*Responsible*) dives in to resolve the issue, working closely with the product development team (*Consulted*) if necessary. The Head of Support (*Accountable*) oversees the process, making sure everything goes smoothly and the issue gets resolved promptly. Once the problem is resolved, the sales team (*Informed*) is updated about the resolution to ensure it can keep the customer informed and manage the relationship effectively.

Implementing a RACI matrix in your tech support processes ensures clear communication, effective decision-making, and ultimately, higher customer satisfaction.

Balancing proactive and reactive approaches in tech support

Navigating the dynamic Salesforce AppExchange ecosystem calls for ISVs to maintain an equilibrium between proactive and reactive techniques in tech support.

Proactive tech support

Proactive tech support seeks to preempt and rectify issues before they affect customers. This involves keeping pace with changes and updates in the Salesforce ecosystem that could potentially influence your application.

Regularly conducting regression testing of your application in response to Salesforce updates is a case in point. By catching possible issues early on, you safeguard your customers from future complications. Staying ahead of the curve regarding upcoming Salesforce changes and training your team to respond to these alterations can forestall many reactive support needs.

Application usage and customer behavior monitoring can also provide insights into potential problem areas. For instance, recognizing recurring difficulties with certain app features can prompt the creation of targeted educational content or even spark feature redesign for a better UX.

Reactive tech support

Reactive tech support enters the fray when a customer faces an issue and seeks assistance. This approach is about handling urgent cases, and while necessary, should not be the entirety of your support strategy.

Fast and effective resolution of customer issues can significantly enhance their perception of your service. However, relying exclusively on reactive support could lead to a backlog of unresolved issues and potentially unhappy customers, especially if your application serves a large user base or has complex functionality.

Reactive support also offers a wealth of data about your customers' experiences. Analysis of reactive support incidents can reveal persistent problems and improvement opportunities in your app.

Communication and support tools

In reactive tech support, one of the crucial components is communication. Using your PBO can help centralize information regarding support cases. If you utilize Communities, it offers the advantage of allowing your customers to create their own cases, empowering them and ensuring transparency. Employing standard Service Cloud features lets you define Case Milestones, ensuring a high-quality support experience for your customers.

For critical issues, regular updates to customers are vital, even if there's not much progress to report. The concept of a "no-update update" is crucial here. Essentially, this involves informing customers that the issue is still being addressed and setting expectations about when the next update will be provided. This kind of transparent communication can bolster customer trust and patience while the issue is being resolved.

Striking a balance

The optimal tech support strategy embraces both proactive and reactive measures. Proactivity minimizes reactive support needs, allowing your team to provide immediate, effective assistance when required. By efficiently addressing reactive support incidents, you bolster customer satisfaction and collect vital information for your proactive initiatives.

SLAs, service-level objectives, and support management

An SLA is a contract between a **service provider** (**SP**) and its customers that sets out the standard of service the customer can expect. However, embedded within the SLA are **service-level objectives** (**SLOs**), which are specific, measurable performance targets that the service must achieve. While SLAs provide the overarching commitment, SLOs specify the detailed expectations within that commitment. Within the Salesforce AppExchange ecosystem, ISVs often have SLAs with their clients, establishing agreed-upon resolution times for different types of support requests.

As an AppExchange partner, it's highly probable that your customers will inquire about your SLAs. Customers need to know that they can rely on you for prompt and effective problem resolution, and SLAs provide them with the necessary reassurances.

Designing your support process

The type of support you offer and the corresponding SLAs you can commit to will depend heavily on the structure of your support team. Some organizations have dedicated teams available 24/7 to handle and resolve customer queries, which enables them to promise quicker response times. Others may only operate between standard business hours in a single time zone, which could result in longer resolution times.

Whatever the structure of your support team, clearly defining your support process and communicating it to your customers is crucial. It helps set realistic expectations and provides a clear roadmap for incident resolution.

Salesforce platform consequences

Especially for AppExchange OEM partners leveraging the Salesforce platform, it's important to be aware of some inherent SLA limitations of Salesforce. For instance, while Salesforce commits to high uptime, there might be instances of downtime or performance degradation. Understanding these nuances can help you manage client expectations better.

Salesforce doesn't use a standard SLA, but a Master Subscription Agreement[1]. It promises to make its services available 24/7 using "*commercially reasonable efforts*". Salesforce has a track record of over 99.9%[2] uptime and offers a community page for real-time system performance info.

Salesforce's downtime can be planned (for maintenance) or unplanned (due to system failures or unforeseen circumstances). Planned downtime, necessary for system upgrades and checks, is usually announced in advance. However, Salesforce can change these dates as needed. Unplanned downtime can be disruptive, as it occurs without notice. Despite Salesforce's promise to retain data during such periods, the experience can be unsettling.

Salesforce downtime can have significant implications for businesses. Planned downtimes can disrupt business processes, especially if maintenance dates change. Unplanned downtimes can lead to business disruptions, financial losses, and loss of customer trust. Even with data safety, the lack of access during these periods can be harmful, especially for businesses heavily reliant on Salesforce.

---

1   https://www.salesforce.com/content/dam/web/en_us/www/documents/legal/Salesforce_MSA.pdf

2   https://engineering.salesforce.com/the-salesforce-trusted-infrastructure-3cfdd72e270/

Support Process KPIs

Key performance indicators (**KPIs**) are essential in any support setting as they help measure the effectiveness of your support process. Here are some critical support KPIs relevant to AppExchange partners:

- **First Response Time (FRT)**: This measures the time taken from when a customer lodges a request to when a support agent first responds. A lower FRT can greatly enhance customer satisfaction.

- **Resolution Time**: This measures how quickly a support issue is resolved once it's been reported. SLAs typically define resolution times.

- **Customer Satisfaction Score (CSAT)**: This score gauges how satisfied customers are with your support services. CSAT surveys can be sent after each resolved case to measure this.

- **Ticket Volume**: This measures the number of support tickets received within a particular time frame. It can help identify peak support times or recurring issues that may need a more comprehensive solution.

- **Percentage of Issues Resolved on First Contact (FCR)**: This measures how often customer issues are resolved on the first interaction without needing any further follow-up.

Utilizing Service Cloud features

Your PBO provides an excellent platform for managing and tracking customer cases, ensuring adherence to SLAs. Salesforce Service Cloud offers various features for effective case management, including the following:

- **Case Management**: Keep track of all customer cases, capture all necessary details, and automate case assignments based on specific criteria. It allows for quick and efficient resolution of customer issues.

- **Milestones**: Set and monitor key case resolution milestones in the customer's timeline. These can help ensure your team meets the expectations set in your SLAs.

- **Entitlements**: Define and manage the support services customers are entitled to based on their contract or license.

Subscriber Support Console

The Subscriber Support Console is a robust platform that allows ISVs to gain detailed insights about their subscribers. It enables your tech support team to view valuable information such as the subscriber's configuration, license status, and data, thereby simplifying the troubleshooting process. Furthermore, if required, subscribers can grant your team login access to delve deeper into their org and resolve issues within your application.

Operationalizing the Subscriber Support Console

With the Subscriber Support Console, you can accomplish several critical functions, as follows:

- **Access subscriber information**: To quickly view subscriber details, you can either click on the subscriber's organization name from the **Subscribers** tab in the **License Management App (LMA)** to navigate to the **Subscriber Overview** page or you can add a direct button at the account or license level. This alternative method allows you to bypass the search and may offer better access control. Here, you can view intricate details about the subscribers and their org setup.

- **Request and obtain login access**: If a direct login to the subscriber's org is required for issue resolution, you can request access using the console. Subscribers can also proactively grant access from within their own org by navigating to **Settings** -> **My Personal Information** -> **Grant Account Login Access** and selecting the name of your AppExchange product. For security reasons, the maximum period for granting access to ISV partners is 1 month. Once granted, you can log in as a subscriber and view their configuration and data to assist with problem resolution.

- **Log in to subscriber orgs**: Login to subscribers' orgs is governed by user permissions and may require **multi-factor authentication (MFA)**. This requirement enhances security by verifying the identity of the user accessing the subscriber's org.

While exploiting the extensive functionalities offered by the Subscriber Support Console, certain best practices can enhance its efficacy and ensure a secure troubleshooting process, as follows:

- **Creating an audit trail**: Logging a case in the **License Management Organization (LMO)** before each login to a subscriber's org will create a trackable record. This trail provides accountability and transparency about when and why access to the subscriber org was needed.

- **Access control**: To preserve the security of customer data and configurations, limit login access to trusted support and engineering personnel. This practice safeguards subscriber's orgs, as logging in grants full read/write access to customer data and configurations.

- **Utilizing debugging tools**: Use Apex debug logs to troubleshoot specific issues. You can generate these logs to view output from your managed package, which can assist in troubleshooting issues particular to that subscriber. Also, you can view and edit data contained in protected custom settings from your managed packages when logged in as a user.

Maximizing revenue with AppExchange Checkout

As we continue our expedition in the Salesforce AppExchange landscape, imagine stumbling upon the valley of AppExchange Checkout, a picturesque scene dotted with automated cash registers. Now, these aren't your ordinary registers; they're sophisticated tools that smooth out and automate the purchase process for your customers right from your AppExchange listing. It's as if we've set up a bustling open-air market in the middle of this vast ecosystem.

But as with any market setup, it's essential to know the lay of the land. You've got to ensure that your product is neatly packaged (distributed as a managed package) and that your booth fits the general market setup because Checkout cannot be used with OEM apps. This section is your tour guide, leading you through the market stalls, pointing out the nuances of AppExchange Checkout, and offering tips and tricks to make your shop the go-to destination for all.

So, roll up your sleeves, grab your register, and let's set up the best market stall in the valley of AppExchange Checkout, making the buying process a gentle breeze for our dear customers. What do you say? Ready to start setting up?

AppExchange Checkout – operational efficiency with automation

Built on Stripe's industry-leading platform, AppExchange Checkout empowers customers to pay for your solution via credit card or bank transfer, thereby enhancing their buying experience. Alongside this, you can incentivize purchases with coupons and trials while managing **value-added tax** (**VAT**) and US sales tax.

A significant feature that bolsters operational efficiency is automatic license provisioning. Every purchase made via Checkout triggers the creation of a license record in the LMA. All actions, including upgrades, renewals, or cancellations, are automatically updated in the license, reducing manual intervention and potential errors.

Pairing AppExchange Checkout with the CMA provides further operational benefits. The CMA brings Salesforce CRM's capabilities to Checkout, providing insights into revenue, subscription status, and more. It also enables sending customizable notifications for key events such as trial expirations and declined payments.

Financial implications and revenue sharing

As of 2023[3], revenue sharing with Salesforce varies based on the payment method. For bank transfers, it's usually 15%, depending if you participate in the Marginal PNR program described in *Chapter 1*. For credit card payments, at the time of writing this book, it's 15% plus a Stripe-imposed $0.30 per transaction fee. For instance, if you sell an app at $50 per user per month and a customer buys 10 licenses via bank transfer, your share with Salesforce would be $75 per month out of the total monthly transaction of $500.

Checkout supports both one-time and subscription payment plans. You can charge on a per-user or per-company basis, providing flexibility in your pricing strategy. While a one-time payment charges customers once at the time of purchase, subscription plans charge customers on a recurring basis, either monthly or annually.

Applying AppExchange Checkout to your business

Implementing AppExchange Checkout requires certain steps. First, you need to set up an account with Stripe. Following this, a product and pricing plan should be created in your Stripe dashboard, setting the cost, currency, and billing frequency for your solution. Bank transfers can be enabled by requesting the payment method in Stripe. Upon approval, you can start receiving bank payments.

You can then enable Checkout on your AppExchange listing. You can also preview the customer experience by modifying the AppExchange listing URL. To cater to international customers, ensure your company is in a country supported by Stripe. If required by your local tax authority, enable VAT in the Publishing Console.

For heightened security, Checkout supports **Strong Customer Authentication** (**SCA**), an identity verification step required for online payments in the **European Economic Area** (**EEA**).

Managing subscriptions effectively

AppExchange Checkout allows you to effectively manage subscriptions. You can handle customer requests related to Checkout subscriptions, such as viewing payment history, adding or removing licenses, and canceling subscriptions. This leads to improved customer service and satisfaction.

---

3   You can confirm if the Checkout pricing has remained the same at this link: `https://developer.salesforce.com/docs/atlas.en-us.packagingGuide.meta/packagingGuide/appexchange_checkout_rev_share.htm`

Limitations of using AppExchange Checkout

While AppExchange Checkout offers a streamlined and automated solution to ease the purchasing experience for your customers, it's essential to recognize its limitations. These include the following:

- **No varied price points for a single listing**: One of the most significant limitations of AppExchange Checkout is its inability to support varied price points for a single listing. This poses a challenge for businesses that operate on a freemium model or those that have multiple pricing tiers. Businesses looking to offer various packages or tiers will need to find alternative ways to present their pricing or consider separate listings for each price point.

- **Inflexible deal customization**: While AppExchange Checkout automates the payment process, this automation comes at the cost of flexibility. It becomes challenging to tailor deals based on a customer's unique circumstances. For instance, you'll encounter the following limitations:

  - **Delayed billing**: You can't offer an agreement with billing postponed to a future date.

  - **Contract modifications**: If a customer's legal department has specific requirements, modifying contract terms via Checkout might not be feasible.

  - **Additional features or support levels**: Upselling or customizing features and support levels for individual customers is not directly supported.

  - **Multi-year contracts**: Checkout doesn't natively support longer-term relationships through multi-year contracts.

- **Geographical restrictions**: AppExchange Checkout relies on Stripe, which means your business must be in a country supported by Stripe. While Stripe has a wide reach, there are still numerous countries where it isn't available. This limitation might hinder businesses aiming for a global audience.

- **Complex tax implications**: Although the system manages VAT and US sales tax, businesses with complex tax requirements or those operating in countries with intricate tax systems might find the automated solutions insufficient.

- **Over-reliance on Stripe**: Since Checkout is built on Stripe's platform, any changes, updates, or issues with Stripe can have a direct impact on your Checkout experience. It's vital to stay updated with Stripe's policies and updates.

While AppExchange Checkout offers many benefits, it's crucial for businesses to weigh these against the limitations. Depending on your business model, customer base, and geographical focus, AppExchange Checkout might be the perfect solution, or you might need to consider alternative methods, described later in this chapter, or supplementary methods to cater to your specific needs.

Leveraging the CMA for operational excellence

As an ISV Partner, a vital part of operational excellence is the effective management and monitoring of your product offerings. Salesforce provides a powerful tool for this purpose: the **Checkout Management App** (**CMA**). The CMA integrates with AppExchange Checkout, presenting valuable data on a user-friendly dashboard and enabling automated email notifications for key activities. Here, we explore the CMA in depth.

Harnessing the power of the CMA dashboard

The CMA dashboard offers a comprehensive view of your AppExchange Checkout data. Preconfigured displays include the following:

- **Monthly revenue**: Tracking financial performance becomes effortless, aiding in financial forecasting and planning
- **New subscribers per month**: Growth trends become visible, informing marketing strategies and customer acquisition efforts
- **Subscription plan by unit**: Reveals customer preferences, offering insights for product development
- **Monthly subscription status**: Monitors trials, purchases, and renewals, enabling proactive customer engagement

The CMA dashboard can be customized using standard Salesforce tools, allowing you to delve deeper into customer data, subscription plans, invoices, and transactions for more precise analytics.

Streamlining communication with email notifications

The CMA enables automated email notifications for typical partner situations, including renewal notices. You can enable, customize, and use these notifications as per your requirements, reflecting your company's brand and identity while staying connected with customers and team members.

Getting started and customizing the CMA

Implementing the CMA involves installing it into your PBO, configuring data access levels, and enabling email notifications as required. You can then customize the CMA further to meet your specific needs. For example, notifications can be augmented with links to additional resources such as setup documentation, or reports can be modified to show annual revenue for a specific offering instead of the default monthly revenue.

Managing CMA settings for enhanced control

Admin users have the power to manage when and to whom the CMA sends emails, change the associated Stripe account, and reimport data manually into the Salesforce org. Furthermore, you can configure logs in the CMA to assist with troubleshooting, providing an additional layer of control.

Efficient channel order management with the COA

Embarking on the journey of operational excellence, the path of an AppExchange Partner resembles the trek of an ambitious mountaineer navigating the COA mountain range. Picture the COA as our go-to climbing gear—reliable, trustworthy, and crucial for scaling these majestic heights. This tool isn't just a hiker's accessory; it's an efficient command center for managing orders.

This section is the Sherpa guiding you through the often rocky but rewarding terrain of efficient order management. We'll walk you through how to pitch your base camp (creating orders), how to plan your ascent (managing orders), and when to radio in for assistance (fixing errors in orders). Just as the thrill of reaching the peak is in overcoming complex climbing challenges, we'll also be untangling complex operational knots along the way.

So, buckle up your harness, check your climbing gear, and prepare to ascend the COA mountain range, from where your operations will stretch out beneath you, as orderly and awe-inspiring as the view from the summit.

What is the Channel Order App (COA)?

The COA is a pre-installed application in your PBO that enables efficient order processing. Its utility varies based on the type of partnership, as outlined here:

- **For OEM**: The COA aids in provisioning Salesforce licenses and in revenue-sharing arrangements
- **For ISVforce**: The COA primarily supports revenue sharing

It's important to note that partners using AppExchange Checkout for managing customer payments should not utilize the COA, as revenue reporting in such cases is automatically handled when customers purchase your AppExchange solution.

Training and access

Given the critical role that the COA plays in order management, Salesforce requires all AppExchange partners to undergo training before using it. This training, provided by the Partner Operations team, ensures that ISVs understand how to leverage the full functionality of the COA. Therefore, the initial steps toward using the COA involve acquiring your PBO, passing the solution security review, and signing up for COA training. This chapter assumes you're familiar with the basics from the mandatory training and aims to dive deeper into the COA's potential for handling complex scenarios and integrating them into your current workflows.

The significance of the COA

After the conclusion of sales to end customers, all orders need to be relayed to Salesforce through the COA. This platform allows partners to place customer orders and report their sales to Salesforce. Following the receipt of your order, Salesforce takes the responsibility of activating or provisioning the product within your customer's org. This process ensures revenue sharing is tracked in line with the terms of your Salesforce partnership agreement.

Order types in the COA

Every application subscription sold to an end customer mandates that an order is submitted to Salesforce via the COA. Such orders must be lodged within a day of receiving the corresponding customer order. The COA offers a range of order types based on various customer scenarios. These include the following:

- **Initial Order**: This is the first order submitted for a fresh customer
- **Add-On**: This pertains to the addition of products or an increase in license numbers for an existing customer
- **Upgrade**: This involves increasing the cost of existing licenses mid-contract or upgrading a customer to a more expensive product during the contract
- **Renewal**: This applies to the renewal of an existing contract not slated for auto-renewal or involves a change in the price of existing licenses upon contract renewal
- **Reduction**: This involves the removal of one or multiple products or a decrease in license numbers on a customer contract
- **Cancellation**: This refers to the permanent removal of all products at the conclusion of a customer contract
- **New Cloud**: This relates to placing an order for an additional, distinct cloud service for an already-established customer

Picking the right order type

The following questions will help you determine the correct order type based on key variables, such as customer status, license quantity adjustments, effective dates, and pricing modifications:

- Is your order for a new or existing customer?
- When do you want the order to be effective?
- How are you adjusting the license quantities?
- What is the new license pricing?
- How are you adjusting current license pricing?

By answering these questions and using the responses to guide your decision, you can accurately identify the right order type to submit.

The following table provides guidance to determine the correct order type based on key variables, including customer status, license quantity adjustments, effective dates, and pricing modifications. By answering the questions and using the responses as a guide, you can accurately identify the appropriate order type to submit:

Customer	Effective Start Date	License Quantity	License Pricing (per License)	Order Type
New	Service Start Date	Increase	Any	Initial
Existing/ New Cloud	Service Start Date	Increase	Any	New Cloud
Existing/ Additional Product	Service Start Date	Increase	No Change	Add-On
Existing	Mid-Contract	No Change	Increase	Upgrade
		Increase	No Change	
		Increase		
	On Contract Renewal Date	Decrease	No Change	Reduction
		Termination	N/A	Cancellation
		No Change	Increase	Renewal
			Decrease	
		Increase	Increase	
			Decrease	
		Decrease	Increase	
			Decrease	

Table 9.1: Order type determination based on key variables

Understanding the difference between upgrades and renewals within the COA can be confusing, but it's important for appropriate order submission. Both types of orders must incorporate all products and licenses that the customer is expected to have in the future.

Upgrades usually occur mid-contract and involve an increase in the overall contract value. They result from an increase in pricing or license quantity and replace all current customer information. The changes brought by an upgrade order go into effect on the service start date.

Renewals, on the other hand, can either increase or decrease the contract's value but only go into effect on the customer's renewal date. They involve changes in pricing with no change in the quantity. Any renewals that result in a decrease in **Annual Contract Value** (**ACV**) must be submitted 30 or more days before the service date.

If the only change to your customer's contract is a change in license quantity, submit an add-on or reduction order. It's important to note that upgrades act as an "early renewal," replacing all current customer information.

Monitoring your order post-submission

After the submission of your order, you can monitor its status within the **Service Orders** tab of the COA. This provides a summary overview, listing the order number, customer name, customer org ID, order value, order type, and order status. To view more detailed information, including order terms and dates, you can select an individual order. Once Salesforce has received and examined your order, they will activate the products and licenses for their customers.

Partner order errors and revisions

Mistakes happen, and when it comes to order submission in the COA, they can be rectified. Partners have the ability to recall any COA orders within 2 hours of the original submission. Any errors discovered after this grace period will require manual intervention via a case.

Here are the steps to initiate the correction process via a case:

1. **Log a case**: Begin the process by logging a case in the Partner Community.
2. **Select a topic and subtopic**: Choose **Channel Order Application & Active Org Provisioning** as the topic and **Partner Order Errors and Revisions** as the subtopic.
3. **Provide order details**: You will need to provide the incorrectly submitted service order number.
4. **Identify the error**: Clearly identify the error in the order and state the correct change that you'd like to see within the order.
5. **Justify the change**: Provide a justification as to why this order needs to be corrected. Keep in mind that edits are subject to Salesforce's approval.

Common errors in order submission can involve the wrong price, quantity, product, or future date being entered.

Automating the ISV order submission process using the COA

For many Partners, submitting a few orders manually each month may not pose a significant burden. However, for larger ISVs that need to submit hundreds or even thousands of orders monthly, automating this process can be a real game-changer.

As you already know, the COA is a managed package installed on your PBO, allowing you to leverage standard Salesforce tools to automate the order submission process. Most of the information required by the COA, such as customer details and sold products, is usually captured during the deal negotiation process. Instead of manually re-entering this information for each order, automating the process offers a more efficient alternative.

Popular methods of automation are presented here:

- **Quick Actions**: You can create Quick Actions on the Opportunity record to create a new customer and define variants for **Add-On** and **Renewal**. This method simplifies the task of submitting new orders by making the necessary actions readily available.

- **Apex Batch**: You can set up an Apex Batch process to automatically submit all orders in a **Draft** status on a nightly basis. This approach is especially beneficial for large-volume orders as it eliminates the need for manual submission.

- **Channel Order Apex API**: You can utilize the Channel Order Apex API to submit orders programmatically. By leveraging the classes in the CHANNEL_ORDERS namespace, this technique offers automation for order submissions, making it ideal for application logic integration or incorporation into other automated workflows.

By taking advantage of these automation options, you can greatly streamline your order submission process, reduce manual errors, and ensure your customers get live more efficiently.

License transfers and swaps

When you need to transfer licenses between two orgs or swap licenses for the same customer, you should log a case in the Partner Community. Make sure you choose **ISV Billing & Order Support** as the product and **License Swap/Transfer** as the topic. In the description, provide all necessary details, including the originating and destination Org ID, quantity, licenses, add-ons to be transferred, and any other relevant details.

Understanding swaps and transfers

To ensure you're handling each scenario correctly, let's delve deeper into the definitions and requirements of swaps and transfers.

License swaps

A swap case is necessary when a partner wants to change a product on their customer's contract with another equivalent product. You can only swap products on the same customer contract with similar products. The conditions of the swap order, including org edition, renewal date, price, and quantity, cannot change. If the swap leads to a price change, it should be submitted as a renewal in the COA. Swaps can only occur on an active customer contract with a valid org ID.

License transfers

On the other hand, transfer cases are required when moving licenses from one org to another for the same customer. Transfer conditions must remain consistent with the original order—this includes customer, renewal date, pricing, and quantity. Transferred licenses must be in **Active** status and fall under an active reseller contract. They must be transferred from an active org and can be transferred into active or trial orgs, but not demo or free orgs.

Case guidelines

Regardless of whether you're performing a swap or transfer, all case submissions should include the org IDs, any relevant product names, quantities, pricing, and start dates. Following these guidelines and understanding the differences between swaps and transfers will ensure that your license adjustments are processed without issues.

CMA versus COA – choosing the right order solution for your AppExchange business

Now, you're a seasoned adventurer standing at a fork in the road. On one side, the pathway is marked "CMA", and on the other, a sign reads "COA". Each trail promises to lead to the same treasure—the shiny gold of operational excellence. But here's the tricky part—you can't split yourself in two and explore both. You have to choose.

The CMA path is akin to a scenic route through the forest, ideal for those who prefer a relaxing journey with the sight of lovely deer (read: managing payments in a straightforward way). On the other hand, the COA trail is for those who don't mind a little uphill climb to enjoy a more panoramic view (read: comprehensive order management).

So, ISVs, it's decision time. Fear not! You won't be left alone at this crossroads. This guide is your trusty compass, highlighting the unique features of each path and guiding you to choose the one that aligns best with your business journey.

Restrictions with OEM Embedded apps

It is crucial to bear in mind a significant limitation: OEM apps cannot utilize Checkout. Therefore, ISVs engaged in the development of OEM Embedded apps are left with no alternative but to choose the COA as the only viable option. This decision provides OEM partners with the necessary tools to distribute their Salesforce licenses to customers directly.

Decision points for ISVforce apps

For ISVforce, the decision is less clear-cut, as both solutions are available for use. As you learned in this chapter, these are your options:

- **CMA**: This solution is directly linked to Stripe for payment processing and allows for managing orders via AppExchange Checkout

- **COA**: With the COA, you manually submit orders to Salesforce, which can provide a level of control necessary for complex or large customer deals

Overall, the CMA can be a go-to solution for ISVs serving small businesses, especially those with a simple pricing model that aligns with the limitations discussed earlier in this chapter. It integrates smoothly with the LMA and Stripe, automating key processes such as upgrades, payment subscription changes, and revenue sharing. The streamlined functionality and hands-off approach of the CMA often make it the preferred choice. It's important to note that most partners cater to mid-sized and enterprise customers, for whom mandatory payments through Stripe might be a sticking point.

The COA, though often perceived as an older and more labor-intensive solution, retains its relevance, especially for businesses that routinely handle sizable customer contracts desiring a comprehensive package. With the advent of COA automation, some manual processes can be streamlined, making it more user-friendly and efficient. In scenarios where a comprehensive approach is needed, the COA becomes indispensable. It allows you to incorporate your Salesforce offering into a broader customer agreement. However, even with automation, it's essential to note that certain modifications might still require manual intervention, which can be time-intensive.

When you're choosing between the CMA and the COA, consider your business model, customer needs, and the complexity of your deals. If simplicity and automation are your priorities, and all your customers accept payments via Stripe, the CMA is likely the best fit. If you need more control for larger, complex deals, the COA might be your go-to solution. Don't forget, if you're unsure, you can always contact your **Partner Account Manager** (**PAM**) to discuss this matter. Remember—it's an either-or decision, so choose the one that best supports your business goals.

Summary

Congratulations, intrepid travelers! We've successfully navigated the complex terrain of operational excellence. Just like skilled cartographers, we've meticulously mapped the sprawling expanse of efficient processes and workflows, laying down the foundation for a successful expedition. In the dense jungle of customer support, we've carved out a path for exceptional service, ensuring we turn each challenge into an opportunity for customer satisfaction.

Standing atop the twin summits of AppExchange Checkout and the COA, we've learned to conquer operational obstacles and streamline order management. And, at the crossroads of the CMA and the COA, we've harnessed our wisdom to confidently select the most fitting payment solution for our venture. This voyage has not only rewarded us with vital tools but also imbibed us with the knowledge to shape our operational excellence.

Yet, fellow adventurers, our journey continues. We leave the familiar terrain of operations behind and set our compasses toward a new frontier—the realm of analytics and insights. In the next chapter, we'll delve into the depths of AppExchange App Analytics. We'll learn to understand subscriber interactions, use analytics for informed decisions, request and analyze data, and leverage this knowledge for product development. So, rest up, for the next stage of our journey awaits, promising the thrill of discovery and the wisdom of data-driven decision-making.

Part 4:
Scaling for Success

Scaling a business is a lot like planning an expedition up Everest, minus the frostbite and, you know, the physical exertion. The climb starts with a burst of adrenaline. You're amped, fueled by dreams of summit selfies with your app. However, as any mountaineer (or founder) knows, the higher you climb, the trickier the terrain. Oxygen gets sparse, yaks start to look judgmental, and suddenly, you're wondering why you didn't opt for beach volleyball instead.

Fear not! This part isn't about surviving high altitudes but thriving in them. I'll be guiding you through the blizzards of data, sidestepping the crevasses of technical debt, and ensuring that, ultimately, you stand victorious atop the peak of AppExchange. By the end of this part, you will be ready to transform your ideas into profitable and scalable Salesforce applications.

Your trek itinerary includes the following:

- *Chapter 10, Leveraging Analytics and Insights*
- *Chapter 11, Managing Technical Debt*
- *Chapter 12, Navigating the Path to Success*

10

Leveraging Analytics and Insights

Gather around, my fellow trailblazers! We're deep in the AppExchange ruins, uncovering ancient wisdom hidden in a sea of numbers.

Think of data as your archaeological toolkit: it's not about the size of your brush (though the bigger the data, the bigger the brush!) but about how you sweep away the sand grains of obscurity to reveal the golden hieroglyphs beneath. These hieroglyphs are no random chicken scratches; they're the heartbeat of your product's success. A little cryptic, I agree, but nothing an *Indiana Jones* of numbers can't handle.

Now, our dig site is split into zones:

- **The papyrus scroll of Partner Intelligence**: Just as with a piece of ancient parchment, Partner Intelligence unfolds layer after layer of wisdom—from unmasking user patterns to revealing hidden trends and spotting looming competitors in the sandy horizon of AppExchange.

- **Marketplace Analytics**: A toolset to optimize your AppExchange listing.

- **App Analytics**: You'll navigate the realm of AppExchange App Analytics to comprehend feature usage, improve UX, and evaluate new feature reception, benefiting areas such as sales, customer success, and software development, thus empowering you to steer your application's success confidently.

- **The oasis of CRM Analytics**: Here, we combine our in-house data with Salesforce's Oasis of Insight. Expect a refreshing burst of knowledge!

- **The caravan of data-driven decisions**: Guided by our map of insights, we'll navigate our caravan through the desert of competition, all the way to the promised land of AppExchange success.

There's a saying in our archaeological society—we're not just discoverers, we're historians, scribing the story of AppExchange, one grain of data at a time. The terrain may seem hot and sandy, but with a sprinkling of humor and a bucketful of data, there's no pyramid we can't explore.

So, let's dust off our brushes, fill our water skins, and saddle up for this expedition. Fellow data archaeologists, we're about to dig deep into the sands of data-driven decision-making. Let the excavation begin!

AppExchange Partner Intelligence

Think of navigating the AppExchange ecosystem as trudging through the sand-swept landscape of ancient Egypt, minus the inconvenience of sand in your shoes. You wouldn't want to wander aimlessly in the desert without a map, would you? Likewise, traversing the AppExchange landscape without leveraging data is like steering a camel blindfolded—entertaining for onlookers, but not so productive for the camel or its rider.

The concept of AppExchange Partner Intelligence plays a central role here. Going beyond traditional **business intelligence** (**BI**), Partner Intelligence zeroes in on the specific data needs of an AppExchange partner, offering the following:

- Detailed performance metrics for your AppExchange listing

- Insight into your prospects' and customers' behavior

- Comprehensive understanding of the consumption of your managed packages and their contents

There are several tools at your disposal to tap into the benefits of Partner Intelligence: Marketplace Analytics, AppExchange App Analytics, and CRM Analytics. Each has its own specific function and use case, so let's take a closer look at them:

- **Marketplace Analytics**: This tool provides a lens into how prospects and leads interact with your AppExchange listing. To access this, simply log on to the Salesforce Partner Community, navigate to the **Publishing** tab, and click on **Analytics**. All AppExchange partners with listed solutions and the **Manage Listings** permission in the Partner Community can avail themselves of this tool.

- **AppExchange App Analytics**: This tool is like a deep dive into how your customers use your managed packages and their contents. This tool is available for packages that have passed security review and are registered to the **License Management App** (**LMA**).

- **CRM Analytics**: This is the go-to tool for integrating your company's in-house data with your solution's App Analytics data within your Salesforce org. CRM Analytics licenses can be enabled directly within your **Partner Business Org (PBO)**.

While you could use any reporting tool for data visualization, using CRM Analytics would offer an enhanced and integrated experience.

With Partner Intelligence and its array of tools, you can empower your business to make informed, data-driven decisions, driving your AppExchange product toward greater success. Remember how archaeologists meticulously brushed away centuries of dust to unearth the Rosetta Stone? Well, that's what we're going to do throughout this chapter. We'll painstakingly dust off the details of these tools and uncover the multitude of benefits they offer.

So, buckle up and hold onto your fedoras, because we're about to embark on an exhilarating journey of data-driven decision-making across the AppExchange landscape. Let's hope we won't run into any mummies along the way!

AppExchange Marketplace Analytics

In the journey of an AppExchange partner, you'll often find that your role is not limited to what's written on your business card. For those helming established start-ups, you might have an ISV digital marketing specialist or an ISV digital marketing director navigating your AppExchange journey. If you're just setting sail on your AppExchange adventure, you might find that your founder's cap often gets swapped for a "Marketing Specialist" hat. It's a bit like playing dress-up, except the stakes are higher and the costumes are metaphorical.

Regardless of the title on your LinkedIn profile, in this section, let's just assume that you're our marketing specialist, our fearless hero embarking on a quest to optimize your AppExchange listing. Fear not, intrepid adventurer—Salesforce has got just the right gear for you. Meet your new sidekick—AppExchange Marketplace Analytics.

Mastering marketing impact

Think of your AppExchange listing as a party you're hosting. As our marketing specialist, your role is to ensure that your guests (potential conversions) find their way to the party (your listing) and have a great time there (convert!). AppExchange Marketplace Analytics is your party planning assistant, providing you with the insights you need to throw the best shindig in town.

Are you putting up the right signs to guide your guests to your party? Is your party's theme catchy enough to attract the right crowd? Marketplace Analytics provides you with the data you need to optimize your listing's performance and make it the talk of the town.

Understanding your guests

Imagine if you could understand what your guests loved most about your party and which parts they skipped. That's precisely what Marketplace Analytics does. It helps you understand which aspects of your listing are the life of the party and which ones might need a little jazzing up.

Making data-driven decisions

Your job is to ensure that the party keeps going and keeps getting better. You can use the actionable data from Marketplace Analytics to improve your listing based on channel, activity, and keyword-search data.

Key features

AppExchange Marketplace Analytics allows Salesforce partners to delve into various facets of customer interaction with their listings. These include the following:

- The frequency of customers viewing your listing tile on AppExchange's home and search results pages

- The contribution of traffic sources, such as Google Ads, to customer activity on your listing

- The top AppExchange search terms that lead customers to your listing

- The listing resources, such as screenshots and white papers, that customers engage with

- The performance of your **AppExchange Marketing Program** (**AMP**) promotions, which we are going to discuss in detail in *Chapter 12*

These insights can help shape your AppExchange business strategy and identify opportunities for increasing leads, installs, and purchases. In this context, we will examine the following screenshot, which presents a snapshot of Formula Debugger Marketplace Analytics:

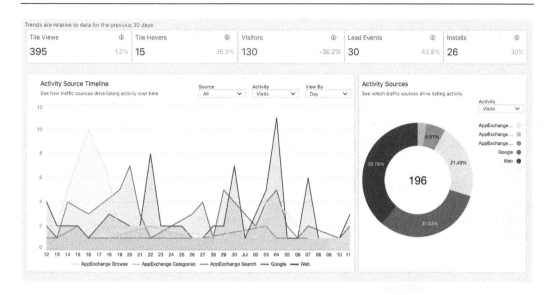

Figure 10.1: A screenshot of the Formula Debugger in action, providing a detailed view of Marketplace Analytics data for optimal AppExchange listing performance

Activity summary

The activity summary section in AppExchange Marketplace Analytics provides key metrics about your listing. It includes a summary of tile views, tile hovers, visitors, lead events, and installs. Trend indicators compare metric performance to a previous time period. By default, Marketplace Analytics shows metrics for the past 30 days, but you can choose another fixed time period or define a custom date range.

Filters

AppExchange Marketplace Analytics offers global and local filters to focus on relevant data. Global filters apply to data in the activity summary and all visualizations, while local filters apply only to data within a single visualization. You can select a specific listing or a fixed time period to analyze, choose traffic sources to show in the visualization, select activity metrics to display, types of lead events to show, or AMP promotions to display.

Visualizations

AppExchange Marketplace Analytics provides various visualizations to track trends and identify opportunities for your listing. One such visualization is the Activity Source Timeline, which shows how internal and external traffic sources contribute to activity on your listing for a specified time period.

Accessing and navigating AppExchange Marketplace Analytics

Access to AppExchange Marketplace Analytics is granted through the Salesforce Partner Community. To provide your team with access, the **Manage Listings** permission must be assigned within the Salesforce Partner Community. This permission not only enables access to AppExchange Marketplace Analytics but also to all Partner Console features, including the ability to create, edit, and publish listings.

Once the necessary permissions are assigned, navigating to AppExchange Marketplace Analytics is straightforward. After logging in to the Salesforce Partner Community, you should proceed to the Partner Console. From there, select **Publishing**, then **Home** > **Analytics**. This will present you with a list of listings from which you can choose the one you wish to view.

Exporting data for further analysis

AppExchange Marketplace Analytics allows you to export your data for further analysis in Salesforce or another tool. The data is exported in a **comma-separated values** (**CSV**) format, with global and local filters applied.

The data provided by AppExchange Marketplace Analytics is available for activities that occurred on your listing from August 2019 onward. It only provides data associated with your published listings. While there is no API for AppExchange Marketplace Analytics, you can export the raw data in CSV format for processing with other tools.

AppExchange Marketplace Analytics does not support the import of external data. However, you can export your data and combine it with your external data using another tool. It's also important to understand that the sum of installs, demos, and test drives might not match the number of leads in AppExchange Marketplace Analytics. This discrepancy can arise due to issues with the **Web-to-Lead** set up in your organization.

Customizing visualizations

Although the layout of the dashboard and the style or formatting of individual visualizations cannot be modified, AppExchange Marketplace Analytics does allow for some customization. From the global filter menu, you can adjust the time period displayed in visualizations. Within a visualization, you can select the activity metrics to be displayed and, for certain visualizations, change the time scale.

Understanding customer interactions

AppExchange Marketplace Analytics records several interactions when a customer installs your solution. For example, when a customer clicks **Get It Now** on your listing, this is recorded as a **Get It Now** click. After the customer chooses a destination for the package and agrees to the terms and conditions, clicking **Confirm and Install** is recorded as an install. However, the number of license records in the LMA may not always align with the number of installs shown in AppExchange Marketplace Analytics, as it depends on the completion of the installation process by the customer.

AppExchange search mechanism

Discoverability is crucial for your product's success on AppExchange, and that often begins with a well-understood search mechanism. AppExchange search, powered by keyword relevance, engagement, listing experience, and **machine learning** (**ML**), offers results tailored to customers' needs. Comprehending these factors can help you optimize your listing and increase visibility.

Keyword relevance

The degree to which the text in your listing aligns with customers' search terms defines its keyword relevance. The better the alignment—especially in the title, tagline, and brief description—the higher the listing's visibility. Appropriate use of keywords that reflect your potential customers' requirements is key here.

Engagement

Engagement is a measure of your listing's popularity based on customer activities such as viewing screenshots, taking test drives, and installing the app. A listing with higher engagement, resulting from more customer interaction, will rank higher in search results.

Listing experience

Listing experience factors in elements beyond keyword relevance and engagement. These include aspects of your Salesforce partnership, such as participation in specific programs, the number of reviews and their quality, and the timeliness of your solution updates.

To get the most out of the AppExchange search mechanism, you can utilize AppExchange Marketplace Analytics. This tool provides insightful data that can help you understand your listing's performance in search results, assisting you in making informed improvements. The following screenshot illustrates this tool, showcasing a snapshot of Formula Debugger Marketplace Analytics:

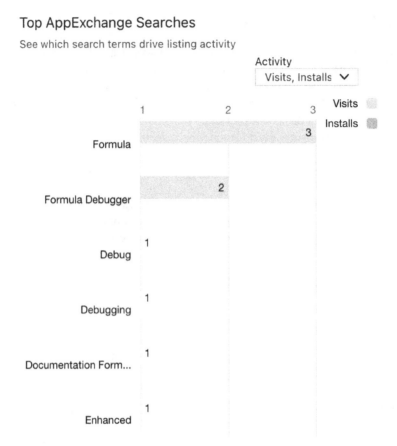

Figure 10.2: A screenshot of Formula Debugger Marketplace Analytics, showcasing its position in the top AppExchange searches

Boosting your listing's discoverability

When it comes to optimizing your listing, keep in mind the importance of the aforementioned factors. For keyword relevance, focus on the business problems your app solves and select pertinent keywords. Enhance engagement by ensuring your listing includes screenshots, videos, and a demo, encouraging user interaction. Improve the listing experience by promptly responding to feedback, regularly updating your listing content, and staying abreast of Salesforce releases.

In conclusion, achieving a robust search position on AppExchange isn't an overnight success but a journey that requires commitment and continuous effort to review and adjust your listing's elements to align with ML and customer preferences.

AppExchange App Analytics

Navigating the AppExchange terrain can often mean trying on various hats, a testament to the versatility demanded by an AppExchange partner. In established businesses, a capable ISV product manager might shoulder the responsibility of decoding the application's usage and user flow. However, if you're spearheading a burgeoning start-up, you might discover the "Product Manager" badge frequently pinned to your entrepreneurial sash.

In this section, let's don a new roleplay costume. Again, forget your designated job title or the role you endorse on LinkedIn; we're stepping into the shoes of a product manager. Your mission, if you choose to accept it, involves uncovering the nuances of feature usage, optimizing the UX, and appraising the reception of new features. Seems like a tall order? Worry not—Salesforce has you covered with the sophisticated AppExchange App Analytics platform.

As our resident Product Manager, here are the key areas you'll be exploring:

- **Understanding adoption**: Identifying patterns of under-usage (potential attrition risks) and over-use (possible contract renegotiation opportunities) of your apps

- **Tracking usage**: Understanding which features are being embraced or overlooked by users, guiding future development and prioritization

- **Optimizing your app**: Analyzing the user journey within your app, highlighting areas of improvement for the UX, and determining the behaviors that yield the best outcomes

To support the areas outlined here, App Analytics data can be utilized at a feature level to inform conversations about features with your team and subscribers. The data revolves around the concept of a `custom_entity`, which represents the components included in your managed package.

For instance, if you've introduced a new feature to manage newsletter subscriptions, your developers may have added a new custom object, a new Lightning page, a new Lightning component, and a new Apex class. As users interact with these components, App Analytics will capture the data, providing invaluable insights that can guide future feature enhancements. This ability to analyze and understand your app's usage at a granular level is a cornerstone of successful product management with AppExchange App Analytics.

Embarking on this journey, you'll also discover that App Analytics can be harnessed beyond product management to benefit various areas of your organization, such as the following:

- **Sales and trials**: App Analytics can track trial usage, understand which features potential customers test, and provide tailored recommendations for a superior trial experience that enhances deal closures.

- **Customer success**: Use App Analytics to promote feature adoption and minimize subscriber churn. By providing comprehensive usage data, App Analytics lets you understand how users are utilizing your solutions, enabling personalized recommendations to drive feature adoption, identify upsell opportunities, and anticipate attrition risks.

- **Software development**: App Analytics offers crucial Apex usage data. By utilizing this data alone or in combination with other sources, you can optimize your code, enhancing its performance and reliability.

You'll be doing all of this while enjoying the benefits of trusted, secure, Salesforce-approved tools that offer a precise insight into how customers are interacting with your application. The road might seem challenging, but with AppExchange App Analytics as your compass, you're more than equipped to steer the ship of your application's success.

Enabling AppExchange App Analytics

Whether you're just setting foot on your AppExchange journey or are well on your way, one of the smartest moves you can make is to request AppExchange App Analytics. "Why the haste?", you ask. Well, the sooner you request it after your application passes the security review, the quicker you start accumulating valuable information about your app's usage.

Keep in mind that some logs are collected exclusively from your customers' orgs, so initially, your data repository might seem like an empty canvas. But remember—Rome wasn't built in a day. With time and increased usage, the canvas will be filled with a spectrum of data, offering you a wealth of information to analyze and act upon.

To activate access to AppExchange App Analytics package usage logs and subscriber snapshots, run `SF CLI` command:

```
sf package update --package "Your Package Alias" --enable-app-
analytics
```

You can anytime deactivate these logs by `SF CLI` command:

```
sf package update --package "Your Package Alias" --no-enable-app-
analytics
```

You can only turn on package usage logs and subscriber snapshots. Package usage summaries are automatically provided.

Once App Analytics is enabled, you'll have a wealth of actionable data at your fingertips. Now, that's a step in the right direction for your app's success on the AppExchange marketplace!

Data types in AppExchange App Analytics

In the domain of AppExchange, data serves as a compass, guiding you through the maze of decision-making processes. AppExchange App Analytics presents three major categories of data types that shed light on your application's performance and user interactions, enabling you to enhance your strategies. These data types comprise the following:

- Package usage logs
- Package usage summaries
- Subscriber snapshots

Let's dive deeper into each of these categories.

Package usage logs

Package usage logs empower you with comprehensive data on user behavior and interactions within your application. These logs encapsulate information about the interactions of users with each packaged component in your application, including every UI, API-based, Lightning-based, and Apex operation. Additionally, they log each **Create, Read, Update, Delete (CRUD)** operation on components and custom objects in your packages. This excludes events from scratch orgs. With package usage logs, you get to analyze user interactions and adoption rates, and consequently make informed decisions concerning feature development.

This data is available for a short window of 45 days from the date the log event occurred. Quick action is required if organizations want to archive or analyze this data.

However, reading package usage log data requires a specific approach. Each line in the log describes an interaction of a user with one of your packaged components. Hence, to comprehend that interaction, one needs to scrutinize each log line, identifying the accessed packaged component, the person interacting with it, and the nature of that interaction.

Package usage summaries

Package usage summaries are your go-to for high-level metrics organized by calendar month. They provide you with an understanding of user access to your package and the operations performed. These summaries capture UI, API-based, Lightning-based, and Apex operations, logging each CRUD operation on components and custom objects in packages. However, they exclude events from sandbox, scratch, and trial orgs.

Package usage summaries are available for download for a significant 10 years from the summary file log date. This extended period ensures that organizations can conduct longitudinal studies and track package usage trends.

These summaries are typically accessible to both partners and subscribers at the start of the following month. For instance, you can obtain a usage summary for May at the beginning of June. As an AppExchange partner, you can request monthly usage summaries using the `AppAnalyticsQueryRequest` object in the SOAP API from the LMO that owns the package.

Subscriber snapshots

Subscriber snapshots provide you with a momentary overview of subscriber activity. They offer a daily snapshot of org, package, and custom entity data, recorded at 00:00 UTC and immediately available for download. You can request a snapshot for a specific date and time or a range of dates and times, receiving one snapshot per valid date and time requested.

By examining these snapshots, you can identify usage trends by org and package. This data allows you to understand the tendencies of your subscribers and make informed decisions to enhance your package. Similarly to package usage logs, snapshot data can be downloaded for 45 days from the snapshot date. Given its nature, it's essential to capture and analyze this data promptly to understand subscriber behavior and attributes at specific moments.

There's one more thing. Not all App Analytics data is gathered in every type of Salesforce environment. The specifics of the data collection can vary significantly based on the org type and status, as shown in the following table:

Data type	Production	Sandbox	Scratch org	Trial
Package usage log	Yes	Yes	No	Yes
Package usage summary	Yes	No	No	No
Subscriber snapshot	Yes	No	No	Yes

Table 10.1: App Analytics data collection across different org types

How to request data

Efficiency is key when handling data in AppExchange App Analytics. While manual data requests might work for ad hoc needs, they could prove to be tedious in the long run. Package Visualizer is a handy tool for such spontaneous data requests, as detailed in *Chapter 2* of this guide. However, to streamline your operations and ensure continuous insights, you should consider scheduling automated queries.

Scheduling and automating your queries

The crux of automation is writing code that will create query request records on your schedule, monitor them, retrieve the data, and store your AppExchange App Analytics data for easy access. For instance, you can store the data in a custom object in your PBO.

There are several automation options at your disposal, including the following:

- Custom API integrations using REST or SOAP API calls
- Salesforce DX automation using the CLI
- Salesforce flows
- Apex

For example, you can automate the retrieval of package usage summaries using Apex scheduled jobs. As you get started, storing logs in your PBO org using Apex would be a sufficient approach. However, when you decide to automate the retrieval of package usage log data, which can significantly increase in volume over time, you should consider a more scalable storage solution, such as Heroku or **Amazon Web Services** (**AWS**).

Automating log downloads using Apex

To streamline the process of downloading logs, you can use Apex to create an automatic process. This will require you to develop a simple solution that should be capable of the following tasks:

- **Regularly make AppAnalyticsQueryRequest requests**: This can be achieved through the implementation of a schedulable Apex class. This class allows you to specify the timing of when these requests should be made, helping to automate the process.

- **Download logs**: This involves performing an `HttpRequest`. This will retrieve the logs from the server and download them to your specified location.

- **Parse retrieved CSV files**: Once the CSV files containing the logs have been downloaded, the next step is to parse them. This involves interpreting the data and transforming it into a more manageable format.

- **Create PackageUsageSummary__c records**: After parsing the CSV files, you'll use this information to create `PackageUsageSummary__c` records. These records can then be stored and used for further analysis.

- **Write Apex unit tests**: Writing unit tests in Apex is critical to ensure the robustness and reliability of your solution. This helps you to detect and fix problems early, thereby improving the quality of your software.

To help you kickstart this development, examples of the aforementioned steps are available at the following GitHub repository: `https://github.com/developerforce/partner-intelligence-basics`. Here, you'll find samples and guides that you can use to set up your Apex implementation for automatic log downloads.

Managing data storage and using external solutions

As the volume of your data grows, it might become challenging to store all of it in your PBO. In your base Salesforce setup, without buying any extra licenses or add-ons, you're given 10 GB of data storage. This sounds like a lot, right? Well, to put it into perspective, this allows for roughly 5 million records. Now, is that a ton? Let's think about it for a moment. Just considering 1 year of package usage summary logs from a single big client could tally up to over 1 million records. Now, keep in mind that package usage logs are much more granular. Plus, chances are you'll have more than just that one client. So, while 5 million might sound like a big number, in the grand scheme of things, it can fill up quicker than you'd think!

In such cases, you should consider using an external solution. For instance, you can leverage AWS to store and manage your data. AWS provides a scalable and secure environment for data storage, which can be particularly useful when dealing with large volumes of data.

PI-Labapp, also known as **Partner Intelligence Starter Pack**, is a free application available via the Salesforce Labs program. It provides ISV partners with usage data about how users interact with their AppExchange solutions. This data can be instrumental in making informed decisions about feature development and identifying potential attrition risks. You can find it on AppExchange: `https://appexchange.salesforce.com/appxListingDetail?listingId=a0N4V00000GmRaNUAV`.

To use the PI-LabApp application, you need a Salesforce PBO username with the API enabled and an existing AWS account. The application includes a `Log pull Config` object that stores the log pull configuration and a `Log pull Activity` object for tracking the log pull activity.

The process of setting up PI-LabApp involves installing the package in your PBO org, assigning permission sets to users, and configuring the log pull records. After setting up Salesforce, you'll need to configure AWS, which includes installing the stack and updating secret keys with PBO login credentials.

Once the setup is complete, you should conduct manual testing to ensure everything works as expected. This involves creating log request records manually in Salesforce and running the step function in AWS. After successful testing, you can enable the Daily Log Pull job, which automates the process of pulling daily log files into the AWS **Simple Storage Service (S3)** bucket.

Finally, to visualize the data, you need to set up AWS Athena. This involves running the Glue crawler to detect the Parquet table from the S3 bucket, running Athena queries, and creating views.

Planning your App Analytics query strategy

The specifics of your query strategy depend largely on the size and scope of your business, as well as the data types you're querying. The strategy you choose must align with your business requirements and goals. It should efficiently provide you with the insights needed to make data-driven decisions about improving UX, optimizing user flow, and enhancing feature adoption. The ultimate aim is to extract maximum value from AppExchange App Analytics, and a well-planned, automated query strategy is an essential step in this direction.

What if App Analytics isn't enough?

As businesses grow, their data and analytical needs evolve. Salesforce's App Analytics is an excellent starting point for all ISVs aiming to understand their application's performance and user behavior. However, there comes a time when the out-of-the-box analytics tools may not provide the granularity and depth of insights desired.

In this case, you can aspire to devise your own fine-granular product usage analytics, looking to dive deeper than what traditional tools can offer. But is crafting a custom analytics solution always the answer?

Indeed, there are notable big ISVs who have opted to create their own logging mechanism, utilizing external systems. Such undertakings are ambitious and can open a treasure trove of detailed insights. However, they come with their own set of challenges:

- **Complexity and time consumption**: Crafting a bespoke analytics solution is no minor endeavor. Designing, developing, and implementing a tailored system can be time-consuming and fraught with unforeseen challenges.

- **Security review concerns**: Salesforce has stringent security review protocols. A custom analytics solution would need to adhere to these protocols, and passing a security review can be a rigorous process.

- **Data privacy and compliance**: Salesforce emphasizes data privacy. ISVs need to be cautious and understand rules around data privacy, especially when tracking user behavior at a detailed level.

Given these considerations, before delving into the development of a custom solution, it's essential to weigh the benefits against the costs and potential pitfalls.

If you find yourself contemplating a custom solution, a valuable first step is to seek external expertise. Engaging with a **Product Development Outsourcer** (**PDO**) Partner can provide a fresh perspective on whether App Analytics truly falls short of your needs. Further details on working with PDOs will be explored in *Chapter 12*.

CRM Analytics

As an ISV partner, it often feels like you're the lone Bedouin navigating the dunes of AppExchange, with each mound of sand representing heaps of data your application produces. And let's be real: raw logs might seem like a hidden treasure to a data scientist, but for most of us, they're more like mirages in the desert—not exactly the oasis of excitement we're after.

But here comes Salesforce, your trusty guide, striding atop a camel across this data desert. Meet your new sherpa on this trek—CRM Analytics for AppExchange App Analytics. With this compass in hand, your previously intimidating mounds of raw data can now transform into navigable trails leading to springs of insightful, actionable intelligence.

CRM Analytics isn't just a sand grain in this desert; it's a powerful mirage buster built on Salesforce's AI-driven analytics platform. With CRM Analytics, you're not just seeing the top of your AppExchange app usage data; you're unearthing hidden artifacts, tracing the tracks of essential metrics, and getting a panoramic view of your customers' behavior.

To join this caravan, simply signal to the stars or, in our case, submit a case to the Salesforce Partner Community. Salesforce rewards your initiative with two free CRM Analytics licenses, like finding two cool water flasks in your travel sack, conveniently available on your PBO.

Understanding CRM Analytics

CRM Analytics is a complex BI product that helps transform raw data into actionable insights. This guide won't make you a BI or CRM Analytics expert, but it will give you a glimpse into the capabilities CRM Analytics can offer to you as an ISV partner. Before delving into the process, let's get familiar with some important CRM Analytics terminology:

- **Analytics Studio**: This is your control center for CRM Analytics, where you can manage and create datasets, lenses, dashboards, and dataflows

- **Dataset**: A collection of related data you import into CRM Analytics, datasets can be derived from Salesforce data or external files

- **Dataflows**: A series of transformations used to prepare datasets, capable of joining, filtering, and augmenting data from multiple datasets or data streams

- **CRM Analytics dashboard**: A visual display of your data comprised of widgets, which are created from lenses

- **Lens**: A saved exploration of a dataset, providing a specific view of your data that can be used to construct dashboard widgets

Integrating and visualizing your data

Having gathered your App Analytics data, the next step involves integrating it with your LMA data within CRM Analytics. This requires you to establish a permission set in your **License Management Org (LMO)**, granting CRM Analytics integration user access to the LMA data.

Creating a CRM Analytics app

For efficient organization and control over sharing of your datasets, lenses, and dashboards, you should create a CRM Analytics app within your LMO.

Importing App Analytics data into CRM Analytics

To store your App Analytics CSV file, you can create a dedicated dataset. Following this, a CRM Analytics dataflow can be built to connect your LMA packages with App Analytics logs.

Visualizing your data using CRM Analytics

CRM Analytics enables you to create lenses, **key performance indicators (KPIs)**, and dashboards for data visualization. Lenses offer a graphical exploration of data in a dataset and form the building blocks for dashboard queries.

Creating a CRM Analytics dashboard

A dashboard can be created using your dataset and lenses, offering a visual representation of your data that simplifies interpretation and understanding.

Adding a dashboard to a package record page

For convenient access and overview, a dashboard can be added to a package record page in the LMA. This provides a direct view of the dashboard and all associated metrics from the package's detail record page:

Figure 10.3: A screenshot of the Formula Debugger LMA, showcasing the integrated CRM Analytics dashboard – a clear and concise visual representation of user interaction and app performance data, aiding in insightful decision-making for the improvement of applications

By integrating and visualizing data using CRM Analytics, you gain valuable insights into user interaction with your applications. This, in turn, empowers you to make data-driven decisions to enhance your applications and serve your customers better.

Driving data-driven decisions

Imagine yourself as the proud owner of an AppExchange caravan. Your cargo? A software product that needs to resonate with the user-travelers you'll meet along the way. You see, these travelers aren't just seeking any old software; they're after solutions that tickle their needs and play a delightful tune on their heartstrings. And as the caravan owner, it's your sacred duty to make decisions that mold your product to their chorus.

In the world of software development, creating a product that not only addresses user needs but also resonates deeply with them is crucial. As an AppExchange ISV Partner, your decisions and product development processes should always be grounded in a profound understanding of your users and their requirements. Adopting such a user-focused approach guarantees not only robust product adoption but also transforms your users into ardent advocates of your solutions.

While it's appealing to make a big splash from the onset, starting on a smaller scale often leads to more effective outcomes. This approach allows for organic account growth, which might take longer but eventually results in a wider and more engaged user base. This method essentially extends the sales cycle but simultaneously facilitates the cultivation of user champions and addresses organization-wide adoption prerequisites such as compliance, support, and metric-based **proof of value (PoV)**.

Data-driven decisions form the cornerstone of a user-centric strategy. By leveraging tools such as AppExchange App Analytics, you can dive deep into usage metrics to understand which features your users find delightful, which aspects need improvement, and where to channel your product enhancement efforts.

For instance, if users show less engagement with a specific feature, this may be a cue for the need to augment in-app guidance or reconsider the feature's design. Conversely, a spike in feature usage could imply positive user reception, indicating that similar updates or features could drive further engagement.

Upon launching a new product, maintaining an open line of communication with your users is crucial. Interpreting App Analytics logs together with their feedback to refine your product and adjust the roadmap not only aligns your offerings with user needs but also fosters a sense of investment and control among your users. Importantly, these strategies for driving data-driven decisions dovetail with the principles of designing customer-centric applications, as detailed in *Chapter 3*. Both approaches place the user at the center of the decision-making process and leverage data to iterate and improve the product continually.

In the words of Jim Barksdale, former CEO of Netscape, *"If we have data, let's look at the data. If all we have are opinions, let's go with mine."* This sentiment perfectly encapsulates the essence of data-driven decision-making—enabling the transformation of your users into champions of your product through continual, data-informed enhancements.

Delving deeper

In the realm of data-driven decision-making, one fundamental truth stands out: there is no silver bullet. What works for one ISV might not be the optimal solution for another. Each organization must introspectively analyze its unique requirements, user base, and goals to decide which metrics to track and how to interpret them.

However, there are some recurring patterns of successful App Analytics implementations. While not exhaustive, the following are a few time-tested measures and techniques that many ISVs have found beneficial:

- **Trends in overall usage by new customers**: Tracking this metric can aid in proactively identifying areas needing additional customer support or training, ensuring more robust product adoption

- **Platform usage metrics**: Understanding if more users access specific features can help you decide where to allocate development resources, considering the balance between legacy support and newer feature integration

- **Churn-rate monitoring**: By predicting churn, you can strategize on retention initiatives, ensuring you're proactively addressing any concerns or issues that might cause a user or organization to switch

- **Growth opportunities**: Identifying which accounts or users are showing increased usage can be an indicator of potential upsell or cross-sell opportunities

- **Operational insights for DevOps and compliance**: Streamlining the management of server incidents and monitoring license assignments can aid in better operational efficiency

- **Collaborative analytics for sales and Customer Success teams**: Equipping these teams with real-time user metrics can help in crafting more personalized sales pitches or support solutions, fostering better relationships with users and clients

Ultimately, while these examples have proven effective for many ISVs, it's crucial to remember that analytics is an evolving field. Regular reviews, iterations, and adjustments based on real-world results and changing user needs will always be the order of the day. Furthermore, if you ever lack direction on which metrics to prioritize, turn to your internal teams. Consult your product team, development team, and sales team. Pose a simple question: *"What information would empower you to perform your role better?"* Often, these insights can guide your analytic endeavors, and by leveraging tools such as App Analytics, you can deliver the requested knowledge, adding value across the organization.

Summary

We've journeyed through the ancient ruins of the AppExchange marketplace, unearthing relics of wisdom and embarking on an expedition through the vast desert of data analytics. We've navigated the papyrus scroll of Partner Intelligence, deciphered the wisdom of Marketplace Analytics, and explored the App Analytics site. At the oasis of CRM Analytics, we refreshed our knowledge, and with our caravan of data-driven decisions, we've charted a course to success.

Throughout this chapter, you have learned to wield our data archaeology toolkit with precision, brushing away the sand of obscurity to reveal golden hieroglyphs of insights. These hieroglyphs, once cryptic, have begun to tell a story—our product's story. We are not just explorers but historians, piecing together the narrative of our AppExchange product, one grain of data at a time. This knowledge, our archaeological treasure, guides us to make informed, data-driven decisions that resonate with our audience and secure our marketplace success.

As we pack away our brushes and data trowels, we prepare for the next challenge looming on the horizon—the ancient, yet relevant, issue of technical debt. Fear not, fellow data archaeologists, for our next chapter will guide us through the labyrinth of managing technical debt for our AppExchange solutions. We'll come to understand its origins, signs, and impacts, and learn effective strategies to navigate this terrain while maintaining the quality, security, and performance of our products. So, secure your archaeological gear and prepare for another expedition. It's time to venture into the unexplored territory of technical debt. Let the journey continue!

11
Managing Technical Debt

Dear adventurous trailblazers, we've bid farewell to the shimmering sands of our data desert, swapping them for the bustling skyscrapers of civilization. As we change our archaeologist hats for shiny business suits, we are stepping into a world that dwells at the confluence of technology and finance. Welcome to the ever-present yet intriguing universe of technical debt.

And remember, where technology and money intersect, debt isn't far behind. Prepare yourself for this new journey. Here's what this chapter has in store:

- **What is technical debt?** Just as credit card debt accrues when you spend beyond your means without immediately paying off your balance, technical debt builds when code is implemented quickly without proper planning or quality assurance. Both situations might seem manageable in the short term, but they can rapidly escalate if not dealt with promptly.

- **Impact on periodic security re-reviews**: Much like how missed payments or high credit utilization negatively impact your credit score, technical debt can affect security re-reviews.

- **Early warning signs of technical debt**: In the same way that receiving overdraft notices is a clear sign of financial strain, certain signs hint at mounting technical debt.

- **Tools and techniques for managing technical debt**: Just as consolidating debt into one loan with a lower interest rate can be an effective method of managing financial debt, there are tools and strategies to manage technical debt.

- **Reducing technical debt by refining your AppExchange application**: Sometimes, if the technical debt becomes too overwhelming, you may need to consider drastic measures, such as a major overhaul of your AppExchange application.

So, pack your bags and fasten your seatbelts. This journey is going to take us through some steep turns and tricky crossroads, but remember, we're trailblazers! From now on, we are like financial analysts of the tech world, navigating the intertwined worlds of code and cost.

What is technical debt?

Technical debt, a term originally coined by Ward Cunningham, software engineer and one of the authors of the *Agile Manifesto*, is a metaphor that software developers and IT professionals use to convey the idea that certain necessary work gets deferred during the software development process. This could involve expedient, short-term solutions that may, in time, impede future development or cause software instability.

Like financial debt, technical debt can accrue "interest" over time – in this case, the interest is the additional time and resources required to fix problems or redesign systems down the road. The longer technical debt remains unresolved, the more "interest" is accrued in the form of decreased productivity, an increased likelihood of bugs, and a slower response to new requirements or changes in the business environment.

In the context of Salesforce ISVs, technical debt can emerge when partners implement quick fixes or workarounds to expedite the release of an app on Salesforce AppExchange, without fully addressing or considering the long-term implications of these choices.

Over my years of working with mature ISVs, I've often found that technical debt is one of the most common reasons for partners seeking help. Successful startups, after an initial phase of rapid customer acquisition, often hit a wall where their development cycles slow down, innovation stagnates, and they're unable to keep up with their initial pace. This is typically the juncture when the accumulating technical debt starts becoming a significant roadblock.

But remember, not all technical debt is negative. When managed wisely, it can act as a strategic tool, enabling teams to deliver quickly and meet crucial business needs. The crucial aspect here is "managing" the debt, which means keeping it at a level where it doesn't overwhelm the development process or compromise the app's long-term value to customers.

The objective of this chapter is to provide you with a comprehensive understanding of technical debt, helping you adopt a proactive approach to manage it, rather than allowing it to manage you. We will explore its causes, impact on software development and business outcomes, and effective strategies to manage and reduce it.

Accumulation of technical debt over time

Technical debt isn't always a result of hasty coding or lack of foresight. It can also be an organic outcome of the changing technological landscape, even when your team is following best practices. This is particularly pertinent to platforms such as Salesforce, which continuously evolve, presenting three major updates annually with new features and modifications.

Salesforce's strategy to sunset older API versions serves as a prime example[1]. The company systematically phases out older API versions, urging the use of newer ones that offer improved efficiency and security. As an ISV, this requires vigilance to ensure your application components using deprecated versions are updated in good time. Although Salesforce typically communicates such retirements well in advance, transitioning to a newer API version isn't trivial. It can involve significant code restructuring, testing modifications, and potential functional changes, all of which contribute to your technical debt.

Further contributing to this organic accrual of technical debt is Salesforce's continual upgrade of its technology stack. The technological shifts from Workflows and Process Builders to more robust Flows, and from Aura Components to **Lightning Web Components (LWC)**, are instances where prior optimal solutions may now be less effective.

Additionally, Salesforce's transition from the Salesforce Classic User Interface to the Salesforce Lightning Experience was a crucial technological evolution to consider. This shift in interface design drastically impacted an application's usability and aesthetics, demanding a significant overhaul of the application's UI/UX design. It was a necessary evolution to meet user expectations and Salesforce's standards, but it also added to the application's technical debt.

All these examples underline the importance of not just introducing new features, but also continuously revisiting and updating existing features to stay in line with Salesforce's evolving standards and technologies. Failing to keep pace with these changes can increase your technical debt, impair your application's performance and maintainability, and slow your ability to innovate. Therefore, a proactive approach to managing technical debt is essential for the sustainable success of your application on the Salesforce platform.

External factors contributing to technical debt

While Salesforce's evolution can indeed contribute to technical debt, it is important to remember that any third-party libraries or technologies your application relies on can significantly affect this too. Changes, updates, and even discontinuation events associated with these resources can lead to an increase in your technical debt.

A notable case of such a scenario involved several prominent ISVs that started developing their user interfaces years before the introduction of LWC on Salesforce. At that time, the decision to use AngularJS for their UI design was well-reasoned, given the capabilities and popularity of the library.

---

1 https://help.salesforce.com/s/articleView?id=000381744&type=1

However, situations changed when AngularJS reached its end-of-life milestone on December 31, 2021. This essentially meant that the AngularJS team no longer provided updates, patches, or security fixes, leaving applications that relied on AngularJS exposed to potential security vulnerabilities and incompatibilities with newer browser updates or other technologies.

Using technologies past their end-of-life date is highly risky because it leaves your application vulnerable to unpatched security issues and potential malfunctions due to a lack of compatibility updates. These issues not only pose a direct threat to your application's security and performance but also impact user trust and confidence in your product.

Consequently, these ISVs found themselves compelled to rebuild substantial portions of their applications in response to AngularJS's end-of-life event. This labor-intensive and time-consuming process significantly increased their technical debt, underscoring the need to monitor and strategically plan for such external factors.

Therefore, managing technical debt extends beyond just your internal development practices and Salesforce's updates. It also requires vigilance in keeping up with changes in the wider technology ecosystem that your application interfaces with, ensuring your application stays secure, performant, and maintainable in the long term.

Types of technical debt in AppExchange development

Technical debt in AppExchange development manifests in various ways, each with unique challenges and solutions. We can categorize technical debt into a few categories:

- **Design or architecture debt**: Design debt occurs when shortcuts taken during the design phase become burdens in the long term. For example, if your solution initially stored monthly summary information on a single record, it may have seemed efficient at first, preserving data storage. But as the demand for more fields per month grows, this design choice can quickly evolve into significant technical debt. Such scenarios call for periodic evaluations and necessary redesigns to mitigate such debt.

- **Code debt**: This form of debt emerges from the code base itself. It can be the result of poorly written code, a lack of sufficient documentation, or deviating from Salesforce development best practices. Regular code reviews, sticking to Salesforce's coding standards, and using static code analysis are some of the ways to manage code debt.

- **Consistency debt**: Often in the pursuit of adopting the latest technologies or methodologies, development teams can introduce a mix of different design patterns, frameworks, and coding styles. For instance, an application that has a haphazard blend of Visualforce, Aura, and LWC can become a nightmare to maintain and debug. While it might be tempting to improve or modernize certain parts of an application, ensuring consistency throughout is crucial. A consistent and well-structured use of Aura, even if considered older, can be more maintainable and efficient than a disjointed combination of the latest tools and styles.

- **Defect debt**: Sometimes, resolving bugs or defects may be postponed due to imminent deadlines. While this might seem a reasonable trade-off at the time, the cumulative effort to address these deferred issues can build up over time, leading to significant technical debt. It's important to allocate time for bug fixing and not let these issues pile up.

- **Infrastructure debt**: Given Salesforce's frequent updates to its development tools and platforms, it's important to stay current to prevent infrastructure debt. For instance, if your **continuous integration/continuous deployment (CI/CD)** process is inadequate, it can slow down your software development life cycle and become a source of technical debt. A well-organized, updated infrastructure and efficient deployment process are essential for preventing this kind of debt.

- **People or skills debt**: The loss of knowledge or skills due to staff turnover can lead to significant technical debt. For example, if the only team member who understood the security review process leaves the company, a re-review request from Salesforce could reveal a serious knowledge gap. To manage this type of debt, it's crucial to invest in continuous training, comprehensive documentation, and knowledge sharing within the team.

With an understanding of the types of technical debt specific to AppExchange development now under your belt, you are equipped with the knowledge to recognize and mitigate its occurrence in your ISV journey. However, as complex as it might seem, technical debt is not always the villain of the piece. When managed effectively, it can be an unexpected ally. So, let's shift our perspective and learn how to use technical debt to our advantage tactically.

Tactical accrual of technical debt

It may sound counterintuitive, but not all technical debt is bad. Sometimes, accruing technical debt can be a tactical decision, made to achieve certain goals more quickly.

Technical debt can be seen as a tool that allows you to move faster in the short term. In a competitive business environment, speed is often critical. Perhaps there's a market opportunity that requires you to act swiftly or a customer demand that needs an immediate response. In such cases, it might be a wise decision to accrue some technical debt to get a product or feature out the door quickly.

The important thing to remember is that such decisions should be taken consciously and with an understanding of their implications. This implies having a plan for repaying the debt as soon as possible. The faster you "repay" your technical debt by refactoring or improving the code, the less "interest" you accrue in the form of additional time, effort, and resources spent on maintenance and troubleshooting down the line.

However, you should be cautious about when and how much technical debt you decide to take on. Taking on too much debt can slow down the pace of development and make the system increasingly difficult to maintain. It can also lead to a decrease in the quality of the product and affect the satisfaction of your customers.

Remember, the key is not to completely avoid technical debt – that would be nearly impossible – but to manage it effectively. This requires a clear understanding of the trade-offs involved, and the discipline to address the debt before it becomes overwhelming.

Technical debt can drive your sales

It might seem overwhelming to confront the concept of technical debt: the potential complexities and costs involved might give you pause. But here's a unique perspective – technical debt can be your ally. Understanding and effectively managing technical debt is one of the reasons why customers might choose your AppExchange app over building their own solution.

Put yourself in the shoes of your potential customer's **Chief Information Officer (CIO)**. Whenever they face the "build versus buy" decision, they need to consider the implications of technical debt. They have to evaluate the costs associated with its management, and the requirement of maintaining a development team to handle it.

This is where the true ethos of Salesforce and the AppExchange comes to the fore: you manage the technical debt and innovation so that your customers don't have to.

As a CIO, the AppExchange provides an opportunity to bring innovative capabilities to users faster, while simultaneously reducing the burden of technical debt. Of course, the debt hasn't really disappeared; it's simply been transferred from the customer to the ISV. This transfer frees up the customer's IT team to focus on delivering high-value, innovative solutions for their business at an unprecedented speed.

Impact on periodic security re-reviews

Remember when we dived into security reviews in *Chapter 6*? It was as exhilarating as your first deep-sea dive into the ocean of code. Now, it's time to take a refreshing plunge again. Salesforce, much like your diligent credit monitoring service, conducts routine security re-reviews. But here's the thing: if your code base has a higher technical debt than a shopaholic with a credit card on Black Friday, these re-reviews start feeling like unexpected credit score checks that always bring bad news.

Now, picture this. You open your email, and it's like getting a letter from your bank saying your credit score needs a review in 3 months. This is easy peasy if your development team was lounging around with feet up, whistling "Sweet Georgia Brown." But we both know that's as likely as finding a unicorn in your vegetable patch.

They're weaving through an ever-evolving roadmap, much like navigating through a city where all the street names are in a foreign language. They're juggling new customers, akin to handling live grenades (figuratively speaking, of course), and ticking off promised features for existing customers as if they were in a game show with a ticking clock.

But just like maintaining a healthy credit score, managing technical debt isn't a one-time spring cleaning effort – it's more of a regular housekeeping chore. It's as routine as brushing your teeth in the morning. Incorporate these tasks into your everyday process, and suddenly, the re-review will seem as ordinary as your monthly credit score check, not a ghost haunting your development process.

Early warning signs of technical debt

Alright, folks, consider this your wake-up call, like that one you get when you find an overdraft notice in your mailbox. They might be easy to ignore when they first start trickling in, but ignore them for long and your bank account starts to look like a desert landscape – all tumbleweeds and cricket noises.

What's that got to do with technical debt? I'm glad you asked! Here's a simplified guide to some red flags that can indicate a growing technical debt issue:

- **Slowing development progress**: Is your team's pace of creating new features noticeably decreasing? This could imply an increasing amount of time spent dealing with complex or problematic code, suggesting the presence of technical debt.

- **Rising bug reports**: Are you seeing a surge in bug reports? This could mean your code base, possibly due to hasty fixes or outdated technologies, is contributing to more frequent errors.

- **Complex code base**: If developers express difficulty in understanding or modifying your code base, it might be due to a convoluted structure or lack of documentation – telltale signs of technical debt.

- **Repetitive rework**: Are developers frequently revisiting and fixing old code? High-quality code should not necessitate constant rework, suggesting technical debt may be at play.

- **Reliance on specific individuals**: Is your code base comprehensible to only a few developers? A shared understanding of your code base is key to avoiding bottlenecks and streamlining the onboarding process for new developers.

- **Struggles with technology integration**: If incorporating new technologies or updating existing ones is a challenge, this could be a sign of substantial technical debt.

By staying alert to these signs, you'll be better equipped to identify and tackle technical debt proactively, maintaining a healthy development process for your product.

The cost of technical debt

While technical debt may allow companies to achieve short-term goals more rapidly, it's crucial to understand that this comes with a cost. Like financial debt, technical debt incurs interest over time in the form of additional resources needed for maintenance, refactoring, and troubleshooting. Moreover, the longer the debt remains unpaid, the more interest it accrues, making it progressively more challenging and costly to repay.

Beyond the direct costs in time and resources, technical debt can also have indirect costs. It can lower the overall quality of the product, leading to a poor user experience. This can, in turn, negatively impact customer satisfaction, which could harm your brand's reputation and potentially lead to loss of business.

Technical debt can also make your code base more complex and harder to understand, which increases the risk of introducing new bugs and makes onboarding new developers more challenging.

The longer the debt remains, the more expensive it becomes to rectify. The reason behind this is tied to two factors – familiarity with the code base and increasing system complexity over time:

- **Familiarity with the code base**: When technical debt is accrued during the development of a new feature or system, the developers working on it are intimately familiar with the context and nuances of the code. Addressing the debt immediately allows them to apply their fresh knowledge to the task, making the process efficient and less costly.

- **System complexity**: As time progresses, your system grows - new features are added, and existing ones are updated or removed. Each change introduces dependencies and interactions that could be affected when resolving technical debt in a particular area. As the system's complexity increases, so does the difficulty and cost of resolving the debt.

In essence, the cost of resolving technical debt is not constant. However, just as managing your financial mess can be approached strategically, handling your code base's technical debt also calls for a well-thought-out digital finance toolbox.

Tools and techniques for managing technical debt

Think about the last time you decided to clean up your financial mess. You took a good hard look at your various loans, credit card bills, and all that jazz, and decided to tackle them head-on, maybe with a solid debt consolidation strategy and some savvy financial planning. Now, what if I told you, managing technical debt could be approached in the same way?

Don't look so surprised! Let's delve into our digital finance toolbox for a minute. Much like sorting through your physical debts, wrangling your code base's technical debt requires a tactical game plan that includes routine health checks, prioritizing the most damaging debts, and taking decisive action.

Technical design review

Before diving deeper into code reviews, it's essential to emphasize the importance of technical design reviews. These reviews, often conducted before any code is written, focus on the overall technical approach, component architecture, and high-level design of large and complex features. By evaluating the technical direction before starting the implementation, teams can ensure that they are on the right path. This reduces the risk of accumulating technical debt due to design flaws.

In a technical design review, stakeholders and team members collaborate to discuss potential challenges, dependencies, and risks. By proactively addressing these issues, the team can make informed decisions, ensuring that the design is not only functional but also scalable, maintainable, and in line with the broader system architecture. Technical design review is especially vital for managed packages development as some decisions can't be undone after adding metadata to the package and installing it on the subscriber's orgs.

Code reviews

Code reviews form a critical part of the development process, and they're especially important when it comes to managing technical debt. During a code review, members of the development team examine each other's code. This process helps uncover any issues that might have been missed during initial development.

Code reviews are an effective method for catching bugs, ensuring code consistency, and preventing the introduction of new technical debt. It's during these reviews that issues such as code smells, poorly designed algorithms, or inefficient processes can be identified and remediated.

When done consistently, code reviews can contribute to higher quality code, improved team collaboration, and a lower level of technical debt. They foster an environment of learning and improvement, where all team members can benefit from each other's insights and perspectives.

Here are some of the key benefits of code reviews:

- **Improvement in code quality**: When code is reviewed by peers, it can result in better readability and maintainability. This is important as it can significantly reduce the occurrence of technical debt.

- **Shared code ownership**: Code reviews can foster a sense of shared responsibility and ownership. This helps prevent a single point of failure if a key team member leaves the organization or changes roles.

- **Knowledge sharing**: Code reviews are a great platform for team members to share their knowledge and expertise. This can lead to better solutions, helping prevent suboptimal design choices that could become sources of technical debt.

- **Mentoring and learning**: For junior developers, code reviews offer an opportunity to learn from more experienced team members. This can help them avoid common pitfalls and grow their skills more rapidly.

Remember, the goal of a code review isn't to find faults with someone's coding abilities but rather to ensure that the best possible solution is found and implemented. For this reason, it's important to approach code reviews with a mindset of collaboration and continuous improvement. This will not only help reduce technical debt but also foster a positive and productive work environment.

Static code analysis

Static code analysis is a powerful approach to enhancing the quality of code and managing technical debt. It is a mechanism that's used to inspect code for potential errors, inefficiencies, and deviations from coding standards without actually executing the code. The process involves matching the source code against a set of predefined coding rules, thus allowing for early identification and rectification of various issues in the codebase.

Utilizing static code analysis can drastically streamline the code review process due to its ability to rapidly detect a wide array of bugs and vulnerabilities. This advantage enables developers to promptly fix these issues without waiting for feedback from a human reviewer. Moreover, the early identification and resolution of issues result in a considerable reduction in development costs.

Static code analysis tools come in both free and paid versions. These tools offer varying degrees of customization to align with specific coding standards and provide varying depths of analysis.

Here are some key points to consider when adopting static code analysis:

- **Error detection**: Static code analysis tools can discover a variety of potential issues, including syntax errors, race conditions, and unused variables, among others. This early detection capability aids in proactive issue remediation.

- **Coding standards**: These tools can be configured to align with specific coding standards, thereby promoting consistency across the code base and adherence to best practices.

- **CI/CD pipeline integration**: To maximize their efficacy, static code analysis tools should be embedded within the CI/CD pipeline. This inclusion allows for automatic code examination every time a new code commit occurs, providing instant feedback to developers before code merges.

- **Code quality metrics**: Beyond detecting potential errors, static code analysis can provide valuable metrics such as cyclomatic complexity, offering a quantitative analysis of code complexity and indicating areas that may require refactoring.

- **Complement to human code review**: While static code analysis significantly increases the efficiency of the code review process, it does not replace the need for human reviewers. Taking care of many common issues allows human reviewers to focus their efforts on the more complex, design-oriented aspects of code review. This approach results in a more thorough and effective review process.

While static code analysis is an incredibly valuable tool for identifying technical debt and enhancing code quality, it should not be viewed as a standalone solution. Instead, it should form part of a comprehensive, well-rounded strategy for managing technical debt, alongside rigorous testing and human-led code reviews.

Salesforce Code Analyzer

Salesforce created and offers Salesforce Code Analyzer, which is a potent tool for source code analysis. As a comprehensive static code analysis tool, it is particularly crucial due to its proficiency in catching the majority of errors that could be flagged during a Salesforce security review. As you already know, packages listed on AppExchange are required to pass a security review, and as part of this process, you are also required to upload your Salesforce Code Analyzer scan reports.

The tool currently supports the PMD rule engine, PMD Copy Paste Detector, ESLint, RetireJS, and Salesforce Graph Engine. These different engines add to their versatility and power in analyzing various aspects of your code base, from generic coding issues to security vulnerabilities.

For developers using VS Code, I strongly suggest installing and using the Code Analyzer plugin[2]. This proactive approach allows individual developers to identify and rectify issues early in the development process, significantly enhancing code quality and efficiency. Additionally, you should integrate Salesforce Code Analyzer into your CI/CD process. This integration allows you to enforce the rules that you define and promotes the production of high-quality code. By setting up Salesforce Code Analyzer in your CI/CD pipeline, every code commit triggers an analysis, ensuring a continuous and consistent level of code quality.

Automated testing

Automated testing is another crucial practice for managing technical debt. It ensures that your code behaves as expected and helps prevent the introduction of new bugs when changes are made to the code base.

Automated tests can range from unit tests, which test individual functions or methods, to integration tests, which ensure that different components of your system work together properly. Higher-level tests, such as end-to-end tests, can simulate user interactions with your application and verify that the entire system functions as expected.

---

2   https://marketplace.visualstudio.com/items?itemName=salesforce.sfdx-code-analyzer-vscode

The key benefits of automated testing include the following:

- **Faster feedback**: Automated tests provide fast feedback on the effect of code changes, allowing developers to catch and fix issues early before they become significant problems.

- **Increased efficiency**: Once written, automated tests can be run at any time, providing constant assurance that your code is functioning as intended. This saves time for the development team as they do not have to manually retest functionality every time a change is made.

- **Reduction in human error**: Manual testing can be error-prone, especially when done repetitively. Automated testing ensures a consistent standard of quality.

- **Documentation**: Well-written test cases can serve as a form of documentation, helping new team members understand how different parts of the system are supposed to function.

Investing in a robust automated testing framework can greatly help in managing and reducing technical debt. It makes refactoring and improving your code less risky as you can quickly verify that your changes haven't unintentionally broken anything. Moreover, it encourages developers to write testable (and therefore usually simpler and cleaner) code from the start, helping to prevent technical debt from accruing in the first place.

Different tools and frameworks are used for each type of testing, and choosing the right ones can greatly influence the effectiveness of your testing strategy. You might want to consider a few types of automated testing:

- **Apex unit testing**: Apex is a proprietary language provided by Salesforce that is used to write business logic for Salesforce applications. Unit tests in Apex are essential to verify the correctness of this logic. These tests are performed at a granular level and help identify issues early in the development process. They are easier to write and execute, and since they are closer to the source code, they make finding and fixing bugs cheaper. These tests are mandatory; Apex code in managed packages on AppExchange must have at least 75% test coverage before the package can be submitted for security review.

- **LWC Jest tests:** Salesforce's LWC framework brings modern web standards to Salesforce development. Jest is a popular JavaScript testing framework, and it's recommended for testing LWC. These tests provide quick feedback on the functionality of individual components and make it easier to identify and fix problems at the component level.

- **End-to-end tests with UI Test Automation Model (UTAM[3])**: End-to-end (E2E) tests simulate the complete user interaction with an application, from start to finish. This kind of testing is typically more challenging to set up and maintain but provides the most comprehensive coverage. Salesforce provides a solution to these challenges with UTAM. UTAM is an open-source tool developed by Salesforce for writing and maintaining E2E tests. Unlike traditional E2E tests,

3   https://developer.salesforce.com/blogs/2022/05/run-end-to-end-tests-with-the-ui-test-automation-model-utam

which are often brittle and hard to maintain due to their tight coupling with the **Document Object Model (DOM)**, UTAM uses a page object model to decouple the test code from the DOM, making the tests easier to write and maintain.

- **Acceptance testing with the Robot framework**: Another option to consider is the Robot[4] framework, which is included in CumulusCI. This provides an alternative to UTAM and offers a versatile and robust approach to testing Salesforce applications.

- **Click and Configure test tools**: There are several vendors in the market offering "Click and Configure" testing tools designed specifically for Salesforce customers. These tools allow users to design test cases by simply navigating and interacting with the application, capturing steps as they go, without the need for extensive programming knowledge.

Choosing the right testing strategy and toolset depends on several factors, including the complexity of your application, your team's expertise, and the specific needs of your project.

However, bear in mind that test code can also accrue technical debt. Tests should be kept clean, readable, and maintainable. They should also be reviewed and refactored as needed, just like the rest of your code base. It's also worth noting that while automated testing is a powerful tool, it doesn't completely replace the need for manual testing, especially for more complex user interactions or visual aspects of your application.

Refactoring

Refactoring is another vital tool in your arsenal for managing technical debt. Refactoring involves changing the structure of code without altering its functionality to improve readability, reduce complexity, and make it more maintainable.

Although the concept sounds simple, refactoring requires a careful and systematic approach. Here are a few steps and techniques involved:

1. **Identify code smells**: Code smells refer to any characteristic in the source code that potentially indicates a deeper problem. These may include long methods, duplicate code, large classes, long parameter lists, or excessive use of globals. Identifying code smells is the first step in refactoring.

2. **Understand the code**: Before starting the refactoring process, it's essential to understand the code fully. Developers should know why the code was written the way it was and what it's supposed to do.

3. **Plan the refactoring**: Not all code smells need to be addressed immediately, nor do they all require the same level of effort to fix. Prioritize the refactoring tasks based on their potential impact on code quality, ease of refactoring, and the level of risk involved.

---

4   `https://cumulusci.readthedocs.io/en/stable/robot.html`

4. **Use the right tools**: Many modern **integrated development environments** (**IDEs**) provide built-in support for refactoring, including functions for renaming, moving, and changing the signatures of methods or classes. Automated refactoring tools can perform these operations accurately and efficiently.

5. **Test after refactoring**: Since refactoring changes the structure of the code, it's crucial to re-run tests after refactoring to ensure that the functionality remains unchanged. A robust suite of unit tests can be especially helpful in this regard as they provide quick feedback on whether the refactoring has inadvertently altered the code's behavior.

6. **Frequent commits**: To keep track of the changes and easily revert if something goes wrong, it's advisable to commit changes to version control frequently during the refactoring process.

7. **Refactor continually**: Refactoring isn't a one-time operation but an ongoing process. As the code base evolves and new features are added, new opportunities for refactoring will arise. Regular refactoring helps keep technical debt in check and makes the code easier to work with.

Remember that the goal of refactoring is not just to make the code "look better," but to make it easier to understand, maintain, and extend in the future. By regularly refactoring your code, you can significantly reduce the buildup of technical debt in your software projects.

Documentation

Documentation is an essential tool for managing technical debt as it provides an accessible, comprehensive record of the software's design decisions, functionality, and operational procedures. By offering clear insight into the software's operation, documentation aids developers in maintaining, updating, and refactoring the system.

When dealing with legacy systems or changes in the development team, the importance of proper documentation becomes more apparent. It serves as a conduit for knowledge transfer, ensuring that incoming team members understand the system's architecture, business logic, and the choices made during the development phase. Without this, newcomers might take longer to understand the system or even introduce errors, thereby inadvertently adding to the technical debt.

Documentation can come in different forms. Let's discuss these in detail:

- **Code comments**: Robert C. Martin, also known as Uncle Bob, once said, "*Good code is its own best documentation. As you're about to add a comment, ask yourself, "How can I improve the code so that this comment isn't needed?" Improve the code and then document it to make it even clearer.*" This statement emphasizes that well-written, clear, and expressive code should not heavily rely on comments. Instead of explaining what the code does through comments, strive to make the code self-explanatory. This approach leads to a more maintainable code base that developers can understand and modify without depending on comments, which could become outdated or misleading over time.

- **System documentation**: This form of documentation provides an overarching view of the system, detailing its design, architecture, and component interactions. It should also outline any third-party dependencies, configuration, and installation procedures.

- **User manuals**: Though not directly tied to the code base, user manuals are valuable documentation resources that clarify the system's intended functionality, assisting developers during software updates or modifications.

- **Architectural diagrams**: These visual aids help developers grasp complex systems more readily.

Effective documentation can significantly reduce the time spent on system comprehension, streamline software maintenance and enhancements, and play a critical role in managing technical debt. However, this documentation must be consistently maintained and updated in tandem with software developments. Outdated or inaccurate documentation can introduce confusion and mistakes, unintentionally escalating the technical debt.

Prioritization

In dealing with technical debt, prioritization is a vital process. Given that not all debt has the same impact, determining what needs to be addressed immediately and what can be deferred is a strategic decision that can greatly influence the project's progress, quality, and overall success.

Prioritization depends on several factors, and a thorough understanding of these can guide an effective debt management strategy:

- **Impact on business**: One of the most significant factors to consider is the debt's effect on the business. Issues that disrupt core functionalities or negatively impact the user experience should be high on the priority list. These could include performance issues, security vulnerabilities, or bugs affecting critical features.

- **Frequency of code use**: Another critical factor is how frequently the problematic code is used or modified. If a specific component with high debt is frequently updated or forms a core part of your application, it may be wise to prioritize its refactoring to prevent the debt from escalating.

- **Ease of refactoring**: The complexity involved in resolving the debt is another aspect to consider. Some debts can be resolved with minor code tweaks, while others may require a significant overhaul of the system architecture. It might be more efficient to quickly address several smaller debts than to get bogged down with one large, complex debt.

- **Risk of accumulation**: Technical debt, if left unaddressed, can accumulate interest in the form of additional complexity, making future changes harder and more error-prone. It's important to identify and prioritize such debts to avoid this pitfall.

The prioritization process should involve all stakeholders, including developers, testers, product owners, and, if possible, business stakeholders. It's essential to remember that addressing technical debt isn't just about "fixing" issues – it's about continuously improving the code base for long-term sustainability. Prioritization is a dynamic process, and as such, it should be revisited regularly as part of your development cycles. By strategically prioritizing the most critical issues, teams can effectively manage their technical debt, improving their code's maintainability, functionality, and overall quality.

Technical debt as part of your product roadmap

While the focus of this chapter is on technical debt, it's worth recognizing that its management plays an integral role within a larger context – the product development roadmap. A product roadmap outlines the vision, direction, and progress of a product over time. It is crucial for aligning teams, setting expectations, and making informed decisions about a product's development.

Product roadmaps typically comprise multiple elements, each with its own set of priorities and objectives. Here are four key categories that are often considered:

- **Innovation**: This involves identifying and capitalizing on significant trends or shifts within your industry. By staying informed about emerging technologies or new product innovations, you can position your product to stay ahead of the curve and seize fresh opportunities.

- **Competition**: In this context, you must understand and respond to features that your competitors possess, that you do not. Identifying and addressing these gaps within your product roadmap can bolster your chances of winning deals and capturing a larger market share.

- **Customers**: This category underscores the importance of pinpointing the needs or pain points of your customers that are currently unmet by your product or roadmap. Actively soliciting customer feedback and conducting user research can unveil new avenues for product development that cater to these needs, enhancing customer value.

- **Technical debt**: Lastly, the category of technical debt focuses on identifying and addressing any quality issues or accumulated technical debt that may be impeding your product development efforts. By resolving these issues and improving the overall quality of your product, you enhance customer satisfaction and diminish the risk of future technical challenges.

In essence, managing technical debt isn't just a standalone task. It should be an integral part of your product roadmap. By categorizing technical debt as a key component of your roadmap, you ensure that it receives the attention it deserves. This systematic attention aids in preventing the debt from becoming unmanageable and increases the overall product quality.

Continuous learning and improvement

The technology landscape is always evolving, and so are best practices for software development. As a result, teams must be committed to continuous learning and improvement to manage technical debt effectively.

Continuous learning involves staying updated with the latest trends and advancements in your technology stack, understanding the evolving nuances of your domain, and incorporating new tools and methodologies into your processes. By keeping abreast of such changes, teams can make more informed decisions about the code they write and the debt they incur.

In an AppExchange development context, it is immensely beneficial to have at least one senior technical individual on your team, preferably a Salesforce **Certified Technical Architect (CTA)**[5]. The CTA can play a crucial role in overseeing the product architecture and making critical decisions that minimize the risk of incurring technical debt. Their vast knowledge and experience can guide the team toward best practices, avoiding pitfalls, and navigating complex architectural challenges.

Furthermore, all developers on your team should aim to achieve the Certified Platform Developer II[6] certification. This certification not only validates the developers' skills and knowledge of the advanced programmatic capabilities of the Salesforce platform but also signals their commitment to mastering the intricacies of Salesforce development.

The entire development team working on Salesforce technologies should regularly follow Salesforce updates and new feature releases. The importance of nurturing a culture of growth within your team cannot be overstated. By encouraging your team members to strive for these certifications and continually improve their skills, you set the stage for high standards in code quality, efficient development practices, and effective technical debt management. The cultivation of such a culture not only promotes individual growth but also results in a stronger, more capable team that can handle the challenges of technical debt adeptly.

Reducing technical debt by refining your AppExchange solution.

Think of technical debt like that credit card bill you've been avoiding. It starts manageable, but suddenly, you're in over your head, and the interest is snowballing. It's an intimidating sight, but don't hit the panic button just yet

There's always that nuclear option – filing for bankruptcy. And in AppExchange terms, that's a complete overhaul of your solution. It's like finally admitting that you shouldn't have bought that jet ski and starting fresh. But remember, just like in real life, this is a drastic measure. It comes with a steep price, and no, I'm not talking about legal fees or a dodgy credit score.

5   https://trailhead.salesforce.com/en/credentials/
    technicalarchitect
6   https://trailhead.salesforce.com/en/credentials/
    platformdeveloperii

Almost two decades ago, software engineer Joel Spolsky criticized Netscape for deciding to rewrite their code base in his influential essay, *Things You Should Never Do*.[7] According to Spolsky, rebuilding a system from scratch underestimates the complexity and the subtleties of the existing system. He argued that the decision was a strategic mistake, leading to a 3-year gap between major releases and a significant loss in market share.

The temptation to start over is a common pitfall for software developers. The notion that the current code is a mess and would be better off being replaced entirely is often misguided. Spolsky emphasizes a fundamental law of programming: "*It's harder to read code than to write it.*" This belief leads developers to want to craft their own solutions rather than understand and improve upon existing ones.

But as Spolsky pointed out, the old code base is a treasure trove of knowledge, fixes, and real-world testing. It embodies the history of the product, the problems it has encountered, and how it has evolved to address those issues. By discarding the old code, you're not only throwing away years of work but also the valuable lessons embedded within it.

Starting over also creates a time and innovation gap, allowing competitors to surge ahead. It also results in the risky situation of maintaining an old code base while developing a new one, hampering your ability to respond to market changes quickly.

For ISV partners, the implications are even more serious. A complete rebuild means publishing the solution as a new managed package, which, in turn, means migrating existing customers to this new package. The Salesforce platform doesn't facilitate easy migrations of this nature. The process involves installing the new package and migrating all customer data related to your package. Given the local customizations that customers may have implemented, this task is fraught with difficulties.

Moreover, your product doesn't exist in a vacuum. As we'll discuss in the next chapter, there is a continuous need for innovation. Choosing to support existing customers on the current version of your package, while developing the new one, means effectively splitting your attention and resources. In this scenario, it's all too easy to neglect necessary updates and improvements to your existing product, affecting your customer churn rate negatively.

Does this mean it's always a poor decision to start a new package from scratch? Not necessarily. Take Salesforce, for example. They chose to sunset their original managed package, B2B Commerce for Visualforce, in favor of creating an entirely new product: B2B Commerce on Lightning Experience.

Before embarking on a drastic measure such as rebuilding your entire solution, consider seeking a third-party expert's opinion. A comprehensive audit of your current package could reveal alternative, less disruptive solutions to your technical debt problem. We'll discuss more about the assistance of **Product Development Outsourcers** (**PDO**) partners, who can help tackle such challenges, in the upcoming chapter. This way, you can make an informed decision that best suits your product's needs, and more importantly, the needs of your customers.

---

7   https://www.joelonsoftware.com/2000/04/06/things-you-should-never-do-part-i/

Summary

In this chapter, we've ventured into the bustling cityscape of technical debt, becoming for a moment financial analysts of the tech world. In this new role, we've grappled with the concept of technical debt, likened to a looming credit card balance that accrues when code is implemented hastily without proper planning or quality assurance. We've seen how this silent and invisible threat, when left unchecked, could escalate quickly and have significant impacts, such as causing hurdles during security re-reviews, much like missed credit card payments would negatively impact your financial credit score.

Equipped with the knowledge of early warning signs, akin to receiving overdraft notices in financial matters, we've learned to detect and address the creeping menace of technical debt. Furthermore, we've explored practical tools and techniques to manage this debt, similar to the relief that comes with consolidating financial debt into a single loan with a lower interest rate. There were even times when the weight of the technical debt was so overwhelming that drastic measures, comparable to declaring bankruptcy, had to be considered, necessitating a complete overhaul of our AppExchange solution for a fresh start.

But the expedition doesn't end here, fellow trailblazers. As we continue our journey, we will step onto the path to success in our next chapter. There, we will delve into the world of continuous innovation, and leverage external expertise to bolster the success of our AppExchange solution. We will discover the prospects and challenges of incorporating artificial intelligence into our application, and discuss success metrics. We've navigated the difficult terrain of technical debt, but now, it's time to use that experience to plot a course toward success. Buckle up and stay tuned for our next exciting expedition!

Further reading

If you're battling with technical debt, *Clean Code: A Handbook of Agile Software Craftsmanship* by Robert C. Martin is a must-read. Martin provides practical strategies to transform messy code into clean, efficient, and maintainable software, effectively reducing technical debt and enhancing system performance.

Navigating the Path to Success

Dear trailblazers, we've journeyed far together, exploring the vast and intricate landscape of the Salesforce AppExchange ecosystem. As we approach the end of this enlightening expedition, this chapter seeks to arm you with the final set of tools and insights necessary for achieving unmatched success in the AppExchange domain. Here's a preview of the critical topics we're about to delve into and their significance for you:

- **The importance of innovation**: Continual evolution is the heartbeat of success in the AppExchange marketplace. We'll dive into why innovation is more than just a buzzword and how it can be your competitive edge.

- **Collaboration with Salesforce**: Salesforce is more than just a platform; it's a partner. Understand the roles and relationships within Salesforce that can amplify your success trajectory.

- **Leveraging external expertise**: The journey gets smoother when you have the right guides by your side. Discover the impact of **System Integrators**, **Product Development Outsourcers**, and **fractional Chief Technology Officers** on your AppExchange voyage.

- **Opportunities and challenges of AI**: In the modern digital era, AI presents both unmatched opportunities and intricate challenges for AppExchange developers. We'll break down its potential and pitfalls to ensure you're well-equipped.

- **Success metrics**: Measurement is the compass that ensures you're on the right path. Grasp the essential KPIs that will validate your strategies and highlight areas of growth in your AppExchange endeavors.

This chapter is not just a summation, but a culmination of all the knowledge and strategies you need not just to navigate but to master the AppExchange terrain. Let's ensure that all the miles we've traveled together culminate in a successful destination.

Innovate or stagnate

Picture this: a hamster named Harry. He's a tiny, furry, and highly ambitious rodent, with a penchant for running fast, wearing a tiny sweatband, and tiny sneakers. Now, imagine Harry on his treadmill, running with all his might, trying to keep pace. That treadmill is the AppExchange world, where innovation and change never cease.

In this competitive landscape, the mantra 'Innovate *or* Stagnate' has never been more relevant. When potential customers are faced with the 'build vs. buy' decision, they are not merely looking to purchase a product as it currently stands. They expect it to evolve, innovate, and align with Salesforce's own innovations.

The cost analysis of building an in-house solution goes beyond the initial development. It includes ongoing maintenance and the addition of new features. If your product doesn't keep pace with innovation, customers may choose to build their own solutions, leading to a potentially high churn rate for your product.

In the previous chapter, we discussed securing resources to reduce technical debt as part of your backlog. However, it's equally important to understand that a lack of resources for innovation can be as damaging as an unattended technical debt. One of the most common reasons why innovative companies fail is due to a prolonged time to innovate. As your product scales, it's very possible that your product teams are entirely consumed with maintenance activities. These can include fixing bugs, implementing capabilities for different parts of the business, addressing technical debt, and more.

While these tasks are necessary and contribute to the overall health of the product, they should not overshadow the need for innovation. If your teams are overwhelmed with 'keeping the lights on' activities, it can stifle creativity and innovation.

Failing to innovate can have dire consequences. Customers may become dissatisfied if they perceive that the product is falling behind the times, leading to increased churn rates. Even worse, a lack of innovation can make your product seem irrelevant in a crowded and competitive marketplace.

It's crucial to maintain a balanced approach. Ensure your teams have the room to pursue more challenging and impactful problems. This way, your product can continue to grow and thrive in the AppExchange marketplace.

Collaboration with Salesforce

Do you know what the best part of being a Salesforce partner is? You're not alone anymore! In the vast and dynamic world of the Salesforce ecosystem, there's an entire network of support awaiting you. As an AppExchange ISV partner, you're part of a thriving community, and a range of Salesforce employees are eager to contribute to your success.

Climbing the ladder of success: grow your business with the AppExchange Partner Program

Imagine yourself on a thrilling expedition, ascending the four key success pillars of the AppExchange Partner Program: *Customer Success*, *Innovation*, *Growth*, and *Impact*. As you conquer each pillar, you move up through the partner tiers, unlocking additional benefits and support from Salesforce. Let's take a closer look at each pillar and how they serve as the stepping stones to achieving AppExchange greatness.:

- **Customer Success**: In the world of AppExchange, customer success is your true north. This pillar emphasizes providing top-notch customer experiences and ensuring your app caters to your users' needs. Key factors to reaching the peak of customer success include delivering exceptional support, maintaining sky-high customer satisfaction ratings, and helping your customers extract value from your application.

- **Innovation**: Don't let your app become a relic! Innovation is crucial in the fast-paced world of technology. As an AppExchange partner, you must stay ahead of the curve, leveraging Salesforce's latest features and capabilities to create groundbreaking solutions. This pillar focuses on developing one-of-a-kind, cutting-edge applications that solve customer challenges and help your offering stand out in the marketplace.

- **Growth**: The *Growth* pillar urges you to expand your business within the Salesforce ecosystem. This includes increasing your customer base, generating more revenue, and expanding your app's reach. By demonstrating consistent growth and a solid sales strategy, you show your commitment to achieving long-term success as an AppExchange partner.

- **Impact**: The *Impact* pillar underscores your overall contribution to the Salesforce ecosystem. Factors such as community engagement, thought leadership, and collaboration with other partners play an essential role here. By making a positive impact on the ecosystem, you help fortify the Salesforce community and display your dedication to the platform's success.

Additionally, given Salesforce's leadership in the *Pledge 1%*[1] program, partners who hop on board with this program earn some extra brownie points.

Partner Trailblazer Score

Partner Trailblazer Score is like your personal AppExchange report card, courtesy of Salesforce. It evaluates your performance across the four essential pillars of *Customer Success*, *Innovation*, *Growth*, and *Impact*. Consider it as a comprehensive tool that offers a detailed insight into your performance, guiding you to the appropriate tier on the AppExchange team. But here's the catch: it's visible only to admins or those with Manage Partnership permissions. The specific guidelines for calculating the score can be found in the Partner portal, as they are outlined in the *Salesforce AppExchange Partner Program Policy*. This policy is updated annually, so the details are not going to be included in the book. To ensure that you have the latest version of the policy, please refer to the Partner portal[2]. Certainly, it's worth highlighting that having a solid understanding of the program's pillars can enable you to make well-informed decisions and steer your company in the right direction.

Below is a table showcasing the scores for different pillars that contribute to the Trailblazer Score. The Trailblazer Score is calculated based on targets spread across multiple categories, detailed in the Consulting Trailblazer Scorecard overview or the AppExchange ISV Partner Program guide. These targets, much like fashion trends, are updated regularly, and partners must meet or exceed them to maintain or improve their score. Take a look at the scores for each pillar in the table below:

Pillar	Element	Total Points
Customer Success	Attrition Rate	200
	Average App Rating	75
Innovation	Technology Adoption	200
	Trailhead Badges	75
Growth	ACV Growth	200
	Total Revenue	75
Lead	Equality	125
	Sustainable Development	50
	Pledge 1%: Bonus points	25

---

1   https://www.salesforce.org/about/pledge/
2   https://partners.salesforce.com/s/education/appinnovators/
    AppExchange_Partner_Program

Please keep in mind that the table's data is accurate as of this writing, for the financial year 2024. The table gives a snapshot of the scores across different pillars, highlighting how our partners are performing in areas that determine their Trailblazer Score.

Partner tiers

Depending on your performance across the success pillars, you'll be assigned one of four partner tiers: Base, Ridge, Crest, or Summit. Each tier comes with specific perks and support from Salesforce.

- **Base tier**: The Base tier is the launchpad for new AppExchange partners, offering access to essential resources, such as the Partner Community, and foundational support for marketing and technical assistance.

- **Ridge tier**: Partners who demonstrate improved performance across the success pillars can climb to the Ridge tier, which offers extra benefits like enhanced marketing support, increased access to Salesforce events, and higher visibility within the AppExchange marketplace.

- **Crest tier**: The Crest tier is a coveted spot for partners excelling in Customer Success, Innovation, Growth, and Impact. These partners receive prioritized support, dedicated account management, and access to exclusive Salesforce resources.

- **Summit tier**: The Summit tier is the pinnacle of recognition for AppExchange partners. These partners have showcased outstanding performance across all success pillars and are considered leaders in the Salesforce ecosystem. Summit partners receive the highest level of support, including strategic planning, executive sponsorship, and exclusive co-marketing and collaboration opportunities with Salesforce.

The table below outlines the partner tiers available based on your performance across the success pillars and the required Trailblazer Score for each tier. These tiers provide specific perks and support from Salesforce to help partners thrive within the AppExchange ecosystem.

Program Benefit Tier	Trailblazer Score Required
Summit	700+
Crest	400 - 699
Ridge	250 - 399
Base	<250

Embark on the thrilling journey of climbing the partner tiers by focusing on the success pillars and continuously improving your Partner Trailblazer Score. As you scale new heights, you can drive your AppExchange business forward and maximize your potential within the Salesforce ecosystem. Happy climbing!

Salesforce team: your allies in success

Let's explore the key roles you will interact with, each designed to assist you in different stages of your partnership, ensuring that you have all the necessary guidance and resources.

Business Development Representative (BDR)

Your initial contact and expert in the AppExchange partner process, the BDR will guide you through the onboarding process, helping you understand the partnership objectives and how your app fits within the ecosystem.

You probably already met your BDR, after you submitted your application, the BDR scheduled a call to discuss the next stages of your partnership. For any pre-submission queries or onboarding assistance, you can reach out to them in the Partner Community's Partner Onboarding Group.

Technical Advisor (TA)

Experts of the Salesforce platform, serving as integral members of the global team responsible for shaping strategy, design, and architecture across the expansive Salesforce technology partner network. TAs play a pivotal role in driving revenue growth within the ISV partner ecosystem, all while ensuring the crucial elements of technical alignment, seamless integration, and harmonious synergy between ISV solutions and the ever-evolving Salesforce platform. Central to their approach is a proactive and collaborative mindset, underpinned by a rock-solid technological foundation and fueled by an unquenchable thirst for continuous learning and innovation. Partnering with a TA opens up a world of opportunities for ISVs. It helps in achieving strategic goals, perfect design, and architectural excellence, which are crucial for success in the ever-changing Salesforce ecosystem.

Partner Account Manager (PAM)

They are your strategic ally as your partnership grows. The PAM works with you to create joint **go-to-market** plans and offers advice on how to expand within the Salesforce ecosystem. As your customer base grows, the PAM provides tailored support, helping you align your product and market strategies with Salesforce's opportunities and customer needs.

Platform Expert Consultations

Navigating the intricacies of Salesforce's extensive platform can be a complex task. Thankfully, as a partner, you have access to personalized guidance through 1:1 consultations with a Salesforce Platform Expert. This specialized service can be your invaluable ally as you work to enhance and innovate your AppExchange product.

Here's what the Platform Expert Consultations include:

- **Tailored technical guidance**: Schedule one-on-one technical consultations with Salesforce experts to receive scalability guidance. These consultations will help you maximize your use of Salesforce technology and potentially improve your Trailblazer Score.

- **Strategic ISV technology guidance**: Gain insights on key ISV technologies like LWC, In-App Guidance, CRM Analytics, 2GP, Platform Cache, and Apex. These strategic insights will guide you through the ever-evolving Salesforce ecosystem.

- **Support with specific tools**: Obtain assistance with running or utilizing the ISV DX Plug-in and get answers to your tech adoption questionnaire. This support ensures that you're fully leveraging the tools provided by Salesforce.

- **Education on ISV technologies**: Receive education on how to use essential ISV technologies such as Trialforce, Push Upgrades, App Analytics, and the ISV Debugger.

- **Collaborative experience**: Enjoy a personalized and interactive experience that encourages discussion and helps get your business-critical questions answered quickly.

To request a consultation, all you need to do is submit a case in the Partner Community. The Platform Expert Consultations are designed to inspire you on your app innovation journey and provide insight into the nuances of key platform features and architectural best practices.

Technology Consultations

The variety of tools, technologies, and best practices can be overwhelming, but fortunately, Salesforce's Technology Consultations are here to assist you. With the guidance of experienced Technical Advisors, you can confidently navigate your development path, ensuring your AppExchange product is aligned with Salesforce's best practices.

What can you expect from Technology Consultations?

- **Tailored technical guidance**: Receive personalized feedback and guidance from Salesforce's ISV Technology Advisors. Their expertise spans across technology, tools, and development best practices, providing you with the insight you need to succeed.

- **Application functionality and architecture feedback**: Engage in meaningful discussions to receive feedback on your application's functionality and architecture. Understanding how your application aligns with Salesforce's architecture principles can be pivotal in your development process.

- **Focused topic areas**: The consultations cover a wide array of topic areas, including:

  - Application architecture
  - Salesforce development

- Security review guidance

- OEM vs. ISVforce

- ISV tools and automation

- New Salesforce technologies

- Industry clouds

Technology Consultations are more than mere discussions; they are strategic collaborations that guide your development journey on the Salesforce platform. Whether you're dealing with application architecture or exploring new Salesforce technologies, these consultations are tailored to provide the precise guidance you need.

Product Roadmap Consultations

Planning your product's technical future can be a challenging endeavor. This is where Product Roadmap Consultations come into play. These strategic consultations offer valuable insights and guidance tailored to your product's vision, aligning your development with Salesforce's innovation.

Product Roadmap Consultations are available to partners at the Crest and Summit tiers. To engage in these valuable consultations, simply contact your Partner Account Manager (PAM). They will facilitate the 2-hour technical consultation with a Salesforce ISV Technology Advisor.

The consultations cover a wide array of topic areas, including:

- **Technical success plan**: A custom-tailored plan to guide your App's current and future technical direction.

- **Product alignment**: Ensure your App's alignment with Salesforce's product roadmap, staying ahead of technological trends.

- **Innovation score enhancement**: Strategic recommendations to boost your innovation score, reflecting your commitment to continuous improvement.

Product roadmap consultations serve as strategic checkpoints in your App's development journey. They offer a rare opportunity to align your product strategy with Salesforce's roadmap, ensuring that your app remains innovative and competitive.

Leveraging events for maximum impact

Ever heard the one about the Salesforce developer who walked into a bar? No? Me neither. But if they did, they'd probably run into an AppExchange guru sipping a martini and sharing platform secrets. The moral of the story: Sometimes, the answers we seek are just a barstool—or a networking event—away. The vibrant ecosystem of AppExchange is not just about code and clicks; it's a bustling bazaar of brainpower.

Salesforce hosts various events such as *Dreamforce*, the *World Tour*, Specialized Events, Basecamps, Community Events, and Salesforce User Groups. These events attract a diverse range of attendees from across the globe and present a unique opportunity for AppExchange partners to promote their products and build networks.

To fully leverage these events, partners need to create a solid pre- and post-event strategy. The strategy should include clear goal setting, content review, booth planning, and a robust follow-up plan.

Before the event, it's crucial to define your goals, which could range from brand awareness and lead generation to relationship building and deal acceleration. Review your marketing materials and ensure your AppExchange listing is up to date. Plan your booth carefully, choosing staff who can effectively demo your product and engage with attendees.

During the event, make your booth stand out with strong visuals and clear messaging. Capture qualified leads and provide a secondary **call-to-action** for interested prospects. Use social media to promote your presence and activities at the event.

After the event, promptly follow up with leads and share your session deck in the content section of your AppExchange listing as a post-event touchpoint. Review the event's success based on your initial goals and learnings to inform your strategy for future events.

Salesforce events also provide opportunities to connect with prospects, customers, and Salesforce employees. It's beneficial to schedule meetings, promote your session or booth, and follow up post-event with personalized messages.

Demo jams: your spotlight to stardom!

Ever dreamed of promoting your app to an expansive audience by showcasing how extraordinary your product is? Well, demo jams are your golden ticket! They are not only one of the most exhilarating parts of every *Dreamforce*, *TrailblazerDX*, and community events but also a thrilling game-show-style stage to prove your app's excellence.

Imagine a stage where 4-6 app partners are lined up, each tasked with giving the most riveting, no-fluff, 3-minute live demo of their app. The pressure is on, the crowd is electrified, and at the end of it all, attendees cast live votes for their favorite demo, and the winner walks away with an exciting prize.

Demo jams are a live spectacle that you can find at events, in webinars (register through `appdemojam. com`), and online via YouTube. Live events are typically held in the bustling atmosphere of the Expo Hall theater during the event.

Demo jams present an incredible opportunity to give a demo to a live audience ranging from 80 to 150 people. According to Salesforce, the demo jam videos can garner up to 11,000[3] views per video, offering significant brand exposure. AppExchange promotes them heavily, and cross-promotion from each partner adds to the reach. It's also an excellent chance to showcase your best demo delivery teammate and have a ton of fun!

The simplicity of demo jams lies in their rules. Your live demo must be strictly three minutes or less. No slides, PowerPoint presentations, or videos are allowed; it must be a live demonstration. And there will only be one winner per demo jam.

Demo jams aren't just a promotional platform; they're a celebration of innovation, creativity, and the compelling power of live demonstrations. Whether you're an AppExchange veteran or a newcomer, participating in a demo jam could lead to your moment in the spotlight. It's about community, learning, and, above all else, having an incredible amount of fun!

---

3   `https://appexchange.salesforce.com/`
    `appxContentListingDetail?listingId=a0N3A00000EJeavUAD`

AppExchange Marketing Program (AMP)

Ever written a brilliant LinkedIn post and thought, 'Gosh, I wish I could put a spotlight on this right now!'? Well, for apps on the Salesforce AppExchange, there's something that comes pretty darn close. Ladies and gentlemen, I present to you: the **AppExchange Marketing Program (AMP)**.

What makes AMP unique is its powerful combination of tools, resources, and insights, specifically designed to maximize the presence of ISV partners on the Salesforce AppExchange. However, it's essential to understand that AMP is a paid program. Please be aware that it can be costly and might not always give a good **return on investment** to smaller ISVs.

AMP goes beyond being just a marketing initiative; it is a strategic investment. Salesforce acknowledges the challenges that ISVs may face in a competitive market and, therefore, offers AMP as a premium suite to provide partners with a competitive edge. It is custom-made to elevate your app, whether you are launching it for the first time or enhancing its existing journey.

Main categories of AMP

The AMP is designed to empower partners with diverse avenues to showcase, promote, and amplify their applications within the Salesforce ecosystem. Here are the main categories that the program offers:

- **Showcase Your Product**: This category enables partners to highlight their applications' unique features, benefits, and value proposition. By creating compelling narratives and using rich visual content, you can captivate potential users and ensure that your product's essence shines through.

- **Promote AppExchange Listing**: Your listing on AppExchange is your primary touchpoint with Salesforce customers. This category offers tools and insights to amplify your AppExchange presence. From optimizing listing content to leveraging promotional slots, this category ensures your app grabs the spotlight.

- **Increase Solution Awareness**: Amplifying your brand's awareness goes beyond AppExchange. This category provides avenues like webinars, joint promotional campaigns, and events, ensuring your solution resonates with a wider audience, both within and outside the Salesforce ecosystem.

- **Educate Salesforce Employees**: A unique component of AMP, this category focuses on aligning Salesforce's internal teams with your product's vision. By educating Salesforce employees about your application, they become ambassadors for your solution, ensuring coherent communication and shared objectives when engaging with potential clients.

Starting with the 60-second solution video is often a smart move. This concise visual can be a powerful introduction to your offering, finding its place on your AppExchange listing, website, or even YouTube channel.

It's essential to manage expectations. While this exposure can significantly boost brand awareness, only a tiny segment (about 5%) of viewers might be in the market for an immediate purchase. The majority are still exploring, evaluating, and considering options.

If you're targeting immediate conversions within a short timeframe, focusing primarily on homepage promotions on AppExchange might not yield the desired results. However, if your sights are set on nurturing leads for conversions in the upcoming quarters, then such promotions can be precious.

AppExchange chat

One particularly interesting feature of the AMP is the AppExchange Chat. This can be enabled directly on your AppExchange listing, providing a new avenue for real-time engagement. In our increasingly digital-centric business landscape, establishing immediate connections with prospects has become more vital than ever. With AppExchange Chat, companies can instantly engage with potential customers the moment they show interest, whether it's to address immediate inquiries or to set up a meeting. This tool is not just about live interactions; if a representative isn't available, the system switches to an automated chat to ensure no prospect goes unattended. Historical data underscores its effectiveness: according to Salesforce, 6% of AppExchange Chat interactions lead to combined human and bot dialogues, 11% transform into new leads, and 5% result in scheduled meetings. For those businesses securing a minimum of 500 listing visits per month, integrating AppExchange Chat can be a strategic move to optimize lead conversion and elevate ROI.

Maximize your AMP return on investment

It might seem curious that we didn't dive into the AMP in our chapter dedicated to AppExchange Listing. The reason is simple yet strategic. AMP is a robust tool, but its efficacy is maximized when deployed at the right moment in your product's journey. Before even contemplating the benefits of AMP, ISVs need to ensure the foundational elements are firmly in place.

AMP can supercharge your efforts, but only when applied to the right problem. Consider the following scenarios to understand where your current challenges lie:

- Can't create demand? If potential customers aren't aware of or interested in your product, you face a marketing problem. The issue could lie in outreach, messaging, or visibility.

- Can't capture demand? If there's interest, but it's directed elsewhere or diffused, you're grappling with a positioning problem. Your product might not be perceived as the ideal solution despite existing demand.

- Can't convert demand? When there's clear interest and your product is in the consideration set, but conversions aren't happening, you have a product problem. Potential mismatches between product features, user expectations, or value delivery might be the culprits.

Once you've nailed down the basics and have a clear understanding of your challenge, AMP can be a game-changer. But remember, it isn't about using AMP to fill gaps or plaster over cracks. It's about elevating an already robust strategy and product offering to new heights. Only with this foundational clarity can you extract the best ROI from your AMP investment.

Leveraging external expertise

Did you hear the one about the lone genius in his garage who took the AppExchange by storm? Me neither. And that's because, while we often glorify the individual achiever, the real heroes of AppExchange are the orchestrators, the maestros who bring together a symphony of external talents.

Navigating the ever-shifting sands of AppExchange isn't a solitary walk in the park. It's more like a group hike up Mount Everest but with fewer frostbites and more API calls. To truly make your mark as an ISV partner, you can't just rely on what's inside the four walls of your organization.

Leveraging external expertise is at the core of AppExchange's life. It provides specialized skills that you might not have even known existed (did someone say "cloud-based juggling integration expert?"), innovative strategies that are outside your current playbook, and diverse perspectives that challenge the status quo. All these ingredients can significantly enhance your delectable journey on AppExchange.

System integrators

System Integrators (**SIs**) in the Salesforce ecosystem are partners who provide implementation services to Salesforce customers, ensuring seamless integration and alignment with other business systems. Forming strategic alliances with SIs can be a potent strategy that can extend the reach of your product. By advising clients to opt for existing AppExchange products, SIs can enhance the value of their services by integrating them with complementary solutions. This approach not only boosts the functionality of the product but also opens up new markets and potential clientele for both SIs and ISVs.

Networking is a crucial aspect of the complex field of technology. Through collaborations with SIs, you can identify potential customers, broker collaborative agreements, and even design joint go-to-market strategies. SIs often possess the connections and insights that can assist ISVs in discovering the right channels and partners for growth.

The technology sector is vast and diverse, with each segment presenting its unique set of opportunities and challenges. By collaborating with SIs, you can break into new market segments that might have been unreachable previously. SIs often hold deep industry-specific expertise, so they can offer you a strategic roadmap to penetrate and succeed in these areas.

Partnerships should be centered on mutual benefits. Collaborating with SIs allows you to create synergies that drive shared success. Whether it's through resource sharing, joint marketing initiatives, or co-developing solutions, these synergies can lead to increased efficiency, innovation, and market penetration.

From the SI perspective, forming strategic alliances with ISVs can be mutually beneficial, but it's your job to emphasize the added value for SIs in such partnerships. Keep in mind, some SIs may not want a cut of the revenue. They prefer staying neutral and will only make recommendations based on what's best for their customers. So, it's important to stay on their radar.

Please note that SIs are not typically Product Development Outsourcers (PDOs) specializing in building AppExchange products. Instead, their expertise lies in seamlessly integrating and combining different subsystems to create a unified solution. By partnering with ISVs and recommending their existing solutions, SIs can enhance the value of their services by providing clients with comprehensive, ready-made applications. This not only saves time and resources for the SI but also expands their market reach and allows them to unlock new opportunities by integrating these solutions with their complementary services. Ultimately, strategic alliances with ISVs can enable SIs to deliver a more competitive advantage and offer their clients a complete and efficient solution.

Product Development Outsourcers (PDO)

If you already know how to partner with System Integrators to grow your business, you might wonder if they could lend a hand in building your AppExchange product. However, the reality is that their expertise lies in implementing solutions for end customers, not in creating commercial apps for AppExchange. So, where can you turn for specialized support and guidance in your product development journey? Salesforce has your back with the **Product Development Outsourcers** (**PDO**) program.

If you've read this book already, you are in a much better place than most ISVs starting their journey. However, it's essential to note that while the lecture provides valuable insights, it doesn't cover all technical details or scenarios. This is where partnering with a PDO can be the best option to get the right answers and overcome any challenges quickly.

Who are the PDOs?

A PDO represents a diverse group of consulting partners who focus on building commercial apps for the AppExchange. Beyond development, they offer valuable services like ideation, go-to-market consulting, prototyping, testing, support, and roadmap planning. PDOs possess the expertise to architect, design, and refine a commercial app, tackle specific areas of ISV partner builds, or augment the partner's in-house development team.

While SIs are essential for implementing solutions tailored to specific business needs for Salesforce customers, PDOs are the go-to partners for AppExchange product development. The Key differentiators are:

- **Understanding of business models**: SIs excel in Salesforce pricing for end customers, while PDOs have in-depth knowledge of the business models available for ISV partners. They focus on creating engaging solutions that end users willingly pay for—products that drive success in the marketplace.

- **Visibility of Org**: SIs build solutions within specific Orgs, but PDOs need to create solutions that can seamlessly integrate into any Org. This flexibility is vital for products distributed on the AppExchange.

- **Project duration**: SIs typically follow project-based development, while PDOs focus on building a product that can evolve and grow throughout its lifetime. This ensures ongoing improvements and adaptability.

- **Expertise in app packaging**: PDOs possess specific expertise in app packaging for the AppExchange, utilizing technologies such as 2GP, **LMA**, **COA**, **FMA**, among others. Understanding what can and cannot be packaged, conducting security reviews, and having package-building proficiency are critical aspects where many SIs often fail. This knowledge plays a vital role in creating a successful product for AppExchange.

Salesforce places significant importance on evaluating PDOs to ensure they possess the necessary skills and expertise to support ISV partners effectively. PDOs report their projects to Salesforce, providing valuable insights into their capabilities and achievements. This section sheds light on how Salesforce evaluates PDOs and the meaning behind the seven specializations that define their expertise.

Seven specializations

Salesforce conducts a thorough evaluation of PDOs, assessing their expertise in different aspects of product development and support through a process of project reporting. In this context, a "Project" denotes the engagement between an ISV partner and a PDO. To gain insights into PDOs' capabilities, these projects are carefully tagged with seven PDO specializations, which encompass various aspects of product development and support that PDOs bring to the table. Let's explore each specialization in detail:

- **Ideation/business model/value prop**: PDOs assist ISVs in defining the right product to build by conducting product discovery, ideation workshops, and designing the business model. They provide advice on how to partner with Salesforce and what partnership model to choose. They also assess the **total addressable market** (**TAM**) and ensure a solid product-market fit.

- **Architecture and UX design**: PDOs work with ISVs to define the technical and user experience design to support their product's epics and user stories. They provide technical review assistance, create mockups, map customer journeys, and develop technical design and architecture documents.

- **Development/QA/release management/security review**: PDOs offer ongoing agile development, test automation, and release automation for the ISV product. They assist with setting up ISV DevOps teams with Salesforce CI/CD best practices and help with security review testing and issue resolution.

- **AppExchange listing, trials, and demo**: PDOs support ISVs after development by assisting in creating their AppExchange listing via the Partner Community. They also help set up demo orgs that utilize trial technology, enabling ISVs to convert leads into closed deals effectively.

- **Product support**: Once the product is released, PDOs provide Tier 2/3 Technical support, ongoing maintenance, and assistance with installation and configuration in key accounts. They establish a product feedback loop to optimize the installation process.

- **Package review and optimization**: PDOs ensure the product is optimized for the long term and utilizes the latest Salesforce features effectively. PDOs offer expertise in packaging strategy and feature management. They address architecture and UX concerns, introduce new Salesforce release technology, and provide guidance on testing and release management.

- **Marketing support**: PDOs assist ISVs in obtaining the necessary data for successful Go-To-Market strategies. They help leverage ISV tools like the Partner Business Org (PBO) and AppExchange Analytics. Additionally, they provide technical marketing input to support customer-facing efforts.

Throughout the evaluation process, PDOs are assessed on three fundamental aspects: knowledge, experience, and quality. These critical components ensure that PDOs possess the expertise required to deliver exceptional results and effectively support their partners. Within each specialization, there are two levels, namely Level I and Level II. To be honored with the prestigious title of PDO Expert, a company must achieve four Level II specializations, showcasing an exceptional level of expertise across various domains.

Choosing the right PDO

If you're an ISV partner aiming to develop a successful AppExchange product, collaborating with one of the Expert PDOs can offer significant advantages.

To explore a list of Expert PDOs and find the perfect partner for your journey, you can visit the AppExchange Portal[4]. As of the book's writing in 2023, there are nine companies listed as Expert PDOs, each demonstrating a remarkable track record of success.

---

4   https://appexchange.salesforce.com/mktcollections/curated/ pdo

Disclaimer: Just a heads up, I've got a personal affiliation with Aquiva Labs[5], one of these elite nine, where I'm responsible for technology strategy and innovations. I totally get why you might think I'm trying to sell you something, but that's not my intention. I just want to provide some examples from my own experiences to make this section less vague, so, I'm sharing this info to be transparent and give you some context.

Leveraging PDO expertise across different company stages

PDOs offer valuable support and expertise to companies at various stages of their AppExchange product development journey. Whether you are a new startup, a mid-size ISV partner, or a mature ISV, partnering with PDOs can provide numerous advantages tailored to your specific needs.

- **For new Startups**: Building the MVP with ease

  For new startups, engaging with PDOs to build the Minimum Viable Product (MVP) version of your app is a game-changing decision. Without a technical founder with a strong Salesforce background, developing the first app can be an extremely challenging task. Recruiting Salesforce developers with AppExchange experience can also be difficult, as it requires a unique skill set beyond standard Salesforce development expertise. By partnering with PDOs, startups can rapidly bring their MVP to life within a short timeframe. This allows them to focus on refining the product and getting it to market faster, rather than spending several months building the development team from scratch.

  Example: It's hard to pick one, because in my experience, it's one of the most common reasons for partnering with PDOs. For instance, one of my European customers, a company with a product offering an editorial management system, joined forces with our team. Their goal? Offer their solution to Salesforce customers, so, to develop an AppExchange app seamlessly integrating their solution with Salesforce Knowledge articles. In the span of a single quarter, we successfully designed and implemented a robust Salesforce app tailored to their customer user interface needs. We also ensured secure integrations with their existing off-platform solution and guided them through the security review process.

- **For mid-size ISV partners**: Maximizing Salesforce platform capabilities

  Mid-size ISV partners, already invested in Salesforce licenses, often desire to leverage the platform's capabilities to the fullest but might be unsure about what they don't know. PDOs can help them explore potential areas for the development and adoption of new features. By collaborating with PDOs, these companies can unlock untapped opportunities, enhance their existing products, and expand their offerings to address a broader range of customer needs.

---

5 `http://aquivalabs.com/`

Example: Let me share with you another story where an existing ISV had a highly successful product comprising an off-platform engine and an AppExchange app tailored for order processing. Their unique selling point was their versatility — you could send your orders in various formats, including email or even scanned PDFs, and they would seamlessly extract vital data and populate your Salesforce objects.

However, when Salesforce made the game-changing announcement about introducing a new 'B2B Commerce on Lightning Experience' product, they faced a disruptive challenge. This ISV, recognizing the need to adapt and evolve, turned to us for guidance on crafting a strategic response to this disruption. After thorough deliberation, they decided to pivot and embrace this new opportunity. They partnered with us, and together, we embarked on the journey of building a brand-new AppExchange app tailored for the new Order Management. This decision to adapt to the evolving Salesforce ecosystem was a pivotal moment for them, and it opened up new opportunities for growth and innovation for their customer base.

- **For mature ISVs**: Overcoming stagnation and challenges

Mature ISVs might encounter challenges that require external expertise to resolve. PDOs can step in by auditing their current products, identifying pain points, assessing and validating product architecture, and providing meaningful recommendations to overcome hurdles. With fresh insights and solutions, these ISVs can break through stagnation and continue their journey of growth and innovation.

Example: One of largest **OEM (Original Equipment Manufacturer)** partners approached us with a significant challenge. Their onboarding process for new customers had become agonizingly slow, averaging a staggering six-plus months. While this extended onboarding period had been manageable when they primarily catered to enterprise-scale customers, it emerged as a formidable barrier as they sought to expand into the mid-size company segments.

Their core offering was a robust cloud HR system designed for multinational organizations, providing the tools needed to efficiently manage a global workforce and respond to changing priorities seamlessly. However, the complexity of their customers' needs was growing exponentially as they ventured into new territories.

The heart of the issue lay in the intricate web of global HR regulations and industry-specific customizations. Picture this: HR requirements for a company operating in Belgium, France, and Luxembourg within the manufacturing industry could be as distinct as a finely tailored suit. Meanwhile, a pharmaceutical company operating in Germany and Austria might require an entirely different configuration.

Now, multiply these variations by the numerous industries their customers spanned and the array of countries they operated in, each with its own unique set of rules and regulations. The result? A profoundly complex challenge that required a precise and adaptable solution.

To address this issue, we initiated a comprehensive audit of their existing onboarding approach. The audit culminated in a series of actionable recommendations categorized into 'low-hanging fruits,' 'quick wins,' and 'major projects.' You might spot this approach, the good ol' 2x2 matrix, a staple of business school wisdom — and yes, I had the pleasure of spending a year at Stanford Graduate School of Business, where they convinced me that squares could change the world. Who knew, right? But, hey, it turns out, with the right perspective, even the most stubborn corners can round up some innovative solutions!

As our next step, we collaborated closely to optimize their Trialforce strategy. Subsequently, we ventured into a partnership to develop a bespoke Salesforce CLI plugin tailored to their specific needs. This plugin empowered their non-technical consultants to automate the provisioning of data and metadata, perfectly customized to meet the unique requirements of each new customer.

The outcome was nothing short of transformative. By streamlining and automating their onboarding process, they achieved a significant reduction in onboarding time for their new customers. This efficiency gain not only saved time and resources but also positioned them for rapid growth in the mid-size market segment, reaffirming the importance of adapting to the evolving needs of their customer base.

- **For all company stages**: Accelerating development regardless of their stage, companies often face situations where they need to accelerate their development efforts. In such cases, partnering with PDOs allows them to access highly skilled development teams ready to initiate new streams of development immediately. The added expertise and capacity provided by PDOs enable companies to tackle new projects and capitalize on market opportunities swiftly.

Example: In the scorching August of 2023, Salesforce dropped a bombshell on a exclusive group of ISVs. They generously offered access to a closed pilot program focusing on Generative AI and an incredible opportunity to flaunt their solutions during the grandest of conferences, Dreamforce. Now, you might be thinking, 'What's the catch?' Well, here it is — the ISVs had a mere few weeks to whip up a proof-of-concept that integrated their existing products with Salesforce's shiny new GenAI Apex APIs.

Enter a partner from the travel industry, seeking our assistance. They were in a difficult situation due to a shortage of in-house developers. The fun part? When I asked one of my colleagues to prepare the draft of the contract specifying that we'd deliver this AI-powered solution, their response was priceless: 'Did you make a typo in the contract's delivery date?'

But guess what? Two weeks later, the impossible became possible. The recording of this AI-enabled demo took center stage in the AppExchange Landing Area of San Francisco.

In conclusion, **Product Development Outsourcers** (**PDOs**) prove to be indispensable partners for companies at different stages of their AppExchange product development journey. From building the MVP for startups, maximizing platform capabilities for mid-size ISVs, and overcoming challenges for mature ISVs, to accelerating development efforts for all stages, PDOs offer tailored solutions and support to propel companies toward success in the competitive Salesforce ecosystem.

Fractional Chief Technology Officer (fCTO)

Building a successful product on the AppExchange requires a harmonious blend of technology and business strategy. To achieve this, having someone dedicated to ensuring that the company's technology decisions align with its business goals is not just beneficial but vital. This is where a **Chief Technology Officer** (**CTO**) steps in as the driving force behind a company's technological journey. However, for startups and smaller companies, hiring a full-time, permanent CTO can pose challenges due to financial constraints or difficulties in finding the ideal candidate. I've encountered way too many early-stage startup CEOs who, in this situation, attempted to build their in-house development teams from scratch, create the software development processes, take on the role of a product owner and manage all the other responsibilities that come with being a CEO. It rarely ends well.

Other may think that changing your lead developer title to CTO will solve all these needs. I've got bad news for you. While your lead developer can be a coding wizard, the CTO's role goes beyond development. It's a business role, albeit at the crossroads where business and technology meet. Please, let your lead developer excel at what they do best - development.

As an alternative solution, you may want to explore the option of engaging a **fractional Chief Technology Officer** (**fCTO**), who can provide valuable expertise on a part-time consulting basis. For AppExchange companies, the most critical requirements from a fCTO are a strong AppExchange product development background, business-oriented mindset and exceptional people management skills. These experienced technology leaders can guide your early-stage company to align its tech strategy with business objectives. The fCTO can become a catalyst for success in the competitive world of AppExchange companies, ensuring that technology is a powerful enabler of business growth.

Don't get me wrong, a full-time CTO is vital for your long-term success. Many ISVs focus on innovation within their products and miss out on genuine innovation opportunities. But if you're tight on budget and can't afford a full-time CTO right now, a fractional CTO with a solid AppExchange background is definitely better than an empty spot on your executive team.

Artificial Intelligence (AI): opportunities and challenges

The book was penned in 2023, shortly after we really started to see a massive boom in the world of **generative AI**. It's fascinating to think that those who read these words in the future will gain insights into this period when the generative AI boom was in full swing. This revolutionary change has the potential to alter the course of history, much like the revolution that artificial light's sharp decline in cost sparked in the early 1800s. When the price of something foundational decreases significantly, the ripple effect can be felt everywhere. The economist William Nordhaus explored this concept when he noted that in the 1800s, it would have cost four hundred times what we pay now for the same amount of light. The subsequent drop in the price of light not only turned night into day but also allowed us to live and work in significant buildings that natural light couldn't penetrate. Similarly, the advent of AI and its integration into AppExchange products have the potential to create a seismic shift in how we develop and use applications. It's akin to the momentous occasion of the first iPhone premiere, which dramatically transformed the landscape of technology and everyday life. Before the iPhone, concepts like Uber, Deliveroo, or Instagram seemed unimaginable, yet they have become ubiquitous in our lives today.

Nowadays, ISV partners are actively exploring ways to leverage AI to enrich their products. AI presents significant opportunities for app development, enabling personalization, automation, and predictive analytics, thus creating more intelligent, user-friendly interfaces. However, the integration of AI into AppExchange products also presents unique challenges. For instance, selecting the best **large language models (LLMs)** for specific use cases can be complex. Additionally, the challenge of pricing arises when customers pay for a seat license, but ISVs pay for usage-based billing for AI-driven features. There's also the challenge of avoiding hallucinations to create reliable features.

Given the rapid evolution of the AI field, with new developments occurring literally every week, it's almost impossible to cover all these aspects in a single book. By the time the book is printed, the information could already be outdated. However, this doesn't mean that we should shy away from embracing AI. Instead, I encourage you to consider AI transformation as a strategic area for partnership with an expert Product Development Outsourcer, as described earlier in this chapter.

Top-tier PDOs keep themselves well-informed about the latest AI-related technologies within the Salesforce ecosystem and the various strategies to incorporate them into AppExchange products. They are often privileged to be invited by Salesforce to join closed pilot programs and offer insights into Salesforce's product roadmaps. Collaborating with a PDO can significantly enhance your journey. You gain access to AI capabilities with the guidance of experts who have conducted thorough research and development, whether it's evaluating different Language Model Models (LLMs) or navigating the common challenges of integrating AI into ISV products. This partnership may enable you to concentrate on your core strengths while tapping into external AI expertise.

Success metrics

As we've been navigating the labyrinth that is the *AppExchange Success Blueprint*, we've unearthed some golden nuggets of strategy for building a flourishing AppExchange business. But, here's the million-dollar question: How do you know if you're actually successful? It's not as simple as a thumbs up or a pat on the back, but let's dive into the world of **key performance indicators** (**KPIs**) that could serve as our trusty compass.

For many early-stage startups, maintaining KPIs may initially seem like a bureaucratic burden, especially when they are focusing on product development and establishing their business. However, overlooking the importance of KPIs can be a costly mistake in the long run. These metrics play a pivotal role in assessing the company's performance, identifying areas for improvement, and showcasing potential growth opportunities.

Investors, whether they are venture capitalists or angel investors, are inherently risk-averse. They want to ensure that they are making informed decisions when investing their capital in a startup. KPIs provide concrete data and evidence of the startup's progress and potential for success. When potential investors evaluate a startup, they will likely inquire about its performance over time, its growth trajectory, and how well it aligns with its stated business goals.

By having well-defined KPIs, startups can demonstrate their ability to monitor and manage their businesses effectively. It shows that they have a clear understanding of their market, customer acquisition, retention strategies, and operational efficiency. This level of insight instills confidence in investors, as they can gauge the startup's ability to achieve its objectives and generate a return on their investment.

Moreover, KPIs help startups stay focused on what truly matters. They serve as guideposts, directing efforts and resources toward the most critical aspects of the business. By regularly tracking and analyzing KPIs, startups can proactively address challenges and adapt their strategies to stay competitive in a dynamic market.

Furthermore, having KPIs in place fosters a culture of accountability and data-driven decision-making. Team members can align their efforts with the company's goals and measure their progress toward achieving them. This transparent and measurable approach enables better communication and collaboration among the team, driving overall performance.

Remember the words of Peter Drucker, "You can't manage what you can't measure." Now, let's delve deeper and explore some commonly used KPIs that shed light on your company's success and performance.

- **Monthly Recurring Revenue (MRR)/Annual Recurring Revenue (ARR)**: These metrics are crucial for any SaaS business, including AppExchange products. They provide insights into earnings trends and future revenue predictions. MRR can be further broken down into different components, such as new sales, expansion, and churned MRR, providing a detailed view of revenue changes.

- **Customer Acquisition Cost (CAC)**: CAC represents the cost of acquiring a new customer. It's calculated by dividing the total sales and marketing costs by the number of new customers. By tracking CAC, businesses can evaluate the efficiency of their marketing strategies and make necessary adjustments.

- **CAC payback period**: This metric measures the time it takes for the revenue from a customer to cover the cost of acquiring them. It's crucial for early-stage SaaS businesses to ensure profitability and sustainability.

- **Churn rate**: This measures the number of customers that stop using your product. Understanding churn rate helps identify issues with product-market fit, service quality, and more.

- **Burn Multiple**: This metric evaluates how much a startup is spending to generate each incremental dollar of ARR growth. A lower Burn Multiple indicates more efficient growth.

- **Gross margin**: Gross margin measures the difference between revenue and the **cost of goods sold (COGS)**, indicating the profitability of a company's products or services.

- **Compound Monthly Growth Rate (CMGR)**: CMGR measures growth in MRR, helping to understand the rate at which your business is growing.

- **Net Revenue Retention (NRR) / Gross Revenue Retention (GRR)**: These metrics measure the revenue retained from existing customers over a given period, taking into account churned revenue and revenue generated from upsells or upgrades.

- **Runway**: This measures how long a company can continue to operate without running out of cash at the current burn rate.

Measuring the success of your AppExchange product involves tracking various KPIs that align with your business model and goals. By focusing on these metrics, you can optimize resources, make data-driven decisions, identify areas for improvement, and ultimately achieve your objectives. Remember, the KPIs you choose should be reviewed and adjusted as your company grows and your objectives evolve.

Summary

In this final chapter of our journey, we embraced the essence of innovation, pinpointing its role as the linchpin of success in the dynamic AppExchange marketplace. We illuminated the significance of building strategic relationships with Salesforce, underscoring the platform as not just a tool, but a critical ally in your endeavors. Moreover, we delved into the power of external expertise, highlighting how System Integrators, Product Development Outsourcers, and Fractional Chief Technology Officers can be invaluable in streamlining your voyage in the AppExchange terrain.

The digital horizon of AI beckoned, presenting a duality of vast opportunities and inherent challenges. We explored this subject, equipping you with the understanding of the potential to integrate AI's capabilities into your AppExchange products, ensuring you remain at the forefront of technological advancements. Lastly, the compass of success metrics was detailed, emphasizing the KPIs that validate your strategies and pinpoint areas ripe for growth in your AppExchange endeavors.

Let's wrap it up

Before we bid farewell to our journey, let's take a moment to review the insights we've gathered along the way. Our adventure has been divided into four distinct parts, each contributing to our understanding of how to thrive in this dynamic landscape, ensuring that you're well -equipped at every step of your journey.

In the first part, we began by diving into the Salesforce ecosystem, understanding its vastness and the benefits of becoming an AppExchange partner. We discussed the importance of crafting customer-centric applications that truly address customer needs and provide value.

The second part saw us diving into the technical intricacies of Salesforce, uncovering ISV-specific features, and mastering the art of seamless integration with external systems while keeping security at the forefront of our considerations. It's possible that you found this part quite technical, especially if you're not a developer. However, this makes it all the more crucial to ensure that every member of your development team is well -versed in this material.

In the third part of our journey, we focused on delivering and managing our applications effectively. We explored release management principles, different software version types, and tools like push upgrades. Onboarding new customers was a crucial aspect, with strategies for engaging experiences, demos, and clear instructions. We also ventured into operational excellence as a means to drive customer satisfaction and revenue growth.

The last part saw us delve into the world of analytics and insights, harnessing the power of data to optimize AppExchange listings and user experiences. We discussed the concept of technical debt and the importance of being prepared for security review re-submissions. Our journey concluded with insights into innovation, collaboration, and success metrics.

As you embark on your own journey, remember that success in the Salesforce AppExchange ecosystem requires a multifaceted approach. Continuously review and apply the knowledge gained in these chapters as you build and scale your product. Embrace customer-centricity, technical proficiency, and data-driven decision-making. Maintain a keen eye on security and quality. Foster innovation and collaboration. These principles will guide you toward lasting success.

Review this book often when you need it, and ensure that you remember the main concepts from every chapter. The biggest risk is not knowing what you don't know. Now, after reading this book, you're at least aware of all the main areas you should become an expert in to build and scale your product successfully. Remember to revisit specific chapters when you encounter issues related to relevant subjects, as this resource will serve as your trusted guide throughout your journey in the Salesforce AppExchange ecosystem.

Let's take a moment to picture this: me, curled up with my laptop, crafting these words, perhaps sipping a (potentially overpriced) latte, imagining the day you—yes, you with the now-magnificent Salesforce prowess—would be reading them. And that moment is... now!

Congratulations! Give yourself a pat on the back—or a slice of cake, whichever feels more rewarding. You've just learned how to morph your ingenious ideas into not just Salesforce applications but profitable and scalable ones. A tad more impressive than assembling an IKEA chair, isn't it?

Now, onto the tiny confession: I had a little too much fun penning down this guide and laughing at my own Salesforce jokes (a niche sense of humor, I know). If you derive half as much joy reading this as I did writing it, we're onto a winner. But hey, the joy doesn't need to end here. Fancy a chat over some more tech jokes or perhaps a more sober discussion about the AppExchange universe? Drop me a line at appexchange@jakubstefaniak.com or ping me on LinkedIn.

Please remember, that's not the end. I mean, it's the end of the book, but it's just the beginning. Equipped with your newfound wisdom, I can't wait to see the AppExchange marvels you'll sculpt. Take the world by storm, one app at a time!

PS. Hey, by the way, if you enjoyed the book, would you mind leaving a review? Maybe on its Amazon page? I get that you're super busy, but it's my first book, and I have a feeling my mom will be refreshing that comments section pretty often. So, if you liked it, I'd love to hear your thoughts. And most of all, you can help save me from those "Why only x reviews, sweetie?" dinner table conversations. Cheers!

Index

Other Books You May Enjoy

If you enjoyed this book, you may be interested in these other books by Packt:

Salesforce End-to-End Implementation Handbook

Kristian Margaryan Jørgensen

ISBN: 978-1-80461-322-1

- Discover the critical activities in Salesforce implementation
- Address common issues faced in implementing Salesforce
- Explore appropriate delivery methodology
- Understand the importance of a change management strategy
- Govern Salesforce implementation through all its phases
- Gain insights on key activities in the continuous improvement phase
- Leverage customer 360 for analytics, AI and automation

Salesforce Anti-Patterns

Lars Malmqvist

ISBN: 978-1-80324-193-7

- Create a balanced system architecture by identifying common mistakes around on- and off-platform functionality and interfaces
- Avoid security problems that arise from anti-patterns on the Salesforce platform
- Spot common data architecture issues and discover intuitive ways to address them
- Avoid the dual traps of over- and under-customization in your solution architecture
- Explore common errors made in deployment setups, test strategy, and architecture governance
- Understand why bad communication patterns are so overlooked in architecture

Packt is searching for authors like you

If you're interested in becoming an author for Packt, please visit authors.packtpub.com and apply today. We have worked with thousands of developers and tech professionals, just like you, to help them share their insight with the global tech community. You can make a general application, apply for a specific hot topic that we are recruiting an author for, or submit your own idea.

Share Your Thoughts

Now you've finished *Salesforce AppExchange Success Blueprint*, we'd love to hear your thoughts! Scan the QR code below to go straight to the Amazon review page for this book and share your feedback or leave a review on the site that you purchased it from.

https://packt.link/r/1835089542

Your review is important to us and the tech community and will help us make sure we're delivering excellent quality content.

Download a free PDF copy of this book

Thanks for purchasing this book!

Do you like to read on the go but are unable to carry your print books everywhere? Is your eBook purchase not compatible with the device of your choice?

Don't worry, now with every Packt book you get a DRM-free PDF version of that book at no cost.

Read anywhere, any place, on any device. Search, copy, and paste code from your favorite technical books directly into your application.

The perks don't stop there, you can get exclusive access to discounts, newsletters, and great free content in your inbox daily

Follow these simple steps to get the benefits:

1. Scan the QR code or visit the link below

https://packt.link/free-ebook/978-1-83508-954-5

2. Submit your proof of purchase
3. That's it! We'll send your free PDF and other benefits to your email directly

www.ingramcontent.com/pod-product-compliance
Lightning Source LLC
Chambersburg PA
CBHW080620060326
40690CB00021B/4764